BATTLING THE PRINCE

SUNY series in New Political Science

Bradley J. Macdonald, editor

BATTLING THE PRINCE

A WOMAN FIGHTS FOR DEMOCRACY

CLAIRE SNYDER-HALL

Keep working for a better world!

Claire

SUNY
PRESS

Cover photo of the author taken by Kelly Sheridan.

Published by State University of New York Press, Albany

For information, contact State University of New York Press, Albany, NY
www.sunypress.edu

Library of Congress Cataloging-in-Publication Data

Name: Snyder-Hall, Claire, author.
Title: Battling the prince: a woman fights for democracy / Claire Snyder-Hall.
Description: Albany : State University of New York Press, [2021] | Series:
    SUNY series in New Political Science | Includes bibliographical references and
    index.
Identifiers: ISBN 9781438484655 (hardcover : alk. paper) | ISBN 9781438484662
    (ebook) | ISBN 9781438484648 (pbk. : alk. paper)
Further information is available at the Library of Congress.

10 9 8 7 6 5 4 3 2 1

For Mikkiavelli

CONTENTS

PREFACE

CLAIRE SNYDER-HALL TO "WE THE PEOPLE," THE 99%—AN OPENING TRIBUTE TO MACHIAVELLI

It is customary these days for those who seek or have sought political office to write memoirs about their lives and experiences.[1] In this volume I share knowledge I have acquired through years of participation as a left-wing, democratic activist in the world of electoral and social movement politics and from my studies.

I offer readers my story within the compass of this small volume, and I hope it will be received with favor. Although this work draws significantly on political theory and research on US politics and history, I have sought not to adorn my work with a lot of jargon or long phrases. Sadly, I cannot tell a feel-good story of a progressive arc of history that inevitably bends toward justice. We can never take that for granted. Yet I recount my sometimes-disheartening experiences because I believe it necessary for political activists, supporters of democracy, and other readers to understand the perilous situation faced right now in the so-called American republic, to recognize habits of powermongering and deference that have developed in our political parties and larger culture, and to accept the enormous difficulty of making change under current conditions.

I trust readers will accept this little literary gift in the spirit in which it is offered—as my attempt to make the world a more just and democratic place, by offering up my experiences and reflections for consideration. With the veil pulled back, we can face our situation head-on and, despite the odds, persist in our hope for a better world.

ACKNOWLEDGMENTS

Writing a book about your personal experiences sounds like an easy task, but I found the process quite challenging. Not only do you need to reflect somewhat detachedly on the events of your own life, but you must also pull out the anecdotes and insights that people other than your friends might find interesting. The extent to which I accomplished that goal can only be evaluated by readers.

This political theory memoir took about five years to craft, and I have a lot of people to thank for help and support along the way. First is Derek Barker of the Kettering Foundation, who suggested in 2015 that I write about my experiences in electoral politics from the perspective of the people-centered, deliberative politics studied at the foundation, and the resulting piece, "Four Years in the Vipers' Nest," delineated a number of themes that became the basis of this book.

The next year, the project got a huge boost from Sarah Surak, who invited me to apply for a Faculty Research Fellowship at the Institute for Public Affairs and Civic Engagement (PACE) at Salisbury University, and I offer heartfelt thanks to her and her codirector Sandy Pope, who suggested the autoethnographic methodology I use in the project, for selecting me as a fellow. Sarah also did me the huge favor of reading the entire final book manuscript and providing helpful comments, for which I am very grateful.

During the 2016/17 PACE fellowship year, I presented a long paper at the fiftieth anniversary conference of the Caucus for a New Political Science, held on South Padre Island, Texas. In particular, I want to thank Clyde Barrow for his enthusiastic encouragement and to those at the conference who engaged the project, particularly Mark Kaswan, the discussant.

An earlier version of chapter 5 was originally published in *New Political Science: A Journal of Politics and Culture*, titled "Battling the Prince: A Political Memoir," and I thank the Caucus for a New Political Science and Taylor & Francis for granting permission to republish.[1] In addition, heartfelt gratitude goes out to Jocelyn Boryzcka, the journal editor, for inviting me to publish that essay, as well as the anonymous reviewers and Chad Lavin, who edited the piece.

After the article came out, a pivotal moment occurred at the APSA meeting when Bradley Macdonald said, "I want to publish your book in the New Political Science book series." I was delighted by the invitation and thank Brad for that encouragement, as well as Michael Rinella, acquisitions editor at State University of New York Press for his support. In addition, I am grateful to Diane Ganeles, the production editor, as well as Anne Valentine and Kate Seburyamo, marketing managers, for all they did to make this volume a reality.

I had the opportunity to present an earlier version of chapter 4, "Good Ole Boys vs. Nasty Women," at the Florida Political Science Association annual meeting and thank Keith Fitzgerald for commenting on the paper and Liv Coleman for organizing the panel.

Preliminary versions of the manuscript benefited from the critical eyes of some dear friends and colleagues, including Lori Marso, Caroline Heldman, Jill Locke, Mary Dougherty, and Don Peterson. When the entire book manuscript was finally drafted, I was blessed to receive detailed and transformative comments from Judith Grant, Vince Lankewish, and the two anonymous reviewers, and I offer all of them deep thanks.

And, of course, my largest debt of gratitude goes to my wife Mikki Snyder-Hall without whom this project simply would not exist. I thank her from deep in my heart for her unwavering support, for literally years of ongoing conversation, for all her insightful suggestions, for reading numerous drafts, and most of all for actually living the events described in the book with me, every step of the way.

THE BIG PICTURE

A THEORETICAL INTRODUCTION

A specter is haunting the United States—the specter of authoritarianism. While that force has long inhabited the realms of household and workplace, government-sponsored authoritarianism has grown over the course of my lifetime, a period when the country was supposedly becoming more democratic. Indeed, over the past fifty-plus years, a punitive, militarized, authoritarian mentality has increasingly animated federal policy, as evidenced by the "war on crime," "the war on drugs," "the war on terror," and now the war on immigrants, all of which have bolstered police, prison, military, and surveillance apparatuses, and aggrandized the executive branch over the legislative.[1] This is a serious problem because authoritarianism is the polar opposite of democratic republicanism, the type of government we are supposed to have in the United States.

Most democracies do not die suddenly because of a dramatic coup d'état but rather erode over time, as ambitious powermongers gain control, and political elites either cannot stop them or choose appeasement, generally the latter.[2] I have worried about the coercive power of the state ever since I became politically active during the Reagan years. In the 1990s, I found the bipartisan support for rigid and unjust, "tough on crime" policies during the Clinton administration—like "three strikes, you're out"—deeply troubling, but when the administration of George W. Bush started torturing people in the Middle East and few objected, I thought our republic had reached its nadir. Then President Obama refused to hold the perpetrators accountable and actually continued, and in some cases expanded, the coercive power of the state, and my dismay increased even more.

1

Subsequently, under the presidency of Donald Trump, the authoritarian threat grew stronger and spread wider. For example, while the Obama administration has been widely condemned for deporting over three million undocumented people, it targeted those convicted of serious crimes and new arrivals. Trump, in contrast, aspired to remove all undocumented immigrants, regardless of any mitigating circumstances, and pursued that goal in a way designed to sow terror in Latinx communities, all over the country. That is, he sent heavily armed Immigration and Customs Enforcement (ICE) agents deep into communities—searching for people even at sensitive locations, like courthouses, schools, and hospitals—to arrest anyone without papers, including those who have lived in the US for decades and have committed no crimes, and then held them in detention camps with inhumane conditions, while they awaited deportation.[3] Meanwhile, down at the border, the Trump administration started snatching little children from the arms of their asylum-seeking parents and keeping them in cages, in an attempt to deter border-crossing, even though they knew many families would never be reunited—a gross violation of human rights. While many people protested in outrage, nearly half of US citizens approved of Trump's anti-immigrant agenda, apparently having no problem with the blatant exercise of arbitrary power by agents of their so-called democratic government.[4]

In the last year of his term, Trump started using blatantly authoritarian tactics against his own citizens, during the Black Lives Matter protests held after the videotaped murder of George Floyd by a white police officer. While the mistreatment of undocumented people is unacceptable in my view, Trump's attacks on US citizens constitutes an escalating level of authoritarianism. In *How Democracies Die*, Steven Levitsky and Daniel Ziblatt present "a set of four behavioral warning signs that can help us know an authoritarian when we see one. We should worry when a politician" denies the legitimacy of his opponents, infringes on their civil liberties, tolerates or encourages the use of violence by his supporters, or rejects the rules of the democratic game.[5] Trump has repeatedly done all those things. For example, on the last day of May 2020 his attorney general ordered National Guard troops to tear-gas a multiracial group of US citizens who were simply exercising their constitutionally protected right to peacefully protest and not breaking any laws. The soldiers used flash grenades, rubber bullets, and low-flying Blackhawk helicopters—war-zone style—to clear Lafayette Square, so the president could walk to a nearby church and pose for a photograph, holding a Bible like a plaque at an awards banquet. Before the photo op, Trump explicitly expressed the desire to "dominate" the streets, threatened to use the "heavily armed" US military against his own people in cities around the country and called for violence and long prison sentences as "retribution" against protesters, whom he called "terrorists."[6] And while this behavior—a "fascist performance," according to Masha Gessen[7]—elicited widespread pushback from military leaders and many others, 41 percent of Republicans said they approved of Trump's tactics in a poll conducted several days after the Lafayette Square offensive.[8]

Then, in July, the Trump administration did something I never thought I would see in the United States, when he ordered unidentifiable federal agents—a secret police—to abduct protesters from the streets of Portland, Oregon, pull them into unmarked vans, and hold them without charges.[9] Also in Portland, US Marshalls extrajudicially executed an anti-fascist protester, who supposedly killed a right-wing extremist, and Trump praised them for it. "We sent in the US Marshalls," Trump said. "They knew who he was; they didn't want to arrest him; and in 15 minutes that ended" with his death.[10] In light of these attacks on the civil liberties and legitimacy of his political opponents and the use of violence to retaliate against them, a September poll found that 86 percent of Republicans in Oregon approved of Trump's response to the Portland protesters, although the majority of voters overall disapproved.[11]

When the 2020 presidential election finally arrived, Joe Biden won by seven million votes, yet seventy-four million people still voted for Trump, the second highest in US history. Indeed, if Trump had not bungled the coronavirus pandemic so badly, and consequently tanked the economy, he likely would have won. After his multiple attempts at voter suppression failed, Trump took his authoritarianism to the next level by refusing to accept the outcome of the democratic election, denying the legitimacy of the incoming president, interfering with the peaceful transfer of power, and encouraging a violent insurrection at the Capitol that has been exposed as a failed attempt at a coup. While this unprecedented attack on US democracy resulted in a wide range of consequences for Trump and created some dissension within his party, 87 percent of Republicans continue to support him.[12] Who knows the ways in which the right-wing attacks on our democracy will continue to unfold after the Trump years or the number of people who will continue to support him?

Authoritarianism has become a very real threat to our democratic republic. This book focuses however, not primarily on governing elites and the right-wing agenda, but rather on our country's overall political culture and the surprising susceptibility of Democrats to authoritarian tactics. When I entered the realm of Democratic Party politics in 2011, after twenty years in the college classroom teaching political theory at a variety of levels and working with the national civic engagement movement and deliberative democracy community, I had a lot of ideas about the ways that democracy should operate, and although I knew that politics-as-usual did not operate according to those ideals, I had no idea about the extent of the crisis in which we now find ourselves. I had long understood the disconnection between citizens and government and wondered if government in the United States really had the consent of the people, a necessary prerequisite for legitimacy. I knew that the government did a lot of terrible things in our name, and that the term *corporate oligarchy* better describes the system of government in the United States than does *democracy* or *republic*.

Yet I also thought the problem rested largely with elites, with our elected officials who care more about their donors and career trajectories than the public good. I expected that everyday people, especially Democrats and self-proclaimed progressives, would have internalized a commitment to democratic values from having lived in a place that many proclaim to be the greatest democracy in the world, and I trusted that the Democratic Party (DP), unlike the "Grand Old Party" of the Republicans (GOP), supported an engaged citizenry, democratic practices, free and open public discourse, and the accountability of elected representatives to the people.

When I stepped into the arena of electoral politics, however, I discovered that things are worse than I thought. Not only do we not have a democratic government, but we have only the thinnest of democratic cultures in our society, even within the Democratic Party itself. Having spent eight years occupying various leadership positions within the party in two very different states—district party chair, candidate for state senate, county executive committee member, precinct captain, steering committee member, state convention delegate, local progressive caucus president, and member of the statewide progressive caucus board—and lobbying Democrats in the state legislature, I have learned that not only does the Democratic Party serve the interests of big donors and the professional class, much more than working or even middle-class people, but Democratic Party operatives and representatives often seem more concerned about shoring up their own power, squashing dissent, and demanding that people fall in line than engaging everyday people or fighting for economic justice for all.[13] We need a strong party, committed to democratic values and practices, that can articulate a vision that mobilizes the people to fight for progressive change, but we do not have one.

Nor do we have the democratic culture needed to undergird the republican institutions that allow us to govern ourselves. As the specter of authoritarianism threatens our republic, the people of the United States stand at a crossroads. As we look to the left, we can see that our deteriorating quality of life is spurring demands for transformative change, as exemplified by the rise of democratic socialism with calls for single-payer health care, higher wages, paid sick leave, a green jobs program, free college tuition, student loan forgiveness, and guaranteed housing, as well as the widespread, multiracial uprising against racist policing and mass incarceration that mobilized in the wake of George Floyd's murder by a white police officer in 2020. On the right-hand side, however, we see quasi-fascist, white supremacist forces strengthening, with people blaming societal problems on minorities and foreigners, resorting to violence and threats, and putting their faith in a demagogic leader who actually proclaimed, "I am the only one who can make America truly great again!"[14] Instead of greatness, however, Trump's reign yielded increasing attacks on republican institutions and democratic norms and fed polarization to the point where Democrats are talking about democracy's death and Republicans about civil war.

In order to move forward in a positive direction, we need a revolutionary party that will address the deteriorating economic situation that makes people amenable to authoritarianism and articulate a vision that mobilizes the people to fight for progressive change. Back in the 1930s, when democracy previously came face to face with its possible demise, Antonio Gramsci, writing from Mussolini's prison, called the people's revolutionary party "The Modern Prince," a mysterious term that allowed him to evade censorship. In this book, I reconnect with Gramsci's vision of a revolutionary party, but I call it the Modern Prince Collective to emphasize the necessary plurality of that entity. Like Gramsci, I argue that building support for a party that truly represents the people will require consciousness-raising to help people see the ways in which the ruling class perpetuates its power culturally and possibilities for transformation.

DEFINING OUR TERMS

Before moving forward with my argument, I want to clarify some of the terms I use in the book. During the "Age of Democratic Revolution" in the so-called long eighteenth century (1788–1815), US founders drew on both civic republicanism and Lockean liberalism in articulating our country's public philosophy.[15] Over time, the less democratic, more individualistic discourse of liberalism became dominant. Indeed, at this point, most politicians in the United States are actually liberals in the philosophical sense, in that they derive their underlying assumptions from the tradition that began with John Locke, who saw people as atomistic individuals, driven by self-interest and possessive of rights, including the right to private property; who viewed the market economy as natural and desirable; and who wanted only limited government that could act as an umpire for competing interests, governing via the rule of law, applied impartially to all.[16] While many in the general public think only Democrats are liberals and Republicans are conservatives, in the philosophical sense, both parties draw on the tradition of liberal individualism, as do libertarians. This can be confusing, so in order to distinguish between the so-called "tax and spend" liberals in the Democratic party and the philosophical liberals in the Republican Party, political theorists started using the term *neoliberal* to refer to those who favor a deregulated market economy and minimal government, as opposed to those who wanted to use the government to create equal opportunity so that all individuals can compete fairly.

Over time, *neoliberal* seems to have replaced *liberal* in popular discourse with some critics calling anyone who supports a market mechanism neoliberal, even left-leaning reformers like Elizabeth Warren. While this may work for those interested in blasting Warren from the left, I do not find it helpful to collapse ideological categories like that. Warren stands to the left of liberal centrists, such as Hillary Clinton and Nancy Pelosi, even if she sometimes waffles or panders, and Clinton and Pelosi stand to the left of people like Mitt Romney and Paul Ryan, who are neoliberals in the original sense. Painting everyone with the brush of neoliberalism obscures important differences.

The Democratic Party includes people who hold a range of positions, including the neoliberal "blue dogs," who resemble the liberal Republicans of yore, and liberal centrists, who favor social equality but staunchly defend capitalism, like Pelosi and Clinton, as well as Barack Obama and Joe Biden (also known as "establishment Dems"), as well as left-leaning liberals, like Elizabeth Warren, who supports highly regulated, welfare-state capitalism, and democratic socialists, like Alexandria Ocasio-Cortez (AOC) and Rashida Tlaib, who reject the underlying assumptions of liberalism.[17] That is why AOC correctly commented, "In any other country, Joe Biden and I would not be in the same party."[18] In other words, the Democratic Party has no overarching ideology. Indeed, some say it is just a conglomeration of interest groups.[19]

The term *progressive* is equally confusing. These days it seems that everyone in the Democratic Party claims the "progressive" label, even people like Pelosi, who refuses to support single-payer Medicare for All or the Green New Deal, which she dismisses as "the Green Dream or whatever they call it."[20] When it comes to defining "progressive," people draw the line in different places, and in my experience, many use the term as a euphemism for pro-gay, but to me it must include support for economic justice, as well as a commitment to social equality in terms of gender, race, sexual orientation, gender identity, and ability. In other words, in my view, left-leaning liberals are progressive, but centrist neoliberals are not.

When I use the term *progressive* in this book, it functions as an umbrella term that includes both left-leaning liberals, like Elizabeth Warren, and democratic socialists, like Bernie Sanders. I do not love the term progressive because of its squishiness, but it is hard to avoid, especially with the DP in the process of splitting into centrist versus progressive camps. When I talk about advancing the "progressive agenda," I refer to issues that could unite left-leaning liberals and democratic socialists. That type of coalition makes sense because ideologies are best understood as existing on a continuum, so a sharp break does not necessarily exist between left-leaning liberalism and democratic socialism, at least when it comes to policies.

The term *republic* is also misunderstood. The modern tradition of republicanism began with Niccolò Machiavelli, author of *The Prince*, whom Gramsci references with the term "Modern Prince."[21] Best known as the quintessential theorist of power, Machiavelli is often depicted as a malevolent figure. In actuality, however, he spent his life advocating republicanism, a democratic form of self-rule that stands in opposition to authoritarianism, royalist or otherwise, and is defined by a commitment to both popular sovereignty and the rule of law.[22] Machiavelli's views were fundamentally "democratic and anti-elitist."[23] He wanted the people to make laws for themselves in popular assemblies and have the arms needed to defend themselves against ambitious, wannabe tyrants.[24]

Machiavelli served for many years in the government of the Florentine republic. When the Medici family overthrew the republic in 1512 and reestablished monarchy, they told Machiavelli, "You're fired," locked him up, and tortured him for weeks for being an enemy of their royalist regime. Released from prison but shut out of power, Machiavelli focused on writing texts and engaging intellectually with political friends. It was during this period that he wrote his most famous book, *The Prince*, about methods of gaining and maintaining power. While on the surface *The*

Prince appears to advocate monarchy, to the contrary, as many scholars have argued, the volume actually offers instructions that, if followed, would lead to the establishment of a republic.[25] The volume instructs the Prince to arm the common people, whom Machiavelli considers more honest, decent, and just than elites, and crush the ambitions of self-styled nobles who seek to aggrandize themselves, their families, and their cronies.[26]

Living under sixteenth-century feudalism, Machiavelli looked to a wise, individual Prince to represent the collective will of the people as the leader of a unified state. In the more democratic twentieth-century, Gramsci did not want a singular ruler to unify the people; instead, he looked to a revolutionary party to organize and express the collective will of the people and enact cultural and economic reforms, an entity he identified as the "Modern Prince."[27] Today in the twenty-first century, as We the People hopefully approach the end of four decades of neoliberal hegemony, we too need a mass party to unify and fight for the well-being of the 99% against the tyranny of the 1%. As stated earlier, I call that new party the Modern Prince Collective—a term meant to invoke both popular sovereignty and collective action. Indeed, to begin a new, more humane era, we must move away from the rule of largely unaccountable elites— one-percenters, career politicians, and other powermongers—and toward a more democratic vision of collaborative rule, historically embodied in the concept of a republic.

When I use the term *republic* throughout this book, I define it as it has been defined throughout most of history, as a democratic form of government, characterized by popular sovereignty, political and economic equality, the rule of law, and freedom from arbitrary power.[28] While the membership category of citizen within traditional republican political theory excluded women, the ideals articulated could, I have argued elsewhere, become gender inclusive.[29] In any event, the long-standing historic definition of republicanism entails a much more robust vision of self-rule—strong democracy—than the reductionist definition proffered by James Madison in Federalist 10, where he calls it "a government in which the scheme of representation takes place" with a "small number of citizens elected by the rest" to govern in their place.[30]

Because the United States was founded as a republic, defined by Madison in reductionist terms, some people in the general public like to assert that "the United States is a republic not a democracy," as if that claim somehow wipes away any appeals to democratic principles. It does not for two reasons. First, in their origins, *democracy* and *republic* were simply Greek and Roman words for the same thing: popular government—the people rule (*demos* + *kratos*) and public thing (*res publica*).[31] Second, even if the term *republic* did mean representative government, that would still be a form of democracy. Indeed, even according to Madison's view, representatives are not supposed to rule in the interest of just themselves, their party, or their donors. He claims representatives will "refine and enlarge the *public* views" and create a *"public voice"* that is "consonant to the *public good"*—and the public ostensibly includes everyone. Representatives of the public must "discern the true interest *of their country*."[32] And since they are elected, they will be held accountable to the people, which means democracy. Consequently, the United States is a republic and also a democracy. Either term is correct, and I use both in this book.

Third, in using the term *republic* and focusing on the United States, I do not mean to condone nationalism. To the contrary, I hope for the emergence of an international federation of constitutional republics, living together in harmony, each a free society, governed democratically within the bounds of the rule of law. Because this vision allows people to govern themselves, a variety of cultures can flourish within this framework. I focus on the "American republic" only because that is where I live and have been politically active, not because I consider it an exceptional beacon for the world.

OUR "MACHIAVELLIAN MOMENT"

Machiavelli, having lived through the destruction of a republic by the return of royalist authoritarianism, knew that a republic, once established, must be carefully protected, lest it deteriorate over time. Contemporary political theorist J. G. A. Pocock argues that every republic ends up facing what he calls the "Machiavellian moment," when it has to figure out strategies to maintain itself as time passes, civic practices weaken, and founding ideals recede in memory.[33]

Today, in the United States, we face our own Machiavellian moment. That is to say, many of the important republican ideals articulated at the founding, albeit in embryonic form, have begun to erode. While not fully implemented because of slavery, white supremacy, and male dominance, in their universalized and idealized form, those revolutionary republican claims include respect for the human dignity and equality of all people, an inclusive popular sovereignty, and protection from arbitrary power in multiple spheres. While those principles were never fully realized in the US context, today they face erosion by the perennial allure of hierarchy, domination, and cruelty, which threaten the future of republican self-rule.

At the close of the Constitutional Convention in 1787, a woman approached Benjamin Franklin and asked, "Well, Doctor, what have we got—a Republic or a Monarchy?" Franklin famously replied, "A Republic, if you can keep it."[34] With that comment, Franklin suggested that many forces pose a threat to the ongoing ability of people to govern themselves for the common good through the rule of law. Coming from monarchical societies, the Founders feared the continuation of royalist thinking, the reestablishment of powerful familial dynasties, feudalist hierarchy, and habits of deference in their new world, and they implemented a number of institutional safeguards to prevent that from happening. While, theoretically, giving the people sovereignty provides the primary safeguard, the Founders also created a divided government that protects liberty by pitting ambitious actors against each other to constrain their power. To quote Madison again, "Ambition must be made to counter ambition."[35] So, for example, in theory members of Congress would never yield their constitutional control over declarations of war to the president, give up their authority to hold him accountable through impeachment, or defer to him in terms of the legislation they pass; members of Congress would jealously guard their own power and prerogatives.

Liberty requires constraints on arbitrary power, but in the contemporary era, will traditional methods still work? The election of Trump made visible the specter of authoritarianism once again. He seems to consider himself above the law, like a king or prince. Will our system of checks and balances effectively constrain him? Will civilian control of the military prevent dictatorship? Do people still have in their hearts a commitment to the democratic values that make a free, self-governing society possible? Did they ever?

A cultural commitment to democratic values is key for a republic's continuation over time. During the Age of Democratic Revolution, republican theorist Jean-Jacques Rousseau argued that constitutional, civil, and criminal law must be supplemented by a "fourth" type of law, "the most important of all" that "is graven not in marble or in bronze, but, in the hearts of the Citizens; which is the State's genuine constitution; which daily gathers new force; which, when the other laws age or die out, revives or replaces them, and imperceptibly substitutes the force of habit for that of authority. I speak of morals, customs, and above all opinion."[36] He believed that engagement in civic practices would instill democratic values, in people's hearts, which is the reason he emphasized participatory citizenship.[37]

As fascism rose within democratic societies in the 1930s, Gramsci also emphasized the important role culture plays in undergirding political power, and the need for cultural change to precede political change. That is to say, Gramsci emphasized that the ruling class maintains its power not predominantly through violence and force but by disseminating its cultural values throughout society, so that everyday people accept them as common sense, as inevitable, a force he calls *hegemony*. Gramsci scholar Carl Boggs explains it this way: "By *hegemony*, Gramsci meant the permeation throughout civil society—including a whole range of structures and activities like trade unions, schools, the churches, and the family—of an entire system of values, attitudes, beliefs, morality, etc. that is in one way or another supportive of the established order and the class interests that dominate it. . . . To the extent that this prevailing consciousness is internalized by the broad masses, it becomes part of 'common sense.'"[38]

This raises the questions, asked by scholar Terry Eagleton: "How is the working class to take power in a social formation where the dominant power is subtly, pervasively diffused throughout habitual daily practices, intimately interwoven with 'culture' itself, inscribed in the very texture of our experience from nursery school to funeral parlour? How do we combat a power which has become the 'common sense' of a whole social order?"[39] Gramsci's framework suggests that given the reality of ruling class hegemony, left organizing must focus first on the "realm of values and customs, speech habits and ritual practices," before we can make significant political change.[40]

Gramsci believes that before revolutionaries can take power, they must work to change people's consciousness—their hearts and minds. This contrasts with his revolutionary predecessor Vladimir Lenin's view that revolutionaries should seize political power first and then work on legitimation. Lenin's position made sense in the context of Czarist Russia where common people did not support the state or the political system. In the United States, however, left activists have to deal with the problem of everyday people thinking our neoliberal, capitalist, oligarchic regime is natural, inevitable, righteous, or at least more desirable than the socialist alternative.

Gramsci emphasizes that if the consciousness of people does not change, then new revolutionary leaders will simply rule over people who have a mentality suitable to the previous regime and over time that will pull society back to the way it was. For example, progressives gaining control in the world of power politics that currently exists in the United States and elsewhere will not lead to radical change because people will continue to be either ambitious powermongers or deferential minions, which still leaves society susceptible to the forces of royalism—or fascism. That is not a foundation upon which a democratic socialist society can firmly stand.

I have learned from my experiences in the realm of US party politics that we need cultural change in this country. People in general do not appear to have a gut-level understanding of and allegiance to democratic values, nor do they clearly oppose authoritarianism. Perhaps this should come as no surprise. Throughout its history, the United States has been fractured by an important rhetorical commitment to equality and popular sovereignty intertwined with deep-rooted practices that perpetuate unjust systems of racial and gender oppression, as well as a capitalist economic system in which the wealth produced by the many becomes the private property of the few. While we loudly tout our democratic bona fides—even taking it upon ourselves to "democratize" other countries with guns and bombs—we actually live in a "bully nation," in which democratic practices are not the norm in our homes, schools, or workplaces.[41] Moreover, few opportunities exist in communities for people to become accustomed to participating in democratic self-rule, beyond simply voting—and many do not even do that. Since practices cultivate habits and beliefs, the generalized lack of commitment to democratic values makes sense.

I am far from unaware of the massive injustices that exist in the world, yet I find myself continually shocked anew when faced with cruelty and injustice. During the Bush-Cheney years, I marveled in horror at the lack of outrage over our government's use of torture at Abu Ghraib and other black sites, a true hallmark of authoritarianism. Being raised with the Cold War narrative that the United States of America respects human rights and the rule of law, I could not understand it when people not only failed to get upset but actually seemed to endorse, even enjoy, the torture and degradation of other human beings. I have had a similar reaction to the police killings of unarmed Black men and women, to the cruelties meted out daily in our prisons, and to the wide range of atrocities perpetrated by Immigration and Customs Enforcement (ICE), particularly the roundups, deportations, family separations, kids in cages, and concentration camps at the border.[42]

I have come to believe that tribalism, cruelty, and authoritarianism do not need to be explained. Sadly, they seem to be the default position of humankind. The values that need to be explained are respect for human rights, due process, and democratic self-rule. Democracy is a fragile achievement that requires the creation of a democratic culture as its underpinning and opportunities for people to develop democratic virtues, such as caring about the public good, critical thinking, truth-telling, and *democratic courage*, which I define as the willingness to stand up to power in defense of democratic values. This definition of democratic courage adds to the four types of courage articulated by Richard Avramenko. He talks about martial courage, based on the willingness to risk one's life; political courage that values the use of reason in the political realm; moral courage that fosters autonomy; and economic courage connected to self-interest rightly understood.[43] My invocation of courage does not track directly onto any of these conceptions. As a child, I was taught by my Christian parents to have moral courage, which involves an allegiance to "goodness—correctness—of character and behavior that arises from the conscience," so that I could strive to be autonomously righteous in an earthly world riddled with sin.[44] The concept of *democratic courage* I advocate in this text is not that, nor is it reducible to the battle of ideas in the realm of reason. I define *democratic courage* as the willingness to stand up to power—in terms of both systems and individuals—in defense of democratic values.

OUR ANTI-CIVIC CULTURE

As noted, the importance of democratic culture has long been of concern to scholars of politics. In 1963, Gabriel Almond and Sidney Verba published the now-classic study *The Civic Culture*, in which they wondered whether democracy would be able to spread worldwide. "The democratic state offers the ordinary man the opportunity to take part in the political decision-making process as an influential citizen," they write. "If the democratic model of the participatory state is to develop in these new nations, it will require more than the formal institutions of democracy—universal suffrage, the political party, the elective legislature. These in fact are also part of the totalitarian participation pattern, in a formal if not functional sense. A democratic form of participatory political system requires as well a political culture consistent with it."[45]

Norms and attitudes matter for democracy, they argue, but they surprisingly eschew the participatory values I view as essential to a healthy democracy. Instead, they stress the importance of citizens having only a passive allegiance to that which they call the "myth of democratic citizenship." That is to say, the civic culture works best, they argue, when the citizen maintains the mere "perception that he can be an influential citizen" but chooses not to engage.[46] This allows space for elites to govern. "A citizen within the civic culture has, then, a reserve of influence. He is not constantly involved in politics, nor does he actively oversee the behavior of political decision makers. But he does have the potential to act if there is need."[47] Or, at least he thinks he does. "That politics has relatively little importance for citizens is an important part of the mechanism by which the set of inconsistent political orientations keeps political elites in check without checking them so tightly as to make them ineffective."[48]

Since the publication of *The Civic Culture*, some scholars believe citizens have transitioned from passive to active; however, in my experience the myth of democratic citizenship is alive and well.[49] We know most citizens do not get involved, and only around half usually vote in presidential elections, yet many people seem to believe that individuals really could rise up and take control, if they chose to do so. For example, in his farewell address to the American public, President Obama said, "Ultimately, . . . our democracy . . . needs you. . . . If something needs fixing, lace up your shoes and do some organizing. If you're disappointed by your elected officials, grab a clipboard, get some signatures, and run for office yourself."[50] State and party will yield, if only people get involved, Obama suggests.

He makes it sound so easy. His democratic optimism remains undaunted by revelations that Democratic Party insiders worked to sabotage the 2016 campaign of Bernie Sanders, who dared to run in the primary against the establishment-selected candidate; by the party's attempts to blacklist individuals and organizations that support progressive challenges in primaries, even in safe Democratic districts or where there is no Democratic incumbent; by arguments about the power of billionaires and the military-industrial-intelligence complex to influence policy-making; or by the barriers to fair elections posed by gerrymandering and voter suppression.[51] While I respect Obama's desire to stimulate civic engagement, making change is not as simple as "Hey! 'Grab a clipboard . . . and run for office.' " A lot of impediments exist, including some from within the Democratic Party itself.

Many of my Facebook friends believe that voting and running for office are the most effective ways to make change, possibly even the only way. Sometimes it seems like their response to every issue is, "Vote!" For example, on the heels of President Trump's illegal and unconstitutional assassination of Iranian major general Qasem Soleimani in January 2020, I posted about the importance of mobilizing an antiwar movement to prevent further escalation, and an online friend suggested that I volunteer to do voter registration for the Democratic Party. Given that the Democratic Party has been generally complicit with militarization and war-making, I failed to grasp the logic of his post.

Many of my Facebook friends aspire to energize people to get more involved, and they want to take over the Democratic Party from the left. Others, however, hold an extremely unrealistic view of individual efficacy, illustrating the "myth of democratic citizenship." For example, when I criticized the superdelegate system during the Democratic primary in 2016 for rigging the system against Bernie Sanders, an academic friend posted on my Facebook page: "Claire, I hope you are going to the convention and will be leading the argument for this kind of structural change within the party rules! You would be a great advocate for taking the party in a new direction!" I found this comment stunningly naïve, especially coming from someone with a PhD in political science. Even if I had still been a local Democratic Party chair and had successfully won the competitive election for one of the few delegate slots, I would not have been allowed to grab the mic at the DNC convention and argue for structural change. It just doesn't work that way. The event is highly scripted and controlled by elites.

While never that naïve, I used to believe that people really could make change, if they just got more involved. Indeed, I spent my entire academic career encouraging students to get involved and writing books and articles about civic participation and democratic practices. Then I entered the realm of electoral politics myself. I could maintain optimism while operating in the realm of theory. In the realm of practice, however, I came face to face with the grim reality of power politics—a realm in which We the People are sidelined and have no party to advocate for us. Yet the hegemonic belief that people could make change, if they really wanted to, functions to keep people invested in a system that disenfranchises them, serving the interests of wealthy donors rather than everyday people.

My currently critical view derives largely from my experiences working inside the Democratic Party in both blue state Delaware and red state Florida. When I combine my experiential learning with what I know from reading on political theory, politics, and history, I no longer have an optimistic view about the ability of everyday people to make change by running for office or working to move the Democratic Party to the left.

Yet it's hard to abandon the idea of working for change inside the party because the DP is often the only game in town.[52] On the other hand, perhaps an alternative might emerge in the future, given the emergence of a visible socialist movement in the United States that can exert pressure from outside the party.

CHAPTER SUMMARIES

This autoethnographic political memoir mines my personal experiences in electoral and social movement politics for lessons on the condition of US politics and culture and combines that knowledge with insights gleaned from reading and observation.[53] While my particular experiences occurred in particular places with particular people, I have found from sharing my stories with folks all over the country that the types of incidents I experienced are far from unique. Consequently, this book is not about blue state Delaware or red state Florida in particular, but about US politics in general.

This memoir uses personal experiences to illustrate the book's larger argument about the state of "our democracy," as well as to tell a hopefully interesting personal story. I have chosen to use archetypal nicknames for some individuals featured in my stories, particularly those I cast in a negative light, because their identities are irrelevant to the points I am making in this book. People close to the drama will know who the characters are, and their identities are discoverable, but for most readers the inclusion of their names would add nothing to their understanding of the book's argument, so why call out the bad actors by name? In fact, using their names would make the stories sound more idiosyncratic than I believe they are. In other words, it is my contention that the incidents I experienced speak to larger political and cultural dynamics and so could have unfolded with different individuals playing those same roles.

In addition, I focus solely on the problems of the Democratic Party in this book because I have no direct experience of Republican Party dynamics. I expect, however, that some of my criticisms of authoritarian tendencies within the DP would resonate with Republicans as well. Indeed, given that Republicans often explicitly support authoritarianism, internal party dynamics might be even worse.

The first two chapters of this book overview my experiences before moving to Delaware and getting involved with the Democratic Party.

Chapter 1 begins with the political situation in the year of my birth and tells a personal and a political story simultaneously. I share the process by which I became an activist as a young person, my embrace of feminism during college, and my activist experiences in the 1980s. Chapter 2 overviews the work I did as a professional political theorist at universities, both inside and outside the classroom. I explain the robust understanding of democracy and socialism I acquired during graduate school, my attempt to contest hegemonic beliefs held by my students, and my efforts to provide civic education to prepare them for active participation in democracy. I also discuss some gender-based challenges I encountered as I attempted to segue my career into higher education administration, before leaving the academy altogether.

The subsequent four chapters recount my experiences with the Democratic Party. Chapter 3 tells the story of running for the Delaware State Senate in 2014, trying to actualize some of the principles I learned from decades of work on democratic theory and practice. Chapter 4 analyzes the campaign with hindsight. As it turns out, during the actual campaign, I could not see the extent to which it was a pre-Trump year, and I also failed to recognize the good ole boy culture that enveloped me and would produce a Trump win two years later. Chapter 5 builds on my discussion of good ole boy culture to make that case that we face a "Machiavellian moment" right now in the United States: The habits of deference people have developed over time now threaten to recreate the royalist mindset that the Age of Democratic Revolution wanted to annihilate. Chapter 6 exposes the quasi-authoritarian culture that exists within the Democratic Party and the barriers to left-wing politics posed by party leaders.

The book concludes with some lessons learned from my experiences in the field. I titled this book *Battling the Prince* because that phrase references three sets of problems that need to be addressed. First, battling the prince means waging war on all the little Prince wannabes in our democratic republic who feel entitled to rule over us with unaccountable power, the bullies who expect deference in the political world, from Trump on down to the local level. Second, battling the prince also refers to the metaphorical Prince inside our heads, the royalist mindset that can develop in any of us who want to make our lives easier by simply deferring to power. Rousseau said we are "born free" yet are "everywhere . . . in chains."[54] Part of that enchainment comes from societal power structures, but some comes from within ourselves. We need both raised consciousness—"wokeness" in today's parlance—and democratic courage to win that battle. Finally, battling the prince refers to my vision of making sure the 1% is battling the Modern Prince Collective. In waging that war, we must remember that we have "nothing to lose" but our "chains," and we have "a world to win."[55]

CHAPTER 1

BECOMING AN ACTIVIST

My story began in 1965, a pivotal year in US politics, and, like every other year, characterized by both positive and negative trends.[1] Although Malcolm X was assassinated on February 21, a week after my birth, in other ways, that year marks the zenith of the civil rights movement with the passage of the Voting Rights Act of 1965 (VRA), directly on the heels of the Civil Rights Act of 1964. Together these acts promised political equality for African Americans, the end of Jim Crow's arbitrary power, and the rule of impartial, color-blind law. Congress also passed the Immigration and Nationality Act of 1965 that eliminated discrimination against immigrants from non–Western European ethnic groups. In addition, the New Left, second-wave feminism, and the lesbian–gay rights movement began their ascent around this time, with people working hard to advance social justice, long before the movements burst into public view on the national stage. These changes, and others not mentioned, held out hope that in the United States of America, all people would finally be free.

The struggle for Black civil rights gained popular support on March 7, 1965, when forty-eight million Americans across the country saw firsthand the brutal treatment of peaceful, unarmed African Americans by law enforcement in the South when ABC News interrupted the Sunday Night movie premiere of *Judgment at Nuremberg* "to show 15 minutes of raw and dramatic footage from the attack on the Edmund Pettus Bridge." That video footage created a "groundswell of northern support" for the Black struggle, and young, white "volunteers poured into Selma."[2] The prospects for an integrated civic life looked promising. Indeed, Gallup polls

19

conducted that spring "showed that 52 percent of Americans identified civil rights as the 'most important problem' confronting the nation, and an astonishing 75 percent of respondents favored federal voting rights legislation.'"[3] When President Johnson signed the VRA into law, "the first of the South's 2.5 million previously disenfranchised eligible blacks were lining up to register to vote under the watchful eyes of federal officials" throughout "the Deep South."[4] The VRA worked so well that in 2013 the Supreme Court decided it was no longer necessary, and it rendered part of the act unconstitutional in *Shelby County v. Holder*, which cleared the way for a return to voter suppression of African Americans, a trend that accelerated under Trump.

Establishing legal equality and the right to vote constituted a huge step forward for Black people, but those two acts did not eliminate racism with a stroke of a pen or erase its legacy. Even after the passage of the VRA, police brutality against African Americans continued. Indeed, a mere three months later, police stopped a car in the impoverished neighborhood of Watts in Los Angeles and ended up beating the two unarmed, Black passengers, a pair of brothers, and also brutalizing their mother, who tried to intervene. On the heels of a long train of abuses, that incident triggered the largest uprising against police brutality and systemic racism in history (until the Rodney King protests), and the State responded with violence and mass arrests by militarized police and the National Guard—authoritarianism on display.[5] Not much has changed. Indeed, fifty-five years later, the videotaped murder of George Floyd by police kicked off the Black Lives Matter movement, the largest protest in history—and the State responded as it did in the 1960s, with pure brutality.

Back in 1965, the United States was also enmeshed in a long-standing ideological battle against Communism that was used to justify a wide range of practices that operated below the radar of most Americans. While I grew up in a stereotypical Cold War family during the 1960s and '70s—a white, middle-class, Protestant family, headed by a gentle patriarch and a mostly stay-at-home mom—unbeknownst to me, our government was facilitating and committing crimes against humanity, even collaborating with former Nazis, in order to beat back the Communist menace in Vietnam, as well as Southern Africa and Latin America. Declassified government documents reveal a lot that occurred without public knowledge during my childhood years and beyond.[6]

Yet as the US government condoned, supported, or participated in everything from torture to assassinations, I attended a public school that offered a civics curriculum that praised our country as a great democracy and a beacon of freedom around the world—myths still widely espoused today. At my school, we were taught that the United States saved the world from the Nazis and now staunchly opposed Communist totalitarianism and the human rights abuses perpetrated by the Soviets. We read *The Diary of Anne Frank* and *The Endless Steppe*, about the horrors of Nazism and Communism, and *Farewell to Manzanar* about the terrible mistake the United States made when it rounded up Japanese Americans and held them in camps, which we were assured would never happen again.[7] As school children, we came to know that the principle of free speech was so important that the First Amendment even protected the rights of Nazis to march through the Jewish neighborhood of Skokie. And while southern states used to require Black citizens to pass an impossible literacy test in order to vote, we did away with that injustice with the VRA. Message received: We were definitely the good guys, and the long arc of history bends toward justice.

The year of my birth, however, also marks the genesis of the New Right that dominates US politics to this day. After Barry Goldwater lost the presidential election by a landslide to Lyndon B. Johnson in 1964, right-wing leaders decided to repackage their "Old Right" agenda (Goldwater economic libertarianism, Klan racism, and the John Birch Society anticommunism) in a way that would be more appealing to the American public. These leaders replaced the Old Right's strident tone, explicit racism, and conspiracy mongering—which seem to have returned thanks to Trump—with the New Right's emphasis on the virtues of the free market, fear of crime, and the need for a strong military.[8] The entry of the Christian Right, comprised of conservative evangelicals, into politics during the 1970s—galvanized against the Equal Rights Amendment (ERA), *Roe v. Wade*, and the burgeoning LGBT rights movement, as well as the Supreme Court–ordered prohibition on school prayer—greatly strengthened the New Right. Together, those constituencies in 1980 helped elect Ronald Reagan, a man who basically supported the Goldwater agenda, and the Right has controlled the government pretty much ever since, while becoming increasingly extreme and antidemocratic.

If we want to build the power of the Left in the United States, I believe we could learn from studying the techniques through which the New Right achieved power. Back in the late '70s and early '80s, conservative Christians infiltrated the Republican Party and moved it to the right, but they also maintained a strong grassroots movement outside the GOP.

The Christian Right did a good job taking its message to everyday people with voter guides distributed at churches and organizing in "what might appear hostile political territory, such as racial/ethnic/religious minority communities or communities known to be liberal strongholds"—finding Black, Latino, and Jewish conservatives and blue-collar union members upset about taxes and liberal mores and peeling them off.[9] I remember hearing commentators note that the Christian Right would simply not vote for candidates who refused to toe the line, and fear of that threat, over time, resulted in a situation in which every Republican politician now supports illegalizing abortion. In later years, the Tea Party had similar success threatening primaries against Republicans who compromise or who fail to wholeheartedly support its agenda. In short, the Right has had great success doing a lot of things that progressive activist groups—like Our Revolution, Justice Democrats, Brand New Congress, and Democratic Socialists of America (DSA)—have started to do since Trump's election in 2016.

GROWING UP CHRISTIAN DURING THE COLD WAR

As soon as I became politically aware, I became a left-wing activist. In thinking about that awakening, I believe the civic and humanitarian values instilled in me during my formative years created the foundation that then became fully activated at the liberal arts college I attended. In addition, because my devoutly Methodist parents emphasized the importance of personal integrity, telling the truth, and living in accordance with one's principles, I was enabled to develop the democratic courage to stand up for what I believe to be right and speak truth to power. My parents did not do hypocrisy. So, when I learned about injustice—the cruelties of racism and misogyny, the vicious role of the US government in Latin American politics, and the death threat posed by the arms race—and encountered opportunities to speak out and take action, I did.

My father was an ordained Methodist minister and European historian, and he supported our family of four with his modest professor's salary. I was born in Delaware, Ohio, when he taught at Ohio Wesleyan, but we moved to Sarasota, Florida, a segregated southern town, in 1969 when he took a job at a newly created liberal arts college, now called New College of Florida. As mentioned earlier, growing up during the Cold War, I was schooled in the mythology around American democracy and our commitment to freedom, equality, and human rights, which I learned in my school's anti-Communist civics classes. Ironically, that quasi-indoctrination ended up playing a profound role in my political awakening because it shaped my expectations about the actions our government should and should not take—expectations I still hold, despite my knowledge of the brutal, antidemocratic reality of US foreign policy.

Even more important to my development, however, were the strong humanistic values, rooted in Christianity, that my parents instilled in me from birth, both explicitly and implicitly. I am very fortunate that my parents always treated my brother and me with love, respect, and kindness. We were never bullied, humiliated, or harshly punished, and so we did not develop an authoritarian mentality that often arises from a punitive parenting style and that correlates with right-wing politics.[10] Instead, our parents encouraged our creativity and focused on our moral and intellectual development.

As a result, I have a deep, unwavering belief in the equal worth and human dignity of every person, in the righteousness of love and compassion, and in the importance of forgiveness and reconciliation. And as a Protestant, I embrace the "priesthood of all believers," which means that every human being can have a direct relationship with the Divine and should not be subordinated to clerical authority. That belief undergirds the demand that human dignity, equality, and freedom of conscience be respected and leads to the idea that people should be able to govern themselves individually in personal matters and collaboratively when it comes to societal concerns. While I did not have a fully conscious understanding of this philosophy as a child, I did believe at a gut level that people should not be subjected to unfair or arbitrary rule. I never considered "because I said so" a satisfactory answer. Does anybody? Indeed, I have an anarchist's heart—perhaps we all do—and in the political realm, I support human dignity, equality, self-determination, empowerment, democracy, justice, and peace—in short, a progressive, left-wing agenda.

My parents were not left-wingers, although they both embraced the strong social justice message of the United Methodist Church. My mom was an FDR liberal, but my father was a registered Republican all his life—a pre-Reagan Republican—although he did identify as a "Christian socialist" in his final years, emphasis on Christian. My parents were not politically active, beyond voting, but they read the newspaper daily and listened to the news on the radio every morning and on TV at night. My parents were mild-mannered people, and they generally did not comment on the news or talk about politics at the dinner table, and as a child, I did not pay much attention to current events. Although I remember hearing "bombing in Cambodia" every night on the TV news, and also some snippets about Watergate, I was just a couple of years too young to have been cognizant of the Vietnam War and its protests, and I had no older siblings or friends to enlighten me.

My father was a quiet man who did not share his opinions all the time, but he had unwavering principles and did speak out against militarism and violence. I knew from a very early age that my dad was a hardcore pacifist who did not believe in violence under any circumstances, even in cases of self-defense. I remember my mother explaining that if my father had been drafted, he would have been a conscientious objector; he would have served the country in a nonviolent capacity but would never pick up a gun, even if it meant jail time. Obviously, we were not allowed to play with war toys.

When I was a bit older, I learned that my father was a huge critic of US foreign policy. He wanted the United States out of the Middle East and favored a complete end to our economic and military support of Israel. In addition to his staunch Christianity, he developed a great admiration for Islam. I remember him commenting in his typical detached, analytical manner during the Iranian Revolution, "This will be interesting." In his elder years, he became a local lecturer on the virtues of Islam and an outspoken critic of George W. Bush and the Iraq War. He condemned Bush from the pulpit during his annual "Prince of Peace" sermon and once led a rally chant: "George Bush is a dangerous man!" He would never in his life consider flying an American flag.

During the 2012 presidential election, I remember Mitt Romney commenting that Obama was not taught to love this country. I remember the comment because it made no sense to me. A person does not have to be taught to love his or her own country; you love your country because it's your home—and you criticize it for the same reason. My parents did not teach me to love the country; they did not have to. But they did teach me to love God and put Him first. In my father's estimation, if there were ever a conflict between that which God requires—what is morally right—and that which the nation requires, it would be cross before crown every time.

As a deeply religious man, my father had great respect for the prophetic tradition—for the idea that a person needs to bear witness and speak truth to power, even if you cannot see an immediate impact. He believed that intention matters, a concept that Jewish tradition refers to as *kavanah*. For example, when he did not want to vote for either Nixon or McGovern in 1972, he explained that withholding your vote as a protest is not the same thing as not voting out of apathy or ignorance. I recently heard a similar point made at a deliberative democracy meeting: A lot of people do not vote in elections, not out of apathy but because "they don't care about what political leaders want them to do."[11] Many are very involved in their communities otherwise, so they should not be considered apathetic. Intention matters.

Along with my father, my mother also taught us the importance of personal integrity and doing the right thing, regardless of other people's actions and even when nobody is watching. When I was in third grade, the teacher gave everyone in the class raffle tickets to sell. Mom told me to give them back and tell the teacher that our family does not believe in gambling. So, despite my natural timidity, I approached the teacher, and in a small voice told her I could not sell the tickets and why. That is an experience I have never forgotten, both in terms of standing up for principles and in terms of the content of the act itself. While I do not personally assume the hardcore antigambling position my mother espoused, I would be hard-pressed to ever vote for casinos or anything like that, due to the way I was raised. It just doesn't seem right. The values instilled early in life run deep.

My mother, who served as a missionary in Japan in the 1950s, had a *stubbornly naïve heart*: When learning of some gross injustice or heartbreaking lack of compassion, she would always exclaim, "I will *never* be able to understand why people are like that!" Born in 1927 and raised in Jim Crow Louisiana, she most certainly witnessed deep racism firsthand, and that is probably the reason she left the state as soon as she finished college and never looked back. Although her sisters joined the Daughters of the American Revolution, my mother denounced that organization for discriminating against African American women.[12] She also refused to take even a sip of alcohol because she "learned early on the horrors of alcoholism." She was a woman of strong, unwavering principles, and she preserved her big compassionate heart and her Christian willingness to forgive for the entire ninety-one years of her life.

Personally, I did not pay attention to politics until the presidential campaign of Ronald Reagan, whom my high school friends and I considered an elderly laughing stock who didn't have a chance. One kid jokingly said they were going to freeze Reagan and defrost him every four years so he could keep running for president. In hindsight that seems a little harsh, given Reagan had only run twice before, in 1968 and 1976. Unfortunately, however, the third time was the charm; Reagan got elected in 1980, my junior year in high school, and held office for eight years.

My history teacher in tenth grade used to lecture us at length about the terrible failures of President Carter and the greatness of candidate Reagan. My father, being a history professor himself, tried to talk about history with my teacher during Parents' Night, but the man would not stop bragging about being a karate coach; he had no discernible interest in history, which outraged my father. At least that teacher was better than my psychology instructor who repeatedly told the class that "all gay men are child molesters and serial killers." That inspired my friend, whose gay brother was repeatedly hospitalized after being gay-bashed, to give our teacher some educational materials, which he angrily refused. I guess that was life in the 1970s before political correctness.

Considering that context, it is no surprise that when I thought I might be gay as a thirteen-year-old, it seemed like a fate worse than death, and so I prayed really hard to Jesus to make me heterosexual. I knew that kids at my school constantly made fun of "lezzies," and I feared becoming a pariah. I could not imagine having a happy life as a gay person. Things were different back then. Homosexual acts were illegal in Florida and many other states and actually remained so, until the *Lawrence v. Texas* decision in 2003. Back in 1977, thanks to the homophobic activism of Miami orange juice queen Anita Bryant, the Florida legislature made it illegal for same-sex couples to adopt children, a law not reversed until 2010. Moreover, it was legal for employers to discriminate against LGBT people all over the country until 2020 when the Supreme Court rendered that unconstitutional in *Bostock v. Clayton County, Georgia*. Hence lesbian and gay Floridians in the 1970s (and beyond) had reason to be afraid, and consequently at age thirteen, I made the deliberate decision to never think about female bodies again but instead to actively focus on guys. I needed a boyfriend stat!

During junior high school, I did not fit in with the so-called popular kids, who came from wealthy families and had material possessions that my parents could not afford and did not value. I clearly remember the day invitations to Cotillion went out. The well-heeled kids were buzzing with excitement, my friends and I excluded. At the time I took it in stride, but a few years later, I coveted an invitation. When I told my father I wanted to attend Cotillion, he said, "I'll see what I can do." Even though he personally scorned that sort of thing, he got me in, which impressed me greatly. As president of the PTA for many years, he had connections!

Excited about the event, I made a special dress for the occasion, using a Butterick pattern and my mom's Singer sewing machine, but once I got to the event, I felt extremely awkward. I am sure the homemade dress did not help any. Consequently, I gave up on the idea of hanging with the upper-class kids and gravitated to the stoner crowd, which included a lot of teens who were not intellectually inclined. For example, many of the boys openly worried about passing the "functional literacy test" required for graduation—the "funky lit," they called it. Again, I did not fit in, but at least I had more fun.

IN THE 1970S, IT ONLY "SEEMED LIKE NOTHING HAPPENED"

While I was focused on adolescent drama, a lot was happening politically during the late 1970s. Contrary to the title of one history of that decade, *It Seemed Like Nothing Happened*, "1977 and 1978 marked the rapid demise of the liberal era."[13] Despite holding the presidency and both houses of Congress, Democrats did not pass their own bills for tax reform, consumer protection, same-day voter registration, health care reform, minimum wage, or labor relations. All of them got defeated. "The precursors of the Reagan revolution were clearly visible."[14] As a consequence of Carter's capitulation during a time in which the DP held unchecked power, an "Anybody but Carter" effort emerged from the left that yielded primary challenges from Jerry Brown and, more significantly, Ted Kennedy.[15] While Carter ended up winning the Democratic nomination with 40 percent of the delegates, Reagan beat him by a landslide in the general election, thanks partly to the so-called Reagan Democrats, the white working-class voters who crossed party lines to support his conservative agenda.

The extreme levels of income inequality that plague the world today started to emerge during the 1970s. Under Carter, business interests began their attacks on unions that accelerated during the Reagan years. Without unions to advocate for them, workers saw wages flatten or decline. In addition, taxes on the wealthiest Americans went down significantly during this same time period. Carter cut the capital gains tax in half, and then Reagan lowered the highest marginal tax rate from 70 percent to 28 percent. This made it possible for CEOs and other industry leaders to keep more of their salaries, which incentivized the push for massive pay increases at the top.

Thomas Piketty documents that income inequality in the United States began skyrocketing precisely because of changes in the tax code.[16] From

1930 to 1980, very high incomes were taxed by as much as 90 percent, not only to finance public goods but also to prevent the emergence of a small cadre of wealthy elites who could essentially become new feudal lords—a trend that may already be happening.[17] The lowering of the top bracket prompted corporate executives to pursue oversized salaries (not tied to productivity) because they could pocket most of the money. While a lot of people accept some level of income inequality, most probably do not realize that in 2018 the top 1% in the United States made $1.32 million on average, while the 99% made only $50,107 on average.[18] Moreover, since inheritance taxes, originally designed to prevent the emergence of familial dynasties, have been derided as "death taxes" and eroded, the currently vast levels of economic inequality will simply increase over time—unless the Left can reverse the tide.

While such extreme inequality is obviously unfair, it also threatens the continuation of our republic over time, contributing to our Machiavellian moment (see the introduction). Currently, the super-wealthy have so much political influence that we arguably already live under an oligarchy. Extreme levels of economic inequality threaten democratic self-rule because, as Aristotle argued in ancient days, citizenship requires participation: ruling and being ruled in turn. High levels of wealth inequality make that impossible, according to Aristotle, because you end up with wealthy people too arrogant to be ruled and poor folks too habituated into servility to rule. Inequality in society generates a dynamic of power and deference, not the foundation for self-rule among equals. Consequently, Aristotle stressed the importance of a large middle class as the basis for a free and equal society.[19]

WAKING UP

Out of all the political turmoil bubbling up around 1980, the Christian Right's Moral Majority caught my attention the most. On the cusp of becoming an adult woman and making my own decisions, I bristled at the idea that my autonomy and personal choices might be curtailed by male authority, whether exercised in the household or by government, and the Christian Right's hierarchical view of gender relations violated my belief in the equality of all people. My first political act was reading to my parents a passage from the local newspaper about the Moral Majority and then dramatically proclaiming, "They represent everything I stand opposed to!"

My parents just stared at me, unable to formulate a response. I cannot recall with certainty the year of that interaction—whether I was in high school or college—but the Moral Majority emerged as a political force around 1980 to help galvanize support for Ronald Reagan and became increasingly prominent during his administration.[20]

In 1982, I started college at the University of Florida (UF), which I attended for two years, before transferring to Smith, a Seven Sisters college in Northampton, Massachusetts, thanks to a generous financial aid package. From my senior year in high school through my sophomore year of college, I dated a white working-class guy, who moved to Florida from Detroit. He's actually the one who took me to my first gay bar, during his gay brother's visit from San Francisco. (The brother clued me in about polyester being uncool, which led to serious improvements in my wardrobe choices!) The night before I left for college, my boyfriend and I attended his heterosexual brother's wedding, where my beau said, "Next time it will be you and me walking down the aisle," a comment that pleased me greatly. I wanted to marry him, but my parents had repeatedly impressed upon me, throughout my childhood, the importance of waiting until after college to take such a step. Indeed, while they never said anything negative about my boyfriend at the time, years later my father informed me that they were worried I was going to marry him and "turn into a Florida redneck."

As it turns out, it was not my boyfriend's professed interest in marriage that changed my life that night but rather a conversation I had at the reception with a young evangelical woman. She wanted me to know that men are created by God to be dominant heads of household, and that as a Christian woman I will have to submit to my husband, as it says in the Bible, which was news to me, having been raised in a liberal denomination. Ironically, her proselytizing did not recruit me to her side but ended up igniting a crisis of faith in me. A few years later, I broke with Christianity completely and lived with no religious practice at all, until 1999, when I started practicing Judaism, before converting in 2002. So, right after starting college, I came to reject Christian authoritarianism in personal as well as political terms, and I did not return to the Church until 2014 when I became an Episcopalian.

My boyfriend also started to become politically aware during college, but in support of Ronald Reagan (although for economic rather than religious reasons). Formerly a long-haired stoner, he cut his hair short and pursued a major in business administration, whereas I wanted to be a "counselor." Luckily, my beloved did not embrace religious conservatism in any way and so his politics did not interfere with our intimacy, although he said he could never officially live with me outside of wedlock because his very Catholic, authoritarian parents would "kill" him; mine would have simply expressed deep disappointment. At first our partisan differences did not matter much, but as I became more political, they started to bother me more. We did not break up because of that. He broke up with me ostensibly so he could play the field, but in actuality, it was probably because I had decided to leave UF for Smith College.

I will never forget, right after Thanksgiving, telling my boyfriend that I wanted to transfer to another college—a decision my parents strongly supported, since they always wanted me to have a good liberal arts education at a small private college up north, but I had rebelled by attending a state university along with my high school friends. My boyfriend and I were lying in bed when I told him I was considering a move. In response, he looked at me and said, "If I could get out of here, I would do it in a minute, and I wouldn't look back. And I'm not promising I'm ever going to marry you." It sounds harsh, but it was honest. By the time fall of 1984 rolled around, however, he did ask me to marry him, but a lot had changed for me by then, and his Republican political views were a deal-breaker. He argued that our differences should not matter because his mom and dad had nothing in common. "Right," I responded, "just ten children and the Catholic religion."

DISCOVERING FEMINISM

As an adolescent, I never felt that I fit in with my peers for a range of reasons—too poor for the rich kids, too mousey for the popular girls, too academic for the stoners, too rebellious for the honors students, and possibly gay to boot—and the anxiety that sense of outsiderness caused obviously transferred with me to Smith College. I remember asking at orientation what kind of music Smith students listen to—a question that now sounds ridiculous—and I found out then that Smith had no typical student. Recognizing the uniqueness of every person, the institution encouraged students to develop themselves as whole people in the context of a rigorous curriculum and an array of extracurricular activities. It took a little adjusting, but I finally felt that I had found my place. Suddenly being intellectually inclined was the norm, and within that milieu, I found my classes very stimulating. "Research shows that women's colleges are particularly effective in producing leaders," and graduates of women's colleges are overrepresented in male-dominated professions across society[21]—and among first ladies. Both Nancy Reagan and Barbara Bush attended Smith College; Hillary Clinton chose Wellesley.

During my years at Smith, feminism animated the discourse on campus. Completely new to me at the time, learning about feminist theory stimulated me on multiple levels, socially, intellectually, and, perhaps most importantly, politically. As I became aware of the many atrocities and injustices perpetrated against women by men, I became increasingly radicalized. Mary Daly's powerful condemnation of male-dominated Christianity in *Beyond God the Father* really resonated with me, given my spiritual crisis at the time.[22] From her books and others, I also learned about the cruel traditions of misogyny that existed all over the globe— including widow-burning in India, foot-binding in China, and genital mutilation in Africa—as well as the seemingly mundane practices of date rape, domestic violence, and sexual harassment, so common in the United States. Exposed to scathing feminist critiques, I found myself gravitating toward more radical solutions than those offered by mainstream "liberal feminism." As I used to explain it, deriving from the Lockean tradition, "liberal feminism" wanted half the politicians, the military, and the CEOs to be women, whereas "radical feminism," growing out of Marxism, aimed to transform society by moving beyond powermongering, militarism, and capitalism, as well as the patriarchal sex/gender system itself.

Feminist legal scholar Catharine MacKinnon articulated the ways in which male dominance and female objectification actually constitute gender as we know it in our society. To be masculine is to enact dominance; to be feminine is to embrace one's own objectification.[23] As MacKinnon so bluntly put it, "Man fucks woman; subject verb object."[24] When seen through a radical feminist lens, traditional courtship rituals suddenly look like sexual harassment or even rape, and traditional marriage resembles prostitution. Perhaps radical feminism is making a comeback, given the controversy that erupted in 2018 when some called the popular Christmas song "Baby It's Cold Outside" a "little rapey," giving pundits on FOX News agita.[25] According to radical feminists, the sex/gender system does not arise naturally; gender is constructed through social practices, cultural traditions, and popular media to benefit men at the expense of women. MacKinnon focused particularly on the ways in which the vast pornography industry helps create and reproduce male dominance and female submission, making the issue of pornography way more than simply a question of censorship versus free speech. At first, I found their so-called "anti-sex" position convincing and embraced the group Women Against Pornography, but I switched to the "pro-sex" side when a friend handed me her tattered copy of *Coming to Power*—the lesbian BDSM book that roiled the movement—and said, "Here, I don't need this anymore."[26]

The 1980s were also the time when critiques of second-wave feminism by women of color rose to prominence, with the publication of *This Bridge Called My Back* and other texts.[27] Every generation of college students probably remembers a particular book that loomed large, and at Smith College it was *The Color Purple* by Alice Walker.[28] Those books and others raised my consciousness about racism and introduced me to the concept of white privilege. Having grown up in a racially segregated southern community and attending a series of schools from fourth grade on that were either essentially all-white or provided little opportunity for interactions across race, including Smith College that enrolled only ninety-five Black students out of twenty-five hundred, I had a lot to learn.

In short, during my two years at Smith, I began questioning all kinds of power relationships in our society. I began by rejecting the power of men over women and whites over Blacks. Next, I learned about "compulsory heterosexuality" and the liberating possibility of "lesbian existence," a topic that nearly caused a brawl in my feminist philosophy class and that spoke to me very personally.[29] Then, I discovered the socialist feminist critique of unjust class power under capitalism. Finally, with more and more categories added to the analytical mix, I found myself logically gravitating toward anarchist feminism. When is it ever legitimate for some people to exercise power over others without their consent?

POLITICAL ACTIVISM

My first opportunity to vote in a presidential election came during my first semester at Smith, and Geraldine Ferraro was on the Walter Mondale for President ticket, a historic first. In the primary, I had voted for the Reverend Jesse Jackson (and would again in 1988). Heir to the civil rights movement, Jackson's multiracial coalition supported single-payer health care, free community college, the Equal Rights Amendment, lesbian and gay rights, pay equity, an end to Reagan's War on Drugs, the anti-apartheid movement, and reparations for slavery. During the 1984 election season, although I had many conversations about electoral politics and the need to vote against Reagan in the dining room at the Laura Scales House, my only interface with any actual campaign involved working with the antinuclear movement.

I will never forget that particular Election Day because this thin-blooded, Florida girl stood on the street in twenty-degree weather with a "Massachusetts Freeze" sign—referring to the nuclear freeze movement, not the weather—until I was so cold I literally could not bend my fingers to unzip my warm, albeit unfashionable, puffy down coat. The nuclear freeze campaign started in 1980 on the heels of the Three Mile Island nuclear disaster a year earlier, and it "sparked one of the largest peace mobilizations in US history."[30] I was all in. When I got back to the Laura Scales House dorm, a conservative woman, who had heard me opining every day for weeks in the dining hall about the outrages of Reagan, looked at me and said, "Have you seen the news?" and then she just started laughing. With trepidation, I walked into the living room to check the television. Sadly, Reagan won by a landslide, winning every single state except Mondale's Minnesota—and DC, which should be a state.

Although I registered in 1983 as a Democrat at age eighteen, I never engaged much with electoral politics, besides voting, until much later in life. Moreover, during my college years, I do not remember anyone ever inviting me to work on a campaign or anything like that. I have no recollection of anyone from either party reaching out to students at my college, although I did see a few stickers around campus for a young man making a first-time run for the US Senate, named John Kerry. In addition, given that my political views, even as initially formed in the early 1980s, stood distinctly to the left of the Democratic Party, I did not think it worthwhile to spend time phoning my representatives or writing them letters. In fact, I still take that position, given that our so-called representatives generally vote in accordance with the interests of wealthy constituents and donors.[31] I also believe most of them already have their minds made up about policy; either they already support my position or they do not care what a left-wing activist thinks. That said, I still sometimes contact my representatives anyway. Moreover, now that we have social media, it is possible to quickly organize masses of people to deluge a representative around a particular issue or engage in public shaming, which arguably has much more of an impact than just writing as an individual.

Instead of focusing on elections, my activism centered on stopping the arms race, that era's existential threat; terminating our country's imperialist support for brutal authoritarianism in Latin America; and ending racist apartheid in South Africa, the three major progressive movements of the times.[32] Even though the New Right had great success with the Reagan Revolution, an active Left also existed in the 1980s. Indeed, "Reagan foreign policymakers faced a broad-based, post–Vietnam War–era peace movement that actively resisted military intervention" in Latin America and the arms race in general.[33] Supporting the peace movement came naturally to me, given my upbringing, but my active engagement with the other two movements began as soon as I found out that the US government supported, and even participated in, torture, disappearances, death squads, assassinations, and overthrowing democratically elected governments; I felt called to action.[34] As happened when I learned about the politics of the so-called "Christian" Right, hypocrisy really bugs me and often prompts me to act.

So, when one of my housemates—a super smart, fresh-faced blonde lesbian—invited me to join her in an action against the war machine, I immediately said yes. She and I, on one very cold New England morning, went into town to meet up with some older activist women for a vigil at the General Dynamics plant, about an hour's drive away. I do not remember many of the details at this point, over thirty years later, but I do clearly recall standing against a chain link fence with the other women, holding protest signs, while a man in a trench coat went around and photographed all of us, I assumed at the time for a government file. I remember feeling a huge sense of empowerment, as I stood there unflinchingly, like I was courageously facing down the enemies of justice, bearing witness like my father had taught me. Then we drove back to town. No doubt the vigil was part of a larger plan of action, but that was the only time I did anything with the older "townie" activists.

The second political action I remember involved participating in a student protest against the CIA when they were on campus recruiting. It was the 1980s, and all the seniors were walking around campus in their navy-blue suits with giant shoulder pads and pussy-bow blouses, applying for high-powered corporate jobs. Our college president, Jill Kerr Conway, had convinced top firms that a good liberal arts education prepares students for success in any arena. So, why not work for the CIA? Indeed, shouldn't the CIA be 50 percent women?

Needless to say, I did not support the corporate agenda or the military-industrial complex, and I did not consider more women working for the CIA a plus. In fact, when I learned that the United States ran the Army School of the Americas that actually trained Latin American military operatives in techniques of torture, like the ones we used in Vietnam (and later Iraq), it shocked and outraged me. When given the opportunity to confront the CIA, I felt anxious inside but boldly took my place anyway. It went down like this: About a dozen of us went into the CIA recruitment session, looking like the typical students we were, but when the time came, we asked questions like, "Will I be able to partici- pate in CIA-sponsored assassinations?" and "Will I get a chance to train people how to torture at the School for the Americas?" Then we all got up and walked out. We appalled a few of our blue-suited classmates, but we made our point, and I again felt very courageous, speaking truth to power. I do not remember if this protest occurred in spring 1985 or the subsequent fall, but 1986 marks the beginning of a nationwide protest to get the CIA off college campuses.[35]

My third major protest took place during February 1986 when hun- dreds of students and I took over College Hall to demand that the college divest millions of dollars from companies with ties to South Africa.[36] This action was part of a second wave of student protests across the country, a divestment movement that began in 1977 with the assassination of Steven Biko.[37] We used to commemorate Biko's murder in one of the South Afri- can protest songs we used to sing with this refrain: "They killed Steven Biko this morning, . . . dying for freedom in South Africa." We aspired to get arrested, so as to make the news—and I was ready—but our new college president, Mary Maples Dunn, denied us that opportunity—and a criminal record. She simply conducted business out of her beautiful home on Paradise Pond, and we continued to block the building until the Board of Trustees agreed to review the divestment process.[38] The national movement continued for the rest of the year, and many of us wore arm- bands to commencement or taped "Divest" to the top of our graduation caps, which upset some of our peers who considered it "inappropriate."

A lot of protests simply aspire to bear witness—an important goal—but, as it turns out, the student divestment movement had a real impact. Not only did Smith College end up divesting $39 million,[39] but "the groundswell of opposition to apartheid led Congress to override President Reagan's veto of the Comprehensive Anti-Apartheid Act of 1986."[40] Overall, by "December 1986, it was estimated that almost $4 billion of investments had been affected" because of student activism, and the movement prompted many new students to become politically connected.[41] The divestment campaign worked, and that, in turn, played a key role in bringing down apartheid. Perhaps that explains the intense fear inspired by the current Boycott, Divest, and Sanction movement against Israel for its treatment of the Palestinians.

In reviewing my early activism and thinking about the impetus of my involvement, I believe that my exposure to injustice and to visions of the means by which the world could become a better place through readings assigned in the liberal arts college classroom resonated with the deep-seated humanitarian values instilled in me by my gentle Christian parents—the equal worth and dignity of every person, opposition to violence, basic fairness, and the commandment to love and serve, for example. In addition, I had been schooled about the superiority of "American democracy" through a Cold War civics class that contrasted our ideals of liberty, political equality, individual rights, due process, and democratic self-rule with the horrors of Nazi and Soviet authoritarianism. Those factors prepped me for participation, but the key activator was being invited to participate in a political action by someone I knew, having the opportunity to engage. In the 1960s, idealistic northern white youth became active in the civil rights movement when they became aware of the racist double standards of Jim Crow *and* saw an opportunity to get involved. A similar thing happened to me: I became active when US hypocrisy became visible to me, *and* I was invited to participate in a protest by an activist friend.

LIVING AT HOME BEFORE IT WAS COOL

Critical of the corporate sector, I did not apply for any jobs, high-powered or otherwise, during my senior year, despite my vague fantasy about moving to Boston. Instead, I moved back to Florida, lived with my parents (although not in the basement, since the state sits at sea level), and continued my activism at the intersection of the peace and feminist movements. I landed a job making a whopping $10,000 a year as a childcare worker at a group home for emotionally disturbed adolescent girls, some of whom needed in-patient psychiatric care but could not get it, since Reagan had cut federal funding for state mental hospitals.

It was during my job interview that I decided to start going by my middle name, Claire, instead of continuing my childhood nickname Becky, short for my legal first name, Rebecca. Although my parents named me after the saint, I reclaimed the name in honor of Claire Lacombe, an activist I learned about during my one history class on the French Revolution. A leader of the Revolutionary Republican Women, Claire Lacombe strode the streets of Paris in pantaloons with a pistol on her belt and forced the reactionary market women to don the tricolored cockade of the Revolution. I took the course because my father said if I were to take only one history course, it should be on the French Revolution, and that course actually laid the groundwork for some of my future graduate work.

Thus, I began my postcollege life as Claire and quickly ascended the tiny ranks of the group home to the case manager position, making $15,000. I had no problem with the low pay, since I lived for free with my parents, until I discovered that the one and only male childcare worker, whom I supervised, made $20,000 a year. My senior research project had focused on gender discrimination—specifically the psychological mechanism through which women acknowledge the existence of discrimination yet deny being a victim of it themselves—and here it was in my first job.[42] When I asked the executive director about it, she said he had negotiated his salary based on past earnings, and he would not work for $10,000 a year. I had no job history beyond cashiering part-time and had not even tried to negotiate a higher salary. When I told my mother about it, she said, "He has a *family* to support, Becky; you don't." She was never a feminist! Shortly thereafter, I moved to another case management job with a different organization.

My activist work, during my postcollege years, had several components. First, I joined my parents' group, the Peace Advocates, a church-based organization, comprised of us three plus two elderly ladies from church, that met weekly at our house. At the time, I was quite enamored with the sanctuary movement, then popular on the left—a national political and religious movement that began in the early 1980s to provide shelter, protection, and support for Central American refugees in church sanctuaries, after the federal government made it harder to claim asylum. We had a lot of great discussions, but it was not an activist group.

One night, my father got a phone call about an hour before the Peace Advocates gathering from a man who said he wanted to attend the meeting, which he saw listed in the local Peace and Justice Center newsletter, and he asked for very specific directions to our location. It was a nice evening, so the five of us sat outside by the pool and waited for him to arrive. A new member, how exciting! As the meeting start time arrived, a black helicopter started circling our home, just flying around and around. After five to ten minutes, I declared it must be a CIA helicopter and dramatically went inside. My mother scoffed—"Don't be ridiculous,

Becky!"—yet the man never arrived. And indeed, we now know that the Reagan administration's Office of Public Diplomacy did in fact monitor "the activities of citizen groups opposed to US intervention in El Salvador. These included the leftist solidarity movement and mainstream church groups."[43] So, I was not crazy! Maybe.

In addition, I got very involved with the Statewide Coalition for Peace and Justice, as part of its Feminist Task Force (FTF). On meeting Saturdays, I would drive forty-five minutes in my burgundy Toyota Corolla—blasting Ferron, Holly Near, or Sweet Honey in the Rock on the cassette player—to the Friends Meeting House in St. Petersburg to participate in a separatist group of mostly older women, some of whom had dropped the patronym and had names like Linda Suzanne or nicknames like Oak. One time I asked Linda Suzanne the reason so many women refused to become feminists. She said, "Claire, we are the descendants of cowards. All the strong women were killed during the witch burnings. Our ancestors sucked cock to survive." OK, then!

During the late '80s, I feared for the future of the country. I read *The Handmaid's Tale* with horror. My first girlfriend, who was seventeen years older than I, thought that if Pat Robertson got elected in 1988, he would put lesbians and gay men into concentration camps or resort to firing squads. She advocated armed resistance—but only at the bar; she was not politically active. At FTF meetings, we debated the justness of armed resistance: no justice, no peace! Believe it or not, one movement leader in my hometown, an older lady who has since passed away, proposed bombing the power company and asked if I would join her. Uh, that would be a hard pass.

EXPLORING FEMINIST THEORY

Writing this memoir has allowed me to reread some of the texts that transformed my thinking as a young twenty-something. Having grown up in a highly segregated community and attending a series of nearly all-white schools, Audre Lorde's book, *Sister Outsider*, educated me about race and class privilege. She asked white feminists, "How do you deal with the fact that the women who clean your houses and tend your children while you attend conferences on feminist theory are, for the most part, poor women and women of Color?"[44] Although I came from a household in which my mother did all the domestic labor—and being culturally middle class, I still clean my own house—Lorde's point still resonated with me intellectually and politically. Written in 1984, *Sister Outsider* became one of the key texts that led to the flourishing of diversity within second-wave feminism.

Looking back, it seems clear that being a part of a marginalized yet politically righteous and morally powerful feminist community amelio- rated my own personal feelings of outsiderness, of not fitting in. Lorde said this about that:

> Those of us who stand outside the circle of this society's definition of acceptable women; those of us who have been forged in the crucibles of difference—those of us who are poor, who are lesbians, who are Black, who are older—know that survival is not an academic skill. It is learning how to stand alone, unpopular and sometimes reviled, and how to make common cause with those others identified as outside the structures in order to define and seek a world in which we can all flourish. It is learning how to take our differences and make them strengths. For the master's tools will never dismantle the master's house. They may allow us temporarily to beat him at his own game, but they will never enable us to bring about genuine change.[45]

Lorde and others certainly helped validate lesbian identity and opened up a space in which I could come out. I guess I exemplify the lament of my conservative Sunday school teacher, who had a lesbian daughter and once said, "Some kids go off to college and come back thinking they know more than the Lord."

The book that I loved most, right after college, was *Going Out of Our Minds: The Metaphysics of Liberation* by Sonia Johnson, who was excommunicated from the Mormon Church in 1979 for supporting the ERA and ran for president in 1984 on the progressive Citizens Party ticket (with endorsements from the Peace and Freedom Party and the Socialist Party USA). It should not be a surprise that she met with the same hos- tility third-party candidates face today. Johnson advocated what academics call "cultural feminism," a strand of feminism that builds on the positive, life-affirming values historically associated with women and encourages the development of a women's community not tied to patriarchy—or should I say, womyn's community? While I no longer embrace the second-wave feminist hope that women around the world might all unite on the basis of gender and create a better world, Johnson's book discusses a number of themes that foreshadow points I make later in this book.

Johnson spent years organizing for the ERA with the National Organization for Women (NOW), leading the more radical side of that effort, engaging in civil disobedience to advance the cause. She recounts the ways in which engaging in civil disobedience develops the capacity for courage in everyday women. For example, she quotes one woman who said after an action, "I am just a housewife from Maryland. But I knelt in the street for over an hour. I could have been arrested. I *would* have been arrested. And I did it for women. I didn't know I had the courage to do anything like that."[46] But she did. Johnson says the action left the women feeling "euphoric" and "high in admiration" for their own bravery.[47]

Johnson's radical tactics ended up putting her on the wrong side of the NOW establishment. It all started at the NOW conference in 1981 when Johnson offered a workshop on civil disobedience and over five hundred women attended. While that sounds positive, it meant that only a few women attended a simultaneous session offered by NOW leaders, and they were not pleased.[48] So the leaders convened a meeting in which women were asked to choose "either-NOW-or-Sonia."[49] Sadly, when authority pushed back, Sonia's supporters abandoned her. Out of the hundreds who had attended her training, all but a few sided with NOW leadership; some even turned on Johnson, blaming her for the conflict.[50] Johnson recounts that the entire experience reminded her of the authoritarianism she experienced in the Mormon Church.[51] She says NOW leaders were "using the same methods of intimidation and fear to control the group," and sadly they had "the same enormous success—the room was full of thoroughly cowed women."[52]

That experience profoundly affected Johnson's thinking about progressive change. She began to understand the ways in which women internalize their own oppression by developing the habits of deference to authority that make patriarchy function smoothly. Johnson explains the phenomenon by quoting Mary Wollstonecraft, a feminist who wrote during the Age of Democratic Revolution: "Considering the length of time that women have been dependent, is it surprising that some of them hug their chains and fawn like the spaniel?"[53] To put it in terms I use later in this book, many women have become accustomed to obeying the "Prince" inside their heads who demands deference to power. In Gramsci's terms, that is how hegemony works: people consent to be dominated.

In *Going Out of Our Minds*, Johnson offers a new approach to feminism that grew out of those painful experiences. First, drawing on the philosophy of aikido, Johnson argues that when you fight directly against what you oppose, you actually give it energy. To use a current example, it often seems that the relentless attacks on President Trump actually empower him. What if the media ignored him instead? What if Democrats focused more attention on espousing a positive, alternative vision instead of reacting to the agenda he sets?

Johnson's cultural feminist vision seeks to do exactly that, by developing a new life-affirming culture on the basis of the values traditionally ascribed to women, and that alternative culture formed the milieu in which my feminist activism in southwest Florida in the late 1980s occurred. We held women-only gatherings, went to women's music festivals, and explored feminist neo-paganism with saging and other rituals. We marched separately during statewide political actions and valorized the women's peace camp at Greenham Common (1981–2000), which was "one of the most significant antinuclear peace mobilizations of the 1980s," and the smaller one at Seneca Falls that had convened in the summer of 1983.[54] We wanted to transform the world.

Like Gramsci, Johnson focuses on the need to change people's consciousness as part of the revolutionary process. "When we envision the future without first changing our present feelings, without undoing our indoctrination, we project all our unexamined assumptions into the future, recreating the old reality, making it inevitable."[55] Cultural change must precede political change. While moving beyond our internalized habits of deference to patriarchy is hard, it is the only thing we have control over, she tells us. "We cannot change the minds of the men in power. . . . We can only change ourselves."[56] The personal is political.

Johnson's experiences taught her that engagement in power politics-as-usual cannot lead to the kind of radical change we need. "*Because the means are the ends*, the problems caused by patriarchy cannot be solved through the patriarchal system with the tools that system hands us."[57] We cannot make change from within the system, using the master's tools. "As long as we think we can change the situation sufficiently through electoral politics, lobbying, demonstrating, letter writing, working for more and better legislation, by some sort of external action, we are not going to be able to feel or think our way out of patriarchy or imagine the new ways; we have to let go *before* there's an alternative to hold on to."[58] Refusing to participate in power politics-as-usual opens our minds to new ideas, but we have to be willing to take a leap of faith.

Looking back at the time I spent as an activist during the 1980s, I can see that we did not stop the war machine or the ascent of right-wing forces, which morphed over time from Reagan's antigovernment rhetoric to George W. Bush's war crimes to the malignancy of Trump's quasi-fascist authoritarianism. We did, however, bear witness, and bearing witness matters. As Lorde argues, we cannot remain silent in the face of evil:

> I have come to believe over and over again that what is most important to me must be spoken, made verbal and shared, even at the risk of having it bruised or misunderstood. . . . What are the words you do not yet have? What do you need to say? What are the tyrannies you swallow day by day and attempt to make your own, until you sicken and die of them, still in silence? Perhaps for some of you here today, I am the face of one of your fears. Because I am a woman, because I am Black, because I am a lesbian, because I am myself—a Black woman warrior poet doing my work—come to ask, are you doing yours?[59]

And it was during this moment in time, two years after college, that I made a choice about my own life's work. After a long internal struggle, I decided not to continue with a career in social work but rather to embrace a life of teaching and learning, just like my father before me, who decided to become a professor rather than a pastor. So, I left Florida for graduate school in 1988 and would not return until 2017 when my mother entered her final years.

CHAPTER 2

MY FIRST CAREER

DEMOCRATIC THEORIST

Exiting the world of social movement feminism, I moved to New Jersey and entered the PhD program at Rutgers University in political science, where I began the transformation from activist to academic political theorist with a specialization in democratic and feminist theory. This process took me away from the women-only spaces of cultural feminism and introduced me to the civic engagement and deliberative democracy community. The heavy workload required by both my doctoral program and the two universities at which I taught after graduation left little time for political activism, but I was able to use my teaching and research to advocate for participatory democracy, feminism, and progressive politics. While I enjoyed being a professor, over time I found that the lack of work/life balance began to wear on me, and so for a range of reasons, I took a leap of faith and gave up a tenured faculty position at a major research university and became a writer-activist, a decision I have never regretted.

THE POLITICAL CONTEXT

When I started graduate school in 1988, the political situation in the United States was grim, similar to the way it looked to me in 2020. There was a destructive right-wing president in the White House, whom many people inexplicably loved, who had engaged in criminal activities with

43

impunity, and who was pushing the world closer to end times. Moreover, with a presidential election looming, the Democrats failed to nominate the dynamic progressive candidate, the Reverend Jesse Jackson, opting instead for the milquetoasty Michael Dukakis, who ran on competence. Consequently, it looked like the Reagan administration would continue its reign with the election of Vice President George H. W. Bush. It appeared that even a strong left-wing political movement had been unable to affect the direction of US politics—to stop the arms race, US imperialism in Latin America, or apartheid in South Africa. Things looked dark.

Then, suddenly, everything began to change. Most importantly, the Cold War ended as the Berlin Wall came down in 1989, followed by the Velvet Revolution, and two years later the Soviet Union collapsed. While the fall of the Eastern Bloc might look like a blow to the socialist cause, the governments in those countries were largely authoritarian and not exemplars of socialism as it is supposed to be, democratic. While some like to claim that Reagan-era militarism and bellicosity won the Cold War, studies show that reforms actually resulted from years of activism and consciousness-changing work inside the USSR and aligned countries. For example, conservative scholar Andrew Bacevich argues that "the courage of the dissidents who dared to challenge Soviet authority," as well as other internal factors, "probably made a greater contribution to undermining the Soviet Union than did the reconstitution of US military power in the 1980s."[1] Progressive scholar-activist David Cortright concurs: "The cold war was ended not by military build-ups but by Mikhail Gorbachev's 'new thinking,' which [began in 1987 and] broke decisively with the logic of militarism, and by the pressures of disarmament activism, which created a political climate conducive to arms reduction and East-West under-standing. . . . The Soviet system collapsed when millions of citizens and human rights campaigners in the East took to the streets in the historic 'velvet revolution' of 1989."[2]

In addition, the other two causes I supported in college also saw sudden, positive change. Aided by the bad publicity of the Iran-Contra scandal, the United States pulled away from its attempts to impose regime change in Nicaragua, albeit probably largely because the Nicaraguan people elected leaders who were friendlier to the United States in the 1990 elec-tion.[3] Moreover, the South African government suddenly released Nelson Mandela from prison in 1990, the apartheid regime began to crumble, and South Africa formed a democratic government in 1994. In all three cases, change came quickly and, to an outside observer, seemingly all of a sudden but in actuality after years of organizing. As Nelson Mandela reportedly said, "It always seems impossible, until it's done."[4]

With the demise of Soviet authoritarianism, democracy appeared to be on the rise all over the world, but as usual progress and reaction went hand in hand. Not willing to deliver the peace dividend the Left expected, government leaders reoriented US foreign policy toward the Middle East and justified continued defense spending for purposes of protecting access to oil, particularly after the Gulf War in 1990.[5] In addition, the valorization of the military and constant praise for the troops (that started with Reagan) became increasingly hegemonic in the 1990s, as Bill Clinton tried to shake the label of "draft dodger" and the Democratic Party its reputation as "national security wimps" by embracing military force and mythologizing those who wield it.[6] Today, "thank you for your service" has become an almost automatic mantra when encountering troops or vets. It was not always thus.

QUESTIONING ALL THAT IS SOLID

Pursuing a PhD in political theory—political philosophy within the discipline of political science—taught me to think more deeply and question the hegemonic beliefs I had acquired over time. As noted previously, hegemonic beliefs are ideas that bolster the power of the ruling class and have become so dominant that they pass as unquestioned common sense, like the idea that it is good for people to work hard for what they have, a theme constantly reinforced on country music radio, for example. That idea has not always existed. As Max Weber argued long ago, the Protestant work ethic—hard work is virtuous—that is now so entrenched in US culture, became dominant at a particular historical time, as European societies transitioned from feudalism to capitalism.[7] Working hard and saving money have not been a universal norm "since the dawn of time," to use a phrase unfortunately espoused in first-year college essays all over the country.

When I started graduate school, I had already learned to think critically about the dominant culture and was open to change, but graduate study would deepen my thinking significantly, and my consciousness shifted quickly. For example, during my very first graduate class, my feminist theory professor, Linda Zerilli—who would become a groundbreaking figure in the field but at the time was a just a junior faculty member—asked us to introduce ourselves and share our interest in feminism. So, I told everyone about my experiences in the women's community in Florida, quite proud of my activist bona fides. When I was done, Zerilli looked at me and said something to the effect of, "Well, that kind of cultural feminism assumes a problematic gender essentialism that is a real bugaboo in my class." And with that intellectual critique, she unmoored me from the political place at which I had settled after college and set me free to imagine the world in new, more creative ways. Zerilli was a great teacher and mentor to me, and she also served as an inspiring role model with her chic New York clothes and cool loft in the West Village.

When I took my first political theory class, Prof. Benjamin Barber's popular "Rousseau Seminar," I had the opportunity to think specifically about democracy for the first time. Having believed since childhood that every human being is fundamentally equal and entitled to a dignified life, I embraced democracy because that is the way that equals govern themselves, and I came to learn that a fully functioning democracy requires a democratic culture to undergird it. In light of my undergraduate interest in the French Revolution, I immediately took to the vision of participatory democracy articulated by Jean-Jacques Rousseau, whose writings inspired the antiroyalist, republicanism of the Jacobins who pushed the Revolution in France forward.[8]

Rousseau saw participatory democracy as the key to reconciling the anarchic freedom of the individual with communal life governed by laws. Famously noting that "man was/is born free, and everywhere he is in chains," Rousseau sought to explain the ways in which political power might be rendered legitimate, that is, compatible with the natural liberty and equality of men—and he did mean men—a question that had weighed on me since my undergraduate exploration of anarchist feminism.[9] To solve this puzzle, Rousseau reasoned that since a person is free when he obeys his own will, he can remain free, while also subject to the law, if he participates in writing the laws. "Obedience to the law one has prescribed for oneself is freedom" because by obeying self-authored law, you are obeying only your own will.[10] Thus, for Rousseau, legitimate government requires popular sovereignty; people must rule themselves.[11] While citizens might delegate responsibilities to political leaders for a period of time, the people can never surrender their sovereignty. Elected representatives and governors remain accountable to the people at all times. The people are boss.

Rousseau's theory of participatory democracy, radical popular sovereignty, and the accountability of elected officials to the people dovetails with similar arguments presented in the US context by Thomas Paine and

Thomas Jefferson around the same time. Both men favored the creation of a republic, in which the people could govern themselves for the common good without being dominated by any set of men, whether the political establishment, clerical authorities, or a local big shot and his cronies. As Paine put it: "There never did, nor never can exist a parliament, or any description of men, or any generation of men, in any country, possessed of the right or the power of binding or controlling posterity to the 'end of time,' or of commanding forever how the world shall be governed, or who shall govern it; . . . Every age and generation must be as free to act for itself, *in all cases*, as the ages and generation which preceded it."[12] Thus, the republican tradition is radically anti-authoritarian. The people are sovereign. No one tells them what to do. They decide for themselves.

Moreover, in this radical republican tradition that led to the founding of the United States, the people retain the right to revolution. That is, when those in power oppose the good of the people or stymie their ability to decide for themselves how to live, the people have the right not only to "petition the government for a redress of grievances," as stated in the US Constitution, but also to organize a revolution. Indeed, as Jefferson put it, "The tree of liberty must be refreshed from time to time with the blood of patriots and tyrants. It is its natural manure."[13]

Getting introduced to the concept of radical popular sovereignty at the tail end of the 1980s, when democracy seemed to be on the rise around the world, excited me intellectually, and I was elated to be able to study with Barber, who was one of the leading scholars in the burgeoning field of "democratic theory." After the Cold War ended, many people accepted Francis Fukuyama's claim that we had reached the "end of history" with the "unabashed victory of economic and political liberalism"—neoliberalism in today's parlance—but Barber spent his entire career contesting that claim.[14] He had written an important book in the 1980s called *Strong Democracy* that criticized liberalism for its reductionist depiction of human beings as atomistic individuals who formed society only to better protect their own selfish interests.[15] The liberal/neoliberal paradigm—think John Locke, Adam Smith, and James Madison—naturalizes the market economy and reduces government to the role of umpire, or, in Barber's words, "zookeeper." It turns the accumulation of private property, the primary source of economic inequality—a fact acknowledged by Madison in Federalist 10—into an inalienable right and, consequently, insolates economic decisions, which often affect entire communities, from democratic control. The liberal tradition reduces democracy to markets and elections.

Barber envisioned democracy as more than simply markets and elections. His vision entails "a self-governing community of citizens . . . who
are made capable of common purpose and mutual action by virtue of
their civic attitudes and participatory institutions rather than by their
altruism or their good nature."[16] In other words, strong democracy provides opportunities for people to experience meaningful participation and
through that participation they internalize democratic values—such as
respect for human dignity, inclusivity, open-mindedness, the freedom to
dissent, and noncoercion. Participation transforms individuals into active
citizens who care about the public good. Clearly, participatory democracy
differs greatly from the politics of profits over people, influence-peddling,
cronyism, divisiveness, toxic partisanship, and payback that tries to pass
itself off as democracy in the United States both then and now.

TALKING VS. FIGHTING: DEMOCRATIC THEORY IN THE 1990S

Democratic theory rose to prominence in the 1990s not only because
of the global trend toward democratization but also in response to the
divisive "culture wars" that officially broke out in the United States when
Pat Buchanan gave his famous speech at the Republican National Convention in 1992. Foregrounding the social issues that had animated the
Christian Right since the 1970s, Buchanan railed against the "Clinton &
Clinton" agenda of "abortion on demand, a litmus test for the Supreme
Court, homosexual rights, discrimination against religious schools, [and]
women in combat."[17] Mocking the plight of the "spotted owl," Buchanan
also attacked vice presidential candidate Al Gore for supporting the agenda
of "environmental extremists who put insects, rats and birds ahead of
families, workers and jobs."[18]

With the internally unifying cause of the Cold War in the rearview
mirror, Buchanan revved the engine of polarization: "There is a religious
war going on in our country for the soul of America. It is a cultural war,
as critical to the kind of nation we will one day be as was the Cold War
itself. . . . We must take back our cities, and take back our culture, and
take back our country."[19] And while he did not mention it in his speech,
Buchanan not only supports the Christian Right but also the racist,
anti-immigrant, anti-Semitic, authoritarian politics of the quasi-fascist
Right, recently reinvigorated by Trump.[20] Buchanan depicts those with views

that differ from his own as enemies who seek to destroy the country—a fringe perspective at the time that has since become the norm.

Democratic theory aspires to move beyond the divisive politics of toxic partisanship, maintaining that when you have a disagreement, you should talk about it, not start a "war."[21] That is the basic contention of deliberative democracy, a strand within the larger field of democratic theory, that prioritizes talking over fighting, whether literally or figuratively. Deliberative democracy gained popularity after the translation into English of Jürgen Habermas's *The Structural Transformation of the Public Sphere* in 1989.[22] Habermas emphasized the importance of rational discourse and the "force of the better argument," meaning that an argument should be evaluated on the basis of its content, not on who said it. Other democratic theorists, like Iris Marion Young, emphasized that the public sphere must also include forms of communication beyond academic-style arguments (which have historically favored male voices), including storytelling, the arts, street theater, and political protests of all kinds.[23]

As I was finishing my coursework, Barber arranged a fellowship for me with the Kettering Foundation, an operating foundation that studies deliberative democracy and other democratic practices, an organization with which I continue to work, almost thirty years later. The foundation understands democracy as entailing a lot more than simply elections. It requires a culture of engagement. For democracy to work as it should, people in communities need to name and frame issues in terms that make sense to them and have an opportunity to deliberate about different ways to address their concerns, teasing out the tensions between different approaches, working through the trade-offs of each option, identifying resources, organizing for action, and learning collectively as they go. Ideally, an engaged public would work as partners *with* elected officials and public administrators to address shared problems.[24]

Foundation president David Mathews contests the commonly articulated idea that US citizens are apathetic, ignorant, and care little about politics, a conclusion some draw from the low percentage of people who vote. Quite to the contrary, argues Mathews, people are not apathetic at all; instead they are " 'mad as the devil' about a political system that has pushed them out of their rightful place in governing the nation."[25] Speaking about the state of US politics in the early 1990s, Mathews argued that US citizens felt they have been "pushed out of the political system by a professional political class of powerful lobbyists, incumbent politicians, campaign managers—and a media elite. They saw the system as one in which votes no longer made any difference because money ruled. They saw a system with its doors closed to the average citizen."[26] Since Mathews made that observation decades ago, the situation he describes has gotten so much worse, particularly in light of the *Citizens United* decision in 2010 that declared that corporations are people and money is speech.

In direct contrast to the neoliberal model of power politics that dominates in the United States, deliberative democracy valorizes a people-centered vision of politics that focuses not on partisan fighting and serving the interests of elites but on nurturing democratic practices and creating policies that help people and communities help themselves and work with their representatives when appropriate. Rather than relying on experts and professionals to govern instead of the people, deliberative democracy wants everyday people to have control over the forces that govern their lives by helping to set the normative direction for public policy, determined through widespread practices of deliberation. People-centered politics does not seek to replace government programs with volunteerism but rather aspires to strengthen the connections between everyday people and those authorized to represent them and increase accountability of elected officials to the people.[27]

While the idea of finding common ground through deliberation might sound utopian in a political era riddled with toxic partisanship and polarization, it seems to me that we need deliberation now more than ever. Properly structured, deliberative forums could play an important role in ameliorating the divisiveness that plagues US culture. For example, consider a comment made by one forum participant: "What you need is a redneck like me and a black fireman over there to come together and talk about crime, and realize the other person is not so bad. We'll leave talking to each other."[28] And while deep-seated divisions will not simply disappear after deliberation, talking together across differences could help build relationships.

Relationships matter in a democratic society because they form the necessary prerequisite for government aimed at the common good. Democratic theorists use the term "social capital" to refer to the "social networks" and "the norms of reciprocity and trustworthiness that arise from them," an argument advanced by Robert Putnam in his 1995 article "Bowling Alone" and his subsequent book with the same title.[29] A lot of politicos tend to dismiss purely social activities as unimportant, but I would argue that those supposedly nonpolitical interactions play an important political role because they build relationships within communities and that solidarity makes subsequent political activism more likely.

The idea that the people ought to take an active role in making laws for themselves or at least providing the normative direction for public policy cuts against the contention that nonelites need experts and professionals to govern in their place and respects popular sovereignty. While definitely not a democratic theorist, conservative commentator William Buckley once commented that he would rather be governed by the first one hundred people in the Boston phone book than by the Harvard faculty. Yet while democratic theory maintains that people are able to govern themselves, even without an advanced degree, education still plays an important role in nurturing civic capacities, like the ability to deliberate—to articulate an argument, understand the implications of various perspectives, and make sound judgments. People also have to learn the meaning of democracy and the reasons that democratic values should be defended, as well as develop self-confidence and the courage of their convictions.

Civic education is vitally important in a democratic society, and studies show that the most effective programs include an experiential learning component, rather than just test-focused memorization.[30] One popular approach to civic education, service learning, links community service to classroom reflection, and Barber helped develop that pedagogy during the 1990s.[31] Because of Barber's pioneering role in the service learning movement, President Bill Clinton selected Rutgers University as the place to launch his AmeriCorps program of national service, one of his signature programs, in 1993.[32] That was a very exciting turn of events, and since I worked at Barber's Walt Whitman Center for the Culture and Politics of Democracy, I got an invitation to the Clinton event and even scored a primo seat.

I will never forget the moment when Clinton finished his speech, and Van Halen's "Right Now" suddenly started blaring from the speakers—"Don't wanna wait 'till tomorrow. Why put it off another day?" And, right on cue, the president walked into the stands and started shaking hands, causing some visible eye-rolling from his Secret Service contingent. While never a Clinton fan myself—in the primary I supported Jerry Brown, who memorably railed against "the smug custodians of global finance"—I deeply enjoyed the experience of shaking Clinton's hand.[33] Believe me, I can attest to his charisma. When we shook hands in a venue filled with ten thousand people, it felt like he and I were alone in the room. The event did not make as much of a splash as we had hoped, due to the first

Trade Center bombing happening around the same time, but it was still a good day for the Ben Barber contingent.

DISCOVERING DEMOCRATIC SOCIALISM

During graduate school, I also discovered democratic socialism, a long-maligned ideology that has gained traction in the public sphere in the wake of the Bernie Sanders campaign in 2016. At Rutgers, I had the opportunity to study Marxism and critical theory with Prof. Stephen Eric Bronner, and I learned from him that Marx and Engels understood themselves as the legitimate heirs of the republican legacy of the French Revolution, taking up the mantle of the Jacobins, the main proponents of liberty, equality, and republicanism during that time.[34] Indeed, as Bronner recounts in *Socialism Unbound*, after the demise of the French Revolution and the defeat of Napoleon, the monarchy reclaimed power in 1815; but then, in 1848, the people rose up again to demand a democratic repub-lic. At first, workers joined with the bourgeoisie in calling for "*political* democracy, predicated on free elections and civil liberties according to the rule of law," but then they realized that political democracy alone would not be enough to ensure a dignified life. Consequently, working people went on to demand a democratic socialist republic that would create more "egalitarian material conditions."[35] In other words, they wanted to extend the republican ideals of liberty, equality, democracy, and protection from arbitrary power into the economic realm. Indeed, you vote once or twice a year; how many days do you work? In response, the bourgeoisie broke away and joined forces with royalists to protect their own property interests, even though that curtailed democracy.

Socialism Unbound, emphasizing the democratic commitments of socialism, originally came out in 1990, right after the fall of the Berlin Wall. In the preface to the second edition, Bronner discusses the speedy pace at which the Left's high hopes for democratization were dashed by the emerging neoliberal order. At the time, Bronner took heat for main-taining a focus on class issues, but in hindsight we can see his prescience. In the wake of the Cold War came not democratic socialism, or even strong democracy, but the "economic inequities, corruption, and material insecurity" that inevitably accompany "a market economy."[36] While people expected the transition from authoritarianism to liberal democracy to provide them with greater control over the forces that govern their lives, economic decisions ended up being made by economic elites, and the quality of life for the many either deteriorated or did not improve. Consequently, decades later, we see the resulting backlash to those shattered dreams of a better, more democratic life with the rise of right-wing populism and quasi-fascism in eastern and central Europe.[37]

While democratic theory circa the 1990s for the most part took class issues off the agenda for discussion, the great thing about democratic discourse is that it never ends. Since 2016 democratic socialism has reentered the public sphere. Bronner's latest book reminds us that socialism should be understood as "an ongoing practical project rather than (as Marx warned against) a model program or a prefabricated ideal. It is a matter of adapting socialism to meet new conditions—not the other way around." That is to say, "preserving a doctrinaire understanding of socialism renders it politically irrelevant. . . . Commitment to principles should not excuse refusing to engage what exists."[38] In other words, we need to use socialist principles to analyze and guide us through new situations, not reduce socialism to an ossified system that gets used like some kind of ideal type—a point a lot of activists on Facebook and Twitter these days would be wise to remember, as public discourse moves forward.

RUNNING ON THE TENURE TRACK

After I graduated with my PhD in 1997, I landed a tenure-track job at Illinois State University (ISU), located in Normal, Illinois, literally in the middle of a cornfield—a huge transition from Park Slope, Brooklyn, where I lived at the time with my second serious partner. The job entailed a heavy teaching load, and I basically spent all my time working. I felt so overwhelmed by my workload that I barely had time to shower. Very few students at ISU cared about politics. The university enrolled around twenty thousand students yet political science had only ninety-five majors. One student in my first-year class of three hundred confided that he had just turned eighteen and really wanted to start voting, but when his friends found out, they made fun of him.

A lot of students also lacked basic knowledge about politics. Believe it or not, some of them, born around 1980, had never heard of the Cold War or the Soviet Union—as opposed to local townspeople who never heard about their demise and continued to opine daily in the local paper about the Communist menace. I was shocked to find that on a multiple-choice test, 13 percent of my first-year class said that Karl Marx was one of our Founding Fathers. When I mentioned this to my bearded, Marxist colleague, he replied, "Good!"

The department had a great Palestinian American chair, who started his Introduction to American Politics course every semester by saying, "The founding fathers were a bunch of racist, sexist, capitalist old men." He told the students, "If you can question God, you can question the founders." The chair worked the halls before every faculty meeting, whipping the vote. He never brought anything up for a vote, unless he knew it would pass. My bearded colleague liked to proclaim about the chair, "He's PLO!" which scared my Jewish partner, a suspicious New Yorker who worked in law enforcement. She and I were fully out as domestic partners and never faced any problems in the department. In fact, we had to laugh when a conservative, older professor started referring to his wife of forty years as his "partner."

Illinois State University was isolated and several hours from Chicago and St. Louis. To give a flavor of the environment, the university sat in a town dominated by a major insurance company, a town in which African American federal officers were asked to prepay for their breakfasts at a national chain restaurant, and in which the local car plant had to settle the largest sexual harassment case in history at the time. My partner and I wanted to move back to an urban area as soon as possible. Fortunately, I got a teaching position at George Mason University (Mason)—the largest public university in Virginia, situated in the suburbs of Washington, DC—and my partner got a good job in the DC area as well.

Mason could have been called Right Wing U. In fact, Bronner asked, "Do you really want to go there Claire? It's generally considered a graveyard for old reactionaries." At that point, I did not care. I just wanted out of the cornfield. I knew Mason had a very conservative economics department and law school, as well as a high-powered libertarian think tank on campus, the Mercatus Center, but I had no idea the extent to which this conservatism pervaded the institution. As it turns out, Mason was deeply entangled with the Koch brothers, who were even allowed to influence academic hiring decisions.[39] Nevertheless, at the time, I was just glad to get out of the farmland and back to the city.

My department, Public and International Affairs, was not particularly conservative, and I did not face any pressure to modify my research or teaching interests at any time over the course of the twelve years I taught there. Although I had a few conflicts with the administration, at various levels, over political issues, I received tenure despite being an out-lesbian who wrote a book on marriage equality right before coming up for tenure in 2004.[40] Given the demographics of Virginia, my students were mostly conservative, including a lot of students with familial or personal connections to the military. In addition, however, the student body included very large Arab and Muslim populations, which added an interesting element to political conversations both inside and outside the classroom, and I learned a lot from them.

BATTLING HEGEMONIC VALUES IN THE CLASSROOM AND ON CAMPUS

Education plays a key role in socializing individuals into the larger culture, but higher education at its best also enables students to interrogate their preexisting beliefs and through critical thinking embrace their own vision of the world, even if that means rejecting dominant values. A good liberal arts education exercises the mind and deepens students' understanding of their own culture and those of others, while also preparing them for lifelong learning. Not reducible to vocational training tied to getting a job, a good liberal arts education provides students with the knowledge, skills, and disposition needed to become active participants in democratic society, as everyday citizens and as leaders. Higher education is a public good.

Despite my own strong commitment to feminism and left-wing politics, I did not aspire to convert students to my way of thinking but rather wanted them to develop their own views through critical thinking. If students end up thinking capitalism is the best political economic system, despite its downsides, that would be acceptable. It would not be acceptable, however, for them to deny that there are any downsides to capitalism, whether out of ignorance or because of ideological zealotry. Likewise, if students decide to defend pornography on free speech grounds, fine, but that acceptance needs to come after hearing, understanding, and considering feminist critiques of pornography as misogynistic and contributive to the toxic ways in which gender gets constituted in our society.

Put differently, I wanted students to question the hegemonic beliefs with which they had been inculcated. For example, because so many people tend to consider the US Constitution sacrosanct, I would frequently cite Barber, who once said, "The US Constitution is simply the will of We the People at a particular moment in time." I also used my former department chair's line about the Founding Fathers—that they were "a bunch of racist, sexist, capitalist old men." When I first started teaching at Mason, I often got pushback from students who said, "That sounds like Communism to me." I will never forget one May first when a baseball cap–wearing young man stood up in the back of the large auditorium in which I taught and said, "Today is May Day, a well-known Communist holiday, as I am sure you know." Then, he promptly sat down next to his giggling ball-capped friends. When I wrote multiple choice exams for the class, I always included a joke as option D. In response to the giveaway question to reward conscientious students, "What did we do the last day of class?" answer D was "we sang songs that Dr. Snyder learned at Communist Youth Camp." Would you believe some students picked that answer?

I also sought to expose my mostly conservative students to left-wing arguments with which they were unfamiliar, particularly in connection to larger debates in society at the time. My first year at Mason, the "global justice movement," which focused on the abuses of multinational corporations and international capitalism, had just burst into the American political scene from the left with the "Battle of Seattle" protest (1999), followed by a major protest in DC (2000).[41] The protests targeted the World Trade Organization, the International Monetary Fund, and the World Bank. In response, I began including a section on the democratic critique of "free trade" in my classes, showing students the film *Mickey Mouse Goes to Haiti* and other videos about sweatshop labor. My students really engaged with the issue of sweatshop labor, as did students all over the country at that time. In fact, "the anti-sweatshop movement [was] the largest wave of student activism to hit campuses since students rallied to free Nelson Mandela by calling for a halt to university investments in South Africa."[42]

The idea that the market economy is natural, righteous, and democratic constitutes one of those hegemonic beliefs that I tried to dislodge in my teaching, but it was tough going.[43] For example, I often assigned Barber's *Jihad vs. McWorld* in my classes because it argues that the market is not democratic and in fact undermines democracy.[44] Barber argues that the proper role of business is to make money; the proper role of the democratic public is to decide what moneymaking practices should be allowed or disallowed. After going over the argument for weeks, I included this question on the exam: "True or false? Barber argues that the market is by definition democratic." Would you believe an overwhelming majority of my students said it was true? I was stunned, but when I told my father about it, he said, "They *know* the market is democratic, and they cannot believe that Barber would say otherwise." That's hegemony.

In fall 2001, my second year at Mason, I decided to organize my Contemporary Political Ideologies class around the left-wing social justice movement, but on the morning of September 11th that all changed when al Qaeda terrorists attacked the United States and shifted the ideological debate to the right. Out: Debates about global justice. In: Debates about Islamofascism. I had no idea about the attack when I obliviously exited my condo that morning. My downstairs neighbor said, "I couldn't turn off the TV." I asked what was happening, and she told me a plane flew into one of the Trade Center towers in New York. What? At first, I thought it must be a terrible accident, and then the second plane hit. Driving to campus on the Capital Beltway felt surreal. While I was in transit, I heard on the radio that a plane hit the Pentagon, which was only five miles from my condo. I called my mother from the car and told her to turn on the TV because the country had been attacked by terrorists. "What channel are you watching?" Just turn it on. President Bush was actually in Sarasota that morning, reading to school children.

When I arrived at my 10:30 a.m. class, my students were just sitting there, stunned. Others, in the hallway, were near hysterics. At that point, I told my class, "We don't know who is responsible for this yet, so let's not jump to conclusions until we get more information." Then, a student in the back started shouting, "This is chickens coming home to roost! When you flout the word of God . . . !" Before he could finish, another conservative student rose from his chair, red in the face, saying, "I am not going to listen to this!" I responded, "Mike, you are welcome to leave, but this is the University, and we will have a civil discourse." He sat back down and, somehow, we all made it through the day, absorbing details as they emerged.

People who lived through the terrorist attacks of 9/11 will never forget that day, but I also remember my left-wing colleague, who studied Latin American politics, stopping me in the hall a few days later to say, "Claire, they are already disappearing people." I am embarrassed to say that I did not believe her. Despite the fact that I cut my teeth protesting US atrocities in Latin America, the *stubbornly naïve heart* I inherited from my mother refused to accept in that moment the things she told me. Later, when the Abu Ghraib photos came out, and I learned about rendition and secret prisons, I remembered our conversation. Those photos shocked and sickened me, but again, it was not the first time US government actors abused people and tortured them to death. In fact, it has since come out that the Chicago police routinely tortured Black suspects for years—1972–1991—right here in the USA, at a domestic black site.[45]

Eighteen months later, the Bush administration invaded Iraq. Visiting my parents in Florida at the time, I will never forget watching US military tanks roll into Baghdad, politically outraged and personally heartbroken because my so-called life partner back in DC was cheating on me, and I knew I had to end the relationship. The breakup turned out to be a good thing, however, because I met my soulmate Mikki Hall ten weeks later, and we married in 2006 (although it was not recognized by the state until 2008). The Iraq War, on the other hand, did not turn out to be a good thing, and it is still being waged, as of this writing (winter 2021), over eighteen years later.

While the devastating attacks on 9/11 came during the early part of my time at Mason, in my last semester there, on May 2, 2011, the US military killed Osama bin Laden. I had a senior seminar that year—the students would have been around ten years old when the Towers fell—and many of them drove into DC that night to celebrate his death. We had a great conversation the next day, and the students shared their experiences of coming of age during the War on Terror, the ways in which it changed their parents, and the ways it affected them. The next day, a "friend" sent me a link to pictures of Osama bin Laden's dead body. If you ever get an email like that, do not click the link. My entire computer got infested with a virus. Doh!

THE AMERICAN DEMOCRACY PROJECT: ENGAGING UNDERGRADUATES

One of the highlights of my career at Mason was being asked to lead the American Democracy Project (ADP) on campus, which I saw as a great opportunity to increase the level of civic education within the student body and strengthen the connection between higher education and public life. The nonpartisan ADP was created in 2003 by the American Association of State Colleges and Universities, in partnership with the *New York Times*, to equip undergraduates "with the knowledge, skills, attitudes and experiences they need to be informed, engaged members of their communities."[46] I took the reins in 2004, right after getting tenure.

Mason called it simply the Democracy Project, however, to take the focus off of the United States.

I had high hopes for the program but was disappointed to discover that students were not interested in attending the programs I organized—mostly panel discussions on hot topics, like immigration reform, gun control, and the Tea Party, as well as the annual congressionally mandated Constitution Day celebration of our freedom—unless it was required for class. Of course, this should come as no surprise. After all, the Democracy Project was a very small program at a university with over thirty thousand students, and it was in no way integrated into the curriculum. Most students did not live on campus, and most of them had jobs, so they were very busy and did not have extra time for unnecessary activities. Consequently, I could only turn out an audience if I convinced a colleague to bring her class to the event—a strategy that worked pretty well, although it meant that mostly government students benefited from the program.

After several years of putting together "cocurricular programming" on public issues, I concluded that the Democracy Project could only be successful on campus if there were some sort of curricular tie-in, which ushered in a new, exciting phase in my civic work at Mason. The new associate provost was very enamored with the idea of integrating civic themes into the general education curriculum, which he oversaw and which was going through a major renovation in preparation for reaccreditation. He and I talked about creating a wide range of lower level courses that connected civic themes to a range of disciplines: The Artist as Citizen, The Scientist as Citizen, The Dancer as Citizen, and so on.

We decided to put together a faculty team to work on creating a set of new courses that focused on civic themes and ended up with only four willing participants. Our original vision was quite grand. We wanted to change the culture of student nonengagement on campus and foster deliberation. We decided that each of us would offer a course centered on civic issues, and the courses would be taught simultaneously. We would have some joint sessions with special guest speakers who would address public issues that were relevant for all four of our classes. The event would be open to the entire campus, as well as the larger community. The four classes would meet occasionally for interdisciplinary discussions among students. Ideally, student groups would "table" outside the event to stimulate student engagement. The public talks would become major events on campus. We decided that the first step would be to pilot the linked courses and speakers' series. Overall, the first-year courses went pretty well, but the project as a whole faced a number of barriers around scheduling, learning objectives, degree requirements, the use of faculty time, and resistance from department chairs.

For the second year, I created a brand-new interdisciplinary senior "seminar" (capped at thirty-five students), that would satisfy the final General Education requirement, organized around the question, "Now that you are graduating and becoming a fully participating member of society, what are you going to do to make the world a better place?" I piloted the course in the fall and then taught it as part of the project in the spring. I wanted to incorporate a civic engagement dimension into the class, so I asked students to choose a public issue they really cared about, analyze it from a values-based perspective, and then write a paper that included a discussion of what they were going to do about it, after graduation. Because it was supposed to be the students' final Gen Ed course, I assigned mostly popular materials from the public sphere—bestsellers, novels, and films—and the students came up with the idea of doing their presentations as short YouTube videos, which were posted online. It worked really well both times I taught it. The students loved the course. They told me that no professor had ever before asked them what they thought about important public issues. In all honesty, teaching those two sections of the senior seminar was the highlight of my teaching career. I was able to use my professional skills to help students see themselves as members of an engaged public, and we discussed issues that really mattered.

LEANING IN

During my last several years at Mason, I started transitioning into higher education administration, partly because I liked the systemic challenge of running academic programs, rather than just teaching, and partly because I wanted to make more money. As public employees in red state Virginia, we faculty members had been repeatedly denied raises, and the DC Metro area was quite pricey. It struck me that at Mason, the dean made $250,000 a year, while my salary floundered at less than a quarter of that. The rising salaries for top administrators and widening gap between their salaries and those of teaching faculty at universities across the country mimics business trends in pay gaps between management and workers. Since I really enjoyed serving as director of the Honors program and then as director of the master's and PhD in political science, I decided to pursue advancement.

Until I let it be known that I wanted a full-time administrative position, I never felt stymied in my career. Being a woman in a male-dominated profession had its challenges, but fortunately I never experienced the toxic #MeToo culture that has recently been exposed all over society—in Hollywood, legislative halls, the military, the hospitality industry, and so forth. When I made the decision that I wanted to transition into higher education administration, I did not believe that sitting quietly and hoping to be noticed would lead to success, so I made my desire for advancement known. It did not go as well as expected.

The first conflict was with my department chair, and it blindsided me. I thought we had a good relationship, even though I had blocked his attempt to install in our department a researcher funded by an unnamed conservative foundation—I assume connected to the Koch brothers, given Mason's entanglement with them. At the time of the conflict, I was graduate director, and the chair asked me to serve as summer chair, which I agreed to do. As we were chatting in his office, he asked me if I had ever considered coming up for chair, which until that moment I had not. I took his question to mean that he thought I would make a good future chair. I thought that he suggested it because he wanted to mentor me. But apparently, he, on the other hand, took my interest to mean I wanted to take his job. Perhaps his question was a test of some kind, and I was supposed to decline. "Oh no. Not me. I would never consider taking on a leadership role." But I took his query as a suggestion, a suggestion I quickly came to like, and I talked openly with him about my aspirations because I thought we were on the same page.

Shortly after our conversation, however, the chair went on an angry rampage against me—triggered by my suggestion at a faculty meeting that the "political theory and law" concentration be divided into "political theory" and "public law and judicial process"—that lasted for weeks. He reportedly started spending every lunch hour at the dining hall, sitting around impugning my character in front of his cadre of young male lunch buddies. It became so bad that I consulted with human resources about ways to handle the situation, and on their advice, I confronted him. The conversation started with my calm statement of fact and expressed desire to have a good working relationship, but he quickly went on the attack. He accused me of showing a "pattern of disrespect" toward my colleagues.

He did not use the quintessentially gendered word "abrasive"—"the one word men never see in their performance reviews"—but one can surmise the synonymity.[47] We then argued loudly for a long time, until we lost steam, and our raised voices were overheard by everyone in the anterior department office. You should have seen their big eyes when I finally came out. As we parted ways, the chair looked at me and said, "Have you lost weight?" I took that to mean our conflict was over, and we lapsed into a quiet détente after that.

When I shared that bizarre experience with a senior female colleague outside my department, who was a bit of a mentor to me, she told me that "men like that can ruin careers." On her advice I decided to take a part-time administrative position in another unit of the college, and then a year later the dean appointed me Director of Interdisciplinary Studies, which was also part-time. I thought my segue into an administrative career was going smoothly. The dean and I had a spirited repartee, and I thought he supported me. I found out different, however, about a year before I decided to leave academia, via an incident I subsequently wrote about in a creative writing class, which I will share here.

CREATIVE INTERLUDE I: LUNCHING WITH THE DEAN

It was a bright sunny day on campus, and the leaves were just starting to turn auburn and gold. It always gave me a good feeling to see all the students rushing from class to class, carrying backpacks and earnestness or casually chatting in groups beside the campus green. Every fall resurrected that back-to-school feeling from my early years, the sharpened pencils in my pencil box, a big pink eraser, a new lunchbox with a cute design—a school bus, Raggedy Ann, or Scooby-Doo, depending on the year.

As I gazed around, I recalled all the semesters that I didn't take the time to appreciate nature's beauty, as I worried about more mundane tasks, the reading I had to do, the papers I had to write, and now the exams I had to grade. I was glad I had started to remind myself to appreciate the turning of the seasons and my good fortune at having a good job that stimulated me, one I had worked hard at, over the course of many years.

At the time, I was actively pursuing a transition into full-time higher education administration. After ten years of full-time teaching, I found myself burned out on the classroom but not on academe. And all was going well. The charismatic male dean had appointed me Director of Interdisciplinary Studies, a part-time position, which to my mind indicated his confidence in my leadership abilities. He trusted my ability to make the program stronger, implement policies to increase rigor, guide students toward graduation, and spend public money wisely. He knew I wanted to transition into administration full-time because I had confided in him. A friend of mine in the Dean's Office assured me that the dean would give me sound advice. I hoped that he might mentor me.

On that particular day, I had taken great pains to look professional because I had to meet with the dean about a complicated issue that had arisen with a review committee I was chairing. When he asked me to chair, he said he was testing me out with an easy assignment, but it had turned out to be anything but easy. His assistant suggested that he and I have lunch. This was my chance to show my leadership skills. I would let him know what was coming down the pike. No surprises on my watch. He needed to know he could trust me.

I was grateful for the chance to meet with the dean one on one because I was planning to apply for the Associate Dean of Graduate Studies position in his office, but the job had not yet been posted. Our lunch would provide the chance to let him know my plans for what seemed like the logical next step in my career. I thought he would consider me a good choice for the position.

Plus, I liked the dean, and I admired him. He was a nationally known scholar who also ran a large unit at a major state university. He wielded a lot of power on campus, and he was the type of man who made you feel special when he talked to you. I liked that he confided in me, telling me more than I needed to know about his dating history, his marital relationship, his cat's bathroom habits, whatever popped into his mind. I liked that he noticed me at graduation, gently adjusting my doctoral hood, as I stood in line, waiting to walk on stage. I liked that he connected with my wife Mikki and always asked about her. I was deeply gratified that he had attended our wedding reception, the one we held in our home after eloping to California when same-sex marriage was legalized. I considered him one of my key supporters on campus.

When noon arrived, we met at the new dining hall, a state-of-the-art facility built in accordance with national trends. George Mason University was on the rise and undergoing a building boom. This sparkling food emporium would no doubt appeal to students, with its multiple food stations serving delicacies from every country and its environmentally correct lack of trays. The dean seemed to take personal pride in the new cafeteria. He gave me a tour of the place, as if he owned it, as if he were responsible for its very existence. The dean was always cocky, and today was no exception. He strutted and smiled, greeting random students as he strode around, but of course none of them knew who he was. To them he was probably just some goofy old man with his pants jacked up too high and a toothy grin. But I knew who he was and the power he held at my institution.

We gathered our lunches, secured a table, and enjoyed our carb-heavy meals in the sunny dining room, surrounded by groups of chattering students. We discussed the committee issue, and the dean advised me on how to handle the problem. We now had a plan. Things were going well. Despite the noisy chaos around us, it seemed like it was just he and I in the room. I decided not to be coy.

"So, I just want to let you know that I am interested in applying for the Associate Dean of Graduate Studies position. I'm just waiting for it to be posted," I informed him, as I casually reached for my iced tea and smiled.

I was expecting him to respond positively, but instead he looked down at his hands. His face darkened and the lighthearted mood between us began to recede.

"Well," he said, looking back up, "if you want a job *like that*, OK, but if you want to become an academic dean, you need to be a full professor." As he spoke, our easy repartee faded, and the hierarchy between us came into focus.

"Yes, I realize that, and I'll be coming up for full next year," I responded, trying to sound confident, assuming that with two books and thirty articles under my belt, I would be in good shape for promotion.

"You just got tenure," he laughed.

"I didn't just get tenure. I got tenure five years ago."

"Well," he said, "if you want to come up for full in *the fastest possible time*, you need a strong record. You need to talk to your chair." As he refocused on me, his eyes hardened, and his jovial grin was long gone.

"I know," I said looking right back at him. "I have spoken with my chair about it."

We paused. Then, suddenly he relaxed. "You know," he said, leaning back in his chair, "I'll never forget the first time I met you."

I exhaled, and my smile returned. Perhaps this conversation was going to get back on track. I looked across the table at him. The sun was shining brightly through the window, and the students were starting to leave for class.

"I noticed you because of your blonde hair." I stared at him, slightly stunned.

"I mean, I know it's not natural," he continued. "Is it?"

"Uh . . ." My brow furrowed as I stared back at him—his large ears, receding hairline, and oversized teeth and lips, suddenly a picture of grotesquery.

"You know I can never tell when a man is hot but a woman . . . ," he uttered, shaking his head ever so slightly. "Look at Sarah Palin. She's a babe," he said, his signature toothy grin returning.

Sensing my shock, he quickly stammered, "I mean, don't get me wrong. I don't agree with her politics, but you've got to admit she's hot. You should know. You like women!"

My head drew back, and I stared at him.

"You know, a lot of women have empty eyes, but not her. She has those sexy, intelligent eyes. You know . . . like yours," he said leaning forward. I didn't know what to say, as he tried to stare meaningfully into my eyes, across the table in the university dining hall on a sunny day in the fall.

Before I could respond, he said, "What do you do again?"

"What do I do?" I asked. "What do I do? I teach political theory and run the Interdisciplinary Studies program." And I report to you, you jackass, I thought, as I felt my blood rise.

"Oh yeah." He looked around distractedly. "I know I went to some book signing thing for you, but I can't remember what the book was about."

He didn't seem to notice my indignation, the tension in my jaw, the heat in my cheeks, or tightness in my chest. I looked him straight in the eye. "I have a book out on the citizen-soldier tradition, a book on marriage equality, and a lot of articles," I responded pointedly. But it didn't matter. He wasn't listening. He was too busy looking out the window.

"Hey, there's a blonde," he exclaimed, actually rising out of his seat and pointing to a young woman who was simply walking across campus, probably on the way to class. It was a bright sunny day outside, but in my mind dark clouds were starting to form.

I walked back to my office, stunned by the encounter, shaded by the new dorm buildings looming over campus. Is that really how the dean thinks of me, I wondered, after all my hard work?

I went through the rest of my day in a daze, but when I got home, I broke down and cried. My dream of a job in the Dean's Office was shattered. The dean had slapped me down, but I didn't understand why. "What do you do again?"

PATRIARCHAL CULTURE

Why did the dean sexualize and belittle me during our lunch meeting? It appears significant that his attack came in direct response to my expressed desire for career advancement. That would not be the only time the dean made inappropriate comments to me instead of commending me for doing good administrative work. The other incident occurred right after I completed a complicated and time-consuming program review, required of all directors, that was very well received by the provost. At the meeting, when the dean heard the provost praise me, the former appeared quite pleased, grinning proprietarily. So, when he asked me to accompany him back to his office after the meeting, I expected that the dean wanted to express gratitude for a job well done.

As we left College Hall, we got into the elevator with one other woman. When she exited, the dean watched her walk away and then said to me: "Women wear high heels to make their legs look sexy, right?" When I replied, "I don't know," he said, "Why don't you know? You're into women." Once again, I had done a good job professionally, and once again he sexualized me, and in that way reestablished his masculine dominance and by extension my feminine subordination. Nothing untoward happened back at his office, but I definitely did not leave with the feeling that my hard work on the program review had advanced my career prospects any. Instead, I felt diminished.

Those interactions with the dean reminded me of the understanding of gender hierarchy that Catharine MacKinnon articulates in her work, which spoke to me during my college years, as explained in the previous chapter. MacKinnon argues that our society's hegemonic view of male-dominated heterosexuality entails the depiction of gender as a hierarchical relation of dominance and subordination, not just difference. According to the Christian Right version of that narrative, women are submissive by nature, designed by God to be men's helpmeets. It's funny that right around the time of my lunch with the dean, I had just published an article on the ideology of "wifely submission" in one of the top academic journals in the field of gender and politics. The article analyzed a long list of marriage advice manuals, recommending submission as the key to a happy marriage. For example, in *The Surrendered Wife*, Laura Doyle advises women to "come to the bedroom as female as possible. That means . . . pretending that you never knew the meaning of ambition, aggression, or . . . control."[48] That way, you can keep your man's interest. Given this cultural backdrop, I would argue that when the dean sexualized our interaction, he invoked that gender hierarchy of male dominance and female submission. He took the dominant subject-position and consequently reduced me to subordinate. While I was in fact his subordinate in terms of job status, by sexualizing our interaction, he triggered a hegemonic cultural narrative that rendered me subordinate by virtue of my feminine nature. In short, by sexualizing me, he rendered me always and forever a lesser being.

Having the dean sexualize and belittle me does not fit into the way professional advancement is supposed to work. In a speech on women's career paths, Smith College president Carol T. Christ says, "Jobs that provide entry to the most prestigious professions—untenured faculty positions, medical residencies, entry positions at law and finance firms—have notoriously long hours. You prove your worth by the time you invest. The heavy commitment of daily time . . . leads to advancement along a linear career path."[49] During my six years on the tenure track, I maintained a grueling pace of work.

Upon achieving the goal of tenure, my workload did not convert into something sustainable. Instead, it got even heavier, partly because of increased teaching, advising, and service responsibilities. Indeed, a survey by the American Political Science Association finds that female faculty are more likely to be asked to do service and less likely to say no, and that service is more likely to be low level and not beneficial to their career advancement.[50] That was definitely true in my case. In addition, the university was talking about implementing post-tenure review with the expectation that faculty would continue to publish at a pre-tenure pace.

Yet despite nearly constant work, instead of advancing along a "linear career path," it seemed that the dean had created a roadblock for reasons that were unclear. I did little besides work, so why shouldn't I get promoted to full professor in the "shortest possible time," rather than languishing for years at the associate level? Studies show that oftentimes women do not advance in their careers because they hold themselves back. "Brought up to nurture and defer to others, women avoid recognition and visibility."[51] Many women fear criticism, and they receive more of it on the job than men do. They have to walk an "impossible tightrope," doing their jobs affectively, while also being likeable to everyone.[52] By making my career aspirations known, I was trying to avoid exactly that situation. I did not—and still do not—believe that sitting silently like a good little girl and waiting to be noticed would get me anywhere.

Perhaps my expressed ambition violated gender norms and that spurred the pushback I got from the dean. We know that women who negotiate salaries and benefits are perceived negatively, even penalized, for doing the same thing a man would do.[53] They are condemned for doing what liberal feminists like Sheryl Sandberg, author of *Lean In*, say they should do. Women are not actually supposed to be ambitious," says Liz Elting, who "started a billion-dollar business out of a dorm room." Instead, she argues, "we're supposed to accept our place, take up as little space as possible, be thankful for what little room we're allowed, and absolutely never make waves lest we be perceived as difficult. . . . Women are supposed to be helpful, pliant, comforting—but never ambitious."[54]

Elting illustrates her argument by citing Hillary Clinton, who was repeatedly vilified for her ambition. "Look at her headlines: 'Is Hillary Clinton Pathologically Ambitious?' 'Flip-flops Show Clinton Is Long On Ambition, Short On Principles.' 'Hillary Clinton's Unbridled Ambition Trips Her Up Again.' 'Don't Destroy the Dems To Satisfy Clinton's Ambitions.' 'The Curse of Hillary Clinton's Ambition.'" In contrast, Elting continues, "Donald Trump, who had never held elective office in his life and whose entire public persona was built around his unceasing desire to win at everything wasn't dogged by claims that he was overly ambitious. And why not? Because ambition in men is assumed, praised, and rewarded."[55] Many people, Clinton included, believe that misogynistic double standards played a large role in her defeat.

With the dean, I faced the classic "double bind." If a woman acts assertive on the job, and leans in like a man would, she gets called "abrasive" or worse. On the other hand, if she appears too feminine, she is not taken seriously.[56] In the eyes of the dean, perhaps I had erred on both sides—an upstart for pursuing an important job yet also frivolous because of my feminine appearance and demeanor. Or perhaps it was nothing I did. Perhaps being the quintessential alpha male, the dean just enjoyed exercising dominance by putting people down, something he had a reputation for relishing.

Kate Manne argues that misogyny in our culture functions to enforce hegemonic gender norms. My experiences were relatively mild, considering all the different ways in which women are put in their place. "As well as infantilizing and belittling, there's ridiculing, humiliating, mocking, slurring, vilifying, demonizing, as well as sexualizing or, alternatively *desexualizing*, silencing, shunning, shaming, blaming, patronizing, condescending, and other forms of treatment that are dismissive and disparaging in specific social contexts."[57] And then, of course, "there is violence or threatening behavior: including 'punching down'—that is, deferred or displaced aggression."[58] For Manne these misogynistic acts work to enforce and reinforce patriarchal social norms. Put differently, misogyny does not arise from people with psychological problems but rather functions to maintain hegemonic gender norms within our culture.

OPTING OUT

The literature on women and work talks a lot about "leaning in," but it also focuses on the phenomenon of women "opting out" of professional jobs that fail to provide enough work/life balance to accommodate childrearing. Back in 2003, Lisa Belkin wrote a high-profile essay in the *New York Times Magazine* about the many highly educated professional women with degrees from prestigious colleges who were choosing not to pursue traditionally male careers, so they could stay home with their children.[59] Anne-Marie Slaughter reignited the opt-out debate in 2012, with her *Atlantic* article "Why Women Still Can't Have It All."[60] Slaughter, a university professor at Princeton and former dean of its Woodrow Wilson School, resigned from a high-powered job in the Clinton State Department, Director of Policy Planning, after only two years because the job left her almost no time to spend with her children.

Surprisingly, given the heavy workloads of most college professors, Slaughter views her academic position as providing all the flexibility she needs to balance work and family, which is hard to believe given her reported productivity: "I have not exactly left the ranks of full-time career women: I teach a full course load; write regular print and online columns on foreign policy; give 40 to 50 speeches a year; appear regularly on TV and radio; and am working on a new academic book."[61] Slaughter seems to have an extremely modest need for family time, since she touts a two-hour dinner break with her family as enough to satisfy her need for balance. While she is a senior faculty member, Slaughter does acknowledge the grinding years on the tenure track when she mentions the case of "Louise Richardson, now the vice chancellor of the University of St. Andrews, in Scotland, [who] combined an assistant professorship in government at Harvard with mothering three young children. She organized her time so ruthlessly that she always keyed in 1:11 or 2:22 or 3:33 on the microwave rather than 1:00, 2:00, or 3:00, because hitting the same number three times took less time."[62] I remember when I was in grad school, one assistant professor reported always having cold cereal for breakfast instead of oatmeal for the same reason, and another reportedly requested her laptop, moments after giving birth to her first child.

Slaughter's account raises two questions for me. First, why does she consider working from dawn to midnight with only a two-hour dinner break with her family an acceptable lifestyle? Second, why do articles about women and work focus almost exclusively on the challenges of childrearing? Women with children certainly do have an additional set of responsibilities that make it more difficult to pursue a career modeled on the traditional male biography, where the career-building years are also the fertile ones. But what about women without children who just do not want to work 24/7? While a full discussion of this topic exceeds the scope of this book, suffice it to say that the hegemonic emphasis on work as the most important thing in life could use some critical analysis. Kathi Weeks provides precisely that in her book, *The Problem with Work: Feminism, Marxism, Antiwork Politics, and Postwork Imaginaries.*[63] The fact that my first reaction to her project was dumbfounded skepticism—What do you mean work is not inherently good, and we should not have to do it all the time?—illustrates the hegemonic power of workaholism among contemporary professionals—or at least in my head.

I did not decide to leave academia because of the way the dean treated me, but his lack of support closed off the last opportunity I saw at Mason for a move into full-time administration. I had already been passed over for a civic engagement leadership position in the Provost's Office, even after my years of uncompensated work as the Democracy Project campus coordinator. In addition, I did not have enough seniority to become department chair—which at Mason came with a very large raise—so there were no moves left to make. Moreover, I did not get the Vice President of Academic Affairs position at Wesley College for which I interviewed—as one of two candidates invited to campus, I got my hopes up—nor did multiple applications for an array of administrative jobs at a range of institutions in the DC area meet with success. Since Mikki and I were not willing to move anywhere my job took me, I appeared to be stuck at Mason with low pay, a heavy workload, and a beastly commute.

My moment of clarity came when I said, "I am not spending the rest of my life commuting on the Capital Beltway."

I never in a million years thought I would leave academia, especially after working so hard to earn my degree, land a job, and get tenure, but I found myself increasingly frustrated at Mason, and my wife Mikki really wanted to relocate to Rehoboth Beach, Delaware, where we had a second home. If we sold our house in Silver Spring and moved to the beach, I could write full-time, which is what I most enjoyed about my academic job. It would also give me more flexibility to spend time in Florida with my father, who had developed Alzheimer's. It was a hard decision, so I decided to go on leave for the 2011–2012 academic year, and then I resigned. I left a perfectly good career, even though I have no children. I just wanted a better quality of life. As a friend likes to say, I gave up tenure because of the traffic.

CHAPTER 3

TALES FROM THE CAMPAIGN TRAIL

I did not plan to run for office when Mikki and I moved to Rehoboth Beach, Delaware—a small town that calls itself "the nation's summer capital" because so many people from DC weekend and summer there, including President Joe Biden. Rehoboth is a blue bubble in a very red county in a solidly blue state. Mikki and I had long loved Rehoboth, which has a disproportionately large and visible community of lesbians and gay men—reportedly the fourth highest number of same-sex couples per capita in the country. Part-time residents since 2003, we had (and still have) a lot of friends in the large and fun-loving women's community there. We like to socialize and particularly enjoy happy hours with live music and dancing, so Rehoboth was perfect for us. Sussex County, however, not so much. As people say, "Outside Rehoboth, it's Alabama."

When we moved to Rehoboth in spring 2011, I was very down on the Democratic Party. Although I voted for Obama in 2008—after supporting John Edwards in the primary because of his focus on economic inequality—I was disappointed with the way the new president dealt with health care, the economy, and the "war on terror." He was not progressive enough and pandered too much to Republicans. When Occupy Wall Street emerged, on September 17, 2011, seemingly from out of nowhere, if I had lived near one of the many occupations that erupted in any of the one thousand cities around the world, I would have actively participated, but my new hometown did not have an Occupy encampment. However, the president of the Progressive Democrats of Sussex County (PDSC) did convene an Occupy Rehoboth rally one chilly afternoon in November at the bandstand. It drew a decent crowd of mostly retirees, but never met again.[1] The running joke was, "We held it at 3 p.m. because we had dinner plans." And so what if we did? The 99% have to eat too!

With no Occupy encampment or Green Party presence in Sussex County, the Democratic Party (DP) appeared to be the only game in town, and so Mikki and I attended a meeting, hoping to meet some cool people. Although neither of us had been active in the party previously, we had gotten involved in electoral politics back in Maryland, during the marriage equality fight. We served for several years as Lobby Day Captains in our district (Montgomery County), which was represented by people who totally supported the cause, so it was a very gratifying experience. We decided to work on the marriage issue, around the time my book *Gay Marriage and Democracy: Equality for All* came out in 2006.[2]

We learned from our lobbying experience that progressive change can happen when people organize. When we began lobbying in February 2006, our longtime Democratic state senator was an incrementalist opponent of marriage equality. As we exited her office after a disappointing exchange, one of our allies said something like, "Don't worry about her. There's a really progressive law professor named Jamie Raskin challenging her in the primary, and he's going to win." Raskin became famous for telling a state senator, "When you took your oath of office, you placed your hand on the Bible and swore to uphold the Constitution. You didn't place your hand on the Constitution and swear to uphold the Bible."[3] Raskin won the state senate election and then went on to Congress ten years later. That experience made Mikki and me hopeful about changing the Democratic Party from within.

With a lot of ideas about the ways in which democracy should function and with little knowledge of the ways in which political parties actually operate, Mikki and I attended our first Democratic Party meeting in a dimly lit hotel room on the side of a major highway. At that point, only elected committee members attended the monthly meetings in the Fourteenth Representative District (14RD), and that night only about five or six people were there. While the 14RD committee could have twenty-one members, only about half the slots were filled. While a third of the positions were earmarked for "young people," the committee members claimed they could not find any. I guess we made a good impression because they quickly elected us to the committee.

Joining the Democratic Party was a bit of a transition for me, after being part of the academic left for decades. Back in the 1990s, in my experience, people often used the term *progressive* to refer to socialists and other leftists not tied to the philosophical assumptions of liberalism—back when the word *socialism* was inflammatory—so when I heard people in Sussex County calling themselves *progressive*, I thought they would share my critical view of Obama, but that was definitely not the case. Not only did all the progressives I met uncritically love Obama, but they also viewed progressive politics as inextricably linked to the Democratic Party. In fact, they often used the term as a euphemism for pro-gay. I did not encounter anyone to the left of the DP. Case in point, the 14RD Democrats, most of whom identified as "progressive," focused almost exclusively on the state legislature, and they loved the Democrat in Name Only (DINO) who represented them in the state house.

PRECURSOR: STATE RACES IN 2012

Everyone on the 14RD committee was optimistic about 2012 because the Rehoboth Beach area had just been awarded a brand-new senate seat, due to population growth, and everyone expected the seat would go blue. The new state senate district included our new hometown, along with two other small towns, Lewes and Milton, and adjacent communities. The district was almost exclusively white (including us) and populated largely by seniors (not including us). The coastal area was (and still is) growing quickly because of all the "transplants" from three major urban areas nearby—DC, Baltimore, and Philadelphia—as well as from New Jersey, Pennsylvania, and New York. The formerly rural area of chicken farms and open land was changing quickly. Because the county commission refused to hire a planner or require developers to pay impact fees, unchecked development was turning a quaint rural area on the shore into crowded, gridlocked sprawl with few decent jobs and skyrocketing housing costs, and the "from-here's" resented the "come-here's" for cultural and economic reasons.

When we came on the scene, the 14RD committee chair was just starting his campaign for the new state senate seat, and everyone expected him to win because he was the Protégé of the district's DINO rep who was slated to become the next Speaker of the House and also had strong support from the neoliberal, Democratic governor. In addition, the Protégé, a successful realtor, had no problem raising money, particularly because he and his older male partner were central players in the wealthy gay male community in town. The Protégé resigned as 14RD chair in January 2012 to focus on his campaign, and the committee elected me to take his place. The president of PDSC served as vice chair, and she became best friends with Mikki and me, and we considered her a rock-solid political ally. I will call her Lady Progressive, for reasons that will be explained shortly.

Mikki and I did not care for the Protégé, largely because we had an unfortunate interaction with him during a real estate deal. We were angry about the events that took place, and it never got smoothed over. In addition, the Protégé supported a centrist neoliberal agenda, whereas Mikki and I wanted to send a progressive to Dover. As party chair for his district during his campaign, I did the things required to support him, but not much more. Our lukewarm support created some hard feelings in the party and the LGBT community, but we could not change the way we felt about him or his platform.

When Mikki and I are unenthusiastic about a particular candidate running in our district, we generally look for someone else to support instead; that way we can still contribute to the Democratic cause, without having to work for someone whose values we do not share. Lady Progressive, who shared our disdain for the Protégé, took the same approach and decided to focus on the state house race in the 20RD, the other half of the new senate district. She and her friend who worked for a US senator before retirement, henceforth called Lady Staffer, identified an older woman—a former educator who now ran a small farm—to run in the 20RD. Let's call her Lady Farmer. My reason for attaching aristocratic titles to these characters will become clear in chapter 5, where I argue that a royalist mindset can develop, even within a democratic republic.

Lady Progressive asked me to help them recruit Lady Farmer to run, so we met with her at the farm. At first, she insisted that a local good ole boy who had run previously should run instead of her. "It's his seat," she repeatedly insisted. We did not agree, and besides he was not interested in running. Lady Farmer, like most first-time female candidates, needed a lot of encouragement to get in the race, so we kept pressing.[4] Finally, after talking it over with her female domestic partner of twenty years, she agreed to run, with the caveat that she would step aside if the local man decided to run again, which luckily did not happen.

Every Sunday during the campaign, Mikki and I joined the three Ladies at the farm for a strategy meeting. Just to give you a sense of the climate in Sussex County outside of the shore towns, one afternoon, we were driving back from the farm in Lady Progressive's Prius when a very large, noisy pickup truck started tailgating us. We just kept driving the speed limit, and then the vehicle peeled out in front of us, spinning up dust, and screeching all four wheels. As it passed us, we could not help but notice that on the back of the truck, spray-painted in giant font, it said, "Lying Socialist Scum!" I guess we all knew to whom that quote referred—the same African American president pictured on the bumper sticker that read, "Does this ass make my truck look big?" Welcome to Sussex!

SADNESS AND JOY

Lady Farmer had a primary challenger that year, a homophobic good ole boy who was a retired fire chief. He knew everyone in Sussex, whereas Lady Farmer had only lived there for ten years. He would be a formidable challenger. We knew we had to turn out the vote to get her past the primary, and Mikki, who is a senior software developer, designed a plan to accomplish that goal that took account of the county's spotty internet service and the fact that many volunteers did not have smart phones. The week before the primary, however, crisis struck.

It was Labor Day weekend, and I was standing in a bar full of half-drunk lesbians, celebrating the end of summer, when my brother Tim called. "Pop's on his way to the ER," he told me. My father, who had advanced Alzheimer's, had been through a series of medical crises after breaking his hip in 2011, and in the past, Tim always told me not to fly down but this time he did not dissuade me. Once at the hospital, Pop was diagnosed with double pneumonia. We knew it was dire.

The next day, Mikki drove me to Philadelphia to catch the first possible flight to Florida, and upon landing I drove straight to the hospital. When I rushed to his bedside, my father's wide face and soft blue eyes lit up. He smiled, and I kissed his cheek. Thank God he still recognized me. Two minutes later, he started gurgling and gasping for air, and the nurse stuck a tube down his throat to suction out the fluid, which made him very uncomfortable. When I said I did not want to catch his pneumonia, the nurse replied, "You can't. It's aspiration pneumonia because he has forgotten how to swallow."

My heart sank. It was my father's decision not to have any tubes, so I knew at that moment that that he was going to die. When I talked to the hospitalist, he said, "Sometimes pneumonia is an old person's best friend." We decided my dad would spend his last days at the Hospice House, in a peaceful, private room. With no food or hydration tubes, he would most likely die within three days.

Two of my father's friends from church—the remaining members of the men's group he led for many years—were in the hospital room when the orderly came to get him. As the gurney wheeled away, the men sang "Jesus Love Me," and Pop's foot tapped along to the melody. The room at Hospice House was beautifully decorated with cushy chairs and homey curtains. The doctor recommended heavy morphine—"This man's in pain!"—so my father remained unconscious for the final three days. Mom stayed with him the entire time, and he passed away early Sunday morning. It was two days before the Delaware primary.

Mikki was with me emotionally every step of the way, but she remained in Delaware to run GOTV for Lady Farmer. Without Mikki, her campaign would have collapsed, and we did not want that to happen, after all our hard work. We considered Lady Farmer a good friend, and Mikki and I both wanted her to win so badly that we willingly sacrificed that time together for the good of the cause. With the help of Mikki's GOTV system, Lady Famer won the primary, shocking the good ole boy contingent.

The very next day, Mikki flew down to join me and the family, as we prepared for the funeral and helped my mother hold it together. Mom asked me to write the obituary "and make it long because he wasn't just a regular person," she told me. I modeled the lengthy piece on the obituary of John Rawls, a groundbreaking political theorist at Harvard who transformed the field with his *Theory of Justice*. I guess that will do! It was so long that the local newspaper charged us $1,100 to run it. The funeral went well; lots of his former students flew in to pay tribute, and the church was packed, which warmed my heart. A few days later, Mikki flew back to Delaware, but I did not return to Rehoboth until October.

ELECTION DAY 2012

Despite the primary victory, Election Day did not go well for Lady Farmer's house race—in which she faced yet another good ole boy, this one a retired cop—or for the Protégé's senate race. The latter's campaign experienced blowback because of some negative mailers, sent out on his behalf by a national LGBT organization, that a lot of people found offensive. Sadly, his opponent, Ernie Lopez, used the flap to highlight his own heterosexuality. Because the Protégé had the support of both the governor and the soon-to-be Speaker, his defeat (43%) shocked the community.

Lady Farmer's campaign took a couple of last-minute hits as well. Her opponent had spent weeks quietly telling everyone that Lady Farmer was a lesbian, which surprised a lot of people and seemed to shame her, a woman in her late sixties, who apparently had never been more than semi-out about her sexuality prior to the campaign. (She subsequently claimed to be bisexual, which surprised a different set of people.) Then, a few days before the election, an influential good ole boy sent an email to his very long list of supporters, gay-bashing her at length. Right before the email went out, the governor did a poll that reportedly indicated a win by Lady Farmer, so when she lost the election (47%), it stunned and devastated her supporters, including us. Although a lot of people blamed the email for changing a win to a loss, in hindsight, I am not convinced she was ever actually winning; I doubt the sample size of voters in Sussex County in the governor's poll was large enough for validity.

In any event, because both Lady Farmer and the Protégé lost in 2012, many people concluded that "no gay can win in Sussex," a belief that would dampen enthusiasm for my candidacy two years later. The contention that homophobia in Sussex County is so strong that no gay person could ever win is actually empirically false. An openly gay man had, in fact, gotten elected, as a Democrat, to one of the county row offices in 2012. According to the candidate, one day on the campaign trail a local man came up to him and said, "Are you that faggot who's running for Clerk of the Peace?" When the candidate responded, "Yes I am," the voter said, "Pleased to meet you. You've got my vote." It probably helped that the candidate served as the attorney for the local Tea Party folks.

DECISION TO RUN

My father's death devastated me, yet I returned to my political work as soon as I got back to Delaware. In January 2013, Lady Progressive asked me to speak at a townhall meeting on gun violence, and I made some remarks based on the research I did on right-wing militias for my first book on the citizen-soldier tradition.[5] Immediately after I finished speaking and returned to my seat, the newly elected chair of the Sussex County Democrats said, "Tell me you're running, and I will stop trying to recruit someone." I demurred. At that point, I thought that someday I might run for office, but I had not considered running so soon.

His suggestion, however, got me thinking and after a lot of long conversations with him and Mikki (who wanted me to run), and Lady Progressive (who said I couldn't win), I decided to run for state senate in 2014. Before locking in though, I took Lady Progressive's advice and phoned the newly elected Speaker of the House, whom she idolized, and asked for his support. He indicated that the Protégé had no plans to run again and said, "If you run, I'll support you."

With the Speaker seemingly on board, Lady Progressive started to warm to the idea of my running. During the month of February, she began actively working on the campaign, even suggesting the Rosie the Riveter imagery we ended up using. Lady Progressive liked the idea of preventing another run by the centrist Protégé, and we all wanted to knock Senator Lopez out of the box before he became entrenched. In addition, I convinced her that we could use the campaign to raise consciousness around progressive issues. Although I was new to the area, I did not see that as an insurmountable barrier because, in my opinion, you do not have to live in a place for twenty years to understand the issues. Besides, we had lots of friends in the community, having been property owners and part-time residents for years before relocating there full-time, and I was chair of the Democratic Party for the district.

With no primary opponent ever emerging, despite persistent rumors, I had the backing of the Democratic Party. I wanted to run a campaign that incorporated some of the ideas I had gotten from my work in the field of deliberative democracy. First, I would talk with voters about the problems they saw in their community and develop an issue platform based on those conversations. Then, I would expand my relationship network by attending community events and asking supporters to invite me into their homes to meet their friends and neighbors, so I could engage them in conversation about the issues.

While I did not start the campaign expecting to win, the numbers did not look that bad. Given the strength of partisanship in US politics over all, I assumed Democrats would vote for me, and there were more registered Democrats than Republicans in the senate district. I also planned to reach beyond the partisan base to left-leaning independents, and also to lesbian and gay Republicans. The numbers said I could win, and while the homophobia of the 2012 election cast a negative pall on my candidacy—an issue people on the Democratic side continued to raise throughout the campaign, including one woman from the Unitarian Church who said, "I sure do wish you were straight"—I did not think we should make generalizations based on the results of one election cycle.

Although I never expected to win, it seemed I had a chance. Senator Lopez opposed marriage equality in a district with one of the largest LGBT populations per capita in the country. He voted against increasing the minimum wage to $8.25 an hour, in an area riddled with low-wage jobs, even though the vast majority of voters supported an increase. He opposed a law preventing homicidal and suicidal people from buying guns, in the wake of the Sandy Hook massacre. And he failed to support a popular bill restoring voting rights to people with felony convictions. Besides taking those controversial votes, Senator Lopez did little else during his two years in office. The only bill he sponsored legalized the sale of alcoholic gelato—which became a bit of a laugh line among my friends.

RUNNING WHILE NOT RUNNING

I did not want to officially launch the campaign until July—after the end of the legislative session on June 30, as was the custom—so I continued to work on progressive causes, focusing on two main issues. First, the marriage equality fight was gearing up. One of my former students from Mason worked for the Human Rights Campaign and was assigned to organize for marriage equality in Delaware. I was so proud when he told people he got into politics because of my Democratic Theory and Practice class. He asked me to co-lead the weekly phone bank, which I did for several months. I also lobbied Senator Lopez as a constituent, asking him to vote for equality, even though I knew that would essentially eliminate the major issue I planned to highlight in my campaign. He told me, "I'm not there yet Claire. I know I will get there one day, but I am not there yet." At the end of June when marriage equality came up for a vote, he voted against it, but it gloriously passed the state legislature anyway. The governor signed it into law immediately. It was an exciting and festive day. Mikki and I had our fifteen minutes of fame when Rachel Maddow ran a film clip that pictured the two of us rejoicing with the crowd. Did you see us on *Rachel* last night?

In addition, Mikki and I also took the lead in organizing in manufactured housing communities against predatory landlords. In Sussex County, most manufactured housing sits on leased land, and a new law allowed landlords to increase the ground rent by an unlimited amount every year. With land increasingly expensive and developers on the prowl, landlords had an incentive to use rent increases to force manufactured homeowners off the land, and when that happened, they usually could not find another place to park their mobile homes, and selling them was unlikely. Mikki and I organized people to join us, going door-to-door with petitions, calling for limits on annual ground rent increases. I also met with community leaders and spoke at community meetings all over the county. We were ecstatic when the law passed, yielding another glorious day.

Unfortunately, however, Lady Progressive, my best friend at the time, whom I considered a rock-solid ally, along with Lady Farmer and Lady Staffer, all mysteriously turned on me sometime in March for reasons about which I can only speculate. Things came to a head the first week of April when Lady Farmer invited us all to the farm for dinner. Lady Progressive came down with the flu at the last minute and did not make it, but Lady Staffer and her wife were there, along with Lady Farmer and her partner. After a very tasty dinner of macaroni and cheese, Lady Farmer launched into a long-winded diatribe against me, detailing the reasons I was not a good candidate and should not run for office. She probably considered it an intervention, but to us it felt like a mean-spirited attack by a woman we considered a dear friend. I was later able to describe the incident in a writing exercise on dialogue for my creative writing class, which I share here.

CREATIVE INTERLUDE II: AMBUSH AT THE FARM—A DIALOGUE

Thanks for having us over for dinner at the farm. As you know I've decided to run for state senate. I'm very interested in talking to you about the campaign and hopefully you will also run. It would be great for us to run together!

Claire, we need to talk. You can't run for office. You can't win! Your opponent is unbeatable. He's everywhere!

Well somebody has to run against him. It might as well be me. I know it's a long shot but the campaign will be a good way to get our issues on the agenda. Are you going to run again? I think you should.

I'm not running, and you shouldn't either. Do you even live in this state?

What? Do I live in this state? Yes, of course! I've lived here for almost four years. You know that! I worked on your campaign, you know, the year my dad died.

Claire, you can't win. You don't even know anybody!

What are you talking about? I know plenty of people! And anyway, that's what a campaign is for, to get to know people, to get your name out there.

Claire, we need a good candidate. You need to build your resume!

My resume? I need to build my resume—or I need to know more people? They are not the same thing.

A lesbian can't win in this district. You know what I went through.

Yes, the homophobia you experienced was terrible, but if I don't run because I'm a lesbian, then they win.

You have no experience.

You had no experience when you ran!

You should run for the school board first.

School board?

Yes, school board. Then later on you can run for senate, once you get some experience.

I don't want to run for school board. Besides, those are two totally different positions. There's no connection between school board and the state senate.

Yes, there is, Claire! That's how things work. You run for school board first, then the senate.

That is not how things work. There's no connection.

You . . . you don't even have a platform!

I do have a platform!

What, Claire? What are you going to run on?

I'm committed to advancing the progressive agenda.

The progressive agenda! Like what? I hope you don't think you are going to run on minimum wage.

I support raising the minimum wage.

You can't run on that! You're crazy. The Chamber will never support you.

I don't expect to get the Chamber's support. That's not my base.

You need to talk to people. Ask them if they think you should run.

I've already made the decision. The county chair asked me to run, and I'm running. Maybe you're right, maybe I won't win. But as I said, it's not just about winning. It's also about getting the issues I care about on the agenda and building capacity within the community.

But I want someone who can win! I am going to find a good candidate to run.

What? You're going to look for someone to run against me? Are you kidding me? After all we did for your campaign when you ran?

A lesbian can't win. You need to think about this. If you decide to run . . .

I am running! How many times do I have to tell you that? I am running! The decision has been made. Are you saying you won't support me?

If you make it through the primary, I will support you then. But I want a good candidate.

Next year? I was hoping you would support me now, perhaps by sharing your volunteer list.

No, absolutely not! Those people are personally loyal to me. They support me!

But you're not running.

I haven't decided. But I won't share my volunteer list, and if I do decide to run, I will not associate with your campaign in any way. We will stay totally separate.

Are you kidding me? How is that going to work when we are running for house and senate in the same district in the same party?

Claire, if you make it through the primary, I will support you then. I will campaign for you and do whatever I can to get you elected. But not before that.

If I somehow make it through the primary, then you will support me . . . so next year . . .

Yes, but I want a good candidate to run.

I am a good candidate!

You can't win. I know this is hard for you to hear, dear. You have no idea what it's like to be gay-bashed. It's the worst thing that can happen to you.

No, the worst thing that can happen is being betrayed by a friend.

THE AFTERMATH

Mikki and I both felt very wounded by our friend Lady Farmer's surprise attack, and it took us a while to digest the incident. When Lady Progressive called the next day to find out how the dinner went, we told her about "the ambush," as we called it. She feigned surprise and vehemently denied knowing anything about it. We didn't think she would lie to us, her two best friends. As it turns out, however, Lady Progressive actually master-minded the entire event. Lady Farmer's partner told me that point-blank when she apologized for her part in the attack, which consisted of asking us if we were going to fly the lesbian flag. She said she tried to talk Lady Farmer out of it, and threatened to boycott the dinner, but decided not to. It also took us a while to understand that Lady Staffer was an architect of the event as well, not just an unwitting bystander. We found out the truth from her wife—an old friend of Mikki's from DC—who exited the room as soon as Lady Farmer started berating me, apparently not wanting anything to do with the confrontation.

When I refused to get out of the race, even after the intervention, Lady Progressive became increasingly angry and hurtful in her criticisms of me, moving from political prognostication to character assassination. Yet for personal and political reasons, I kept trying to smooth things over—hear her out, respond to her arguments, make my case. In May, I invited her to join my campaign inner team—since she liked working as a strategist, I thought that might reignite her interest—and she agreed, so I thought we were cool. Finally, she was back on board!

Having spent my entire professional career advocating democratic theory and practice, I planned to incorporate those themes into the campaign. My first draft of a platform began with a statement of values: "The values a person holds indicate how she will approach complicated political issues. As a teacher and student of American political thought, Claire has long advocated a return to the values of the **American Republic** in its best sense. Those values include **Liberty** (personal autonomy and freedom from arbitrary power), **Equality** (under the law for everyone), **Popular Sovereignty** (giving people control over the forces that govern their lives), **Public-Spiritedness** (the disposition that considers the good of the community along with individual rights), **Participation** (of citizens in the governing process), and **Accountability** (of elected officials to the People)." The document also included a long list of possible campaign issues, including a lot of democracy reform issues (straight off the Common Cause website) that I considered important, such as decreasing the amount of money in politics, increasing transparency in government, redistricting reform, lobbying reform, and early voting, as well as progressive issues like affordable health care, public education, sustainable development, fair treatment for manufactured home owners, and combatting sea level rise. I planned to see which of these gained traction after talking directly with voters.

When Lady Progressive arrived at the meeting, I felt optimistic about reconciling. Then, she denounced me in front of the entire group, telling my inner team all the reasons I should not run and could not win. Next, she took a red pen and dramatically crossed out every issue on my proposed platform. "You don't need a platform," she proclaimed. "Lopez has no platform. No one in Sussex County has a platform." The idea of not having a platform seemed ludicrous at the time, but I have subsequently learned that most state legislative candidates around the country do not in fact have platforms.[6] Nevertheless, I could not imagine running without a platform. What would I tell people when they asked why I was running?

After multiple attempts to reconcile with Lady Progressive got rebuffed, I finally gave up on the possibility of smoothing things over and, unfortunately, the conflict continued. Lady Progressive and Lady Farmer spent the entire rest of the campaign—almost a year and a half—doing everything they could to undermine me. They badmouthed me behind my back, spread lies about me, told people who wanted to volunteer for both me and Lady Farmer that they had to choose (even though my senate district encompassed her house district), tried to sabotage my fundraising efforts, and a lot of other things. We tried our best to keep the conflict out of public view, but the Ladies let people know and of course blamed the whole thing on me. The week before the election, Lady Progressive told a retired Methodist bishop that Mikki flipped her the bird, which, if you know Mikki, is absurd. Her enemies get the deep freeze not the middle finger. It's very difficult to combat a whisper campaign, so we did our best to follow the advice of a politically well-seasoned friend: "Just keep your head down and keep working." And in the end, we did win some people over with our tireless work ethic.

Why did the Ladies turn on me so viciously? Based on subsequent events, if I had to guess, I would say that the Speaker decided he wanted me out of the race and enlisted Lady Progressive to do his dirty work. That exact thing actually happened when I briefly decided to run for school board in spring 2012, and the Christian Right–supporting wife of the Speaker's best friend decided she wanted to run. So, it was probably the Speaker, but it could have been something else. Maybe Lady Farmer had already decided to run (despite her many denials) and somehow saw me as a threat. Perhaps Lady Progressive wanted to run for the state senate seat, and I squeezed her out. Or maybe it's simply that Lady Progressive told me not to run and was incensed that I disobeyed her. I will never know for sure, but the events detailed in chapter 5 point to the Speaker.

PROVINCIALISM AND THE QUASI-FEUDAL MENTALITY

Once my campaign got started, it surprised me to discover that elections in Sussex County were not issue based but mostly popularity contests, and that politicians tended to run on the basis of their biographies—how long their family has lived in the county, how long they have been married, the number of children they have, things like that—rather than on actual issues. At candidate forums, I heard numerous candidates, given only five minutes to speak, spend precious time recounting each grown child's current profession. Family connections seemed to matter a lot, and members of the "old families" had particular clout. Indeed, Senator Lopez's wife was the granddaughter of a longtime state senator, a retired police captain, which no doubt eased his rise to power. People accepted Lopez with no problem, which is a bit surprising, since he is not white, being of Puerto Rican descent.

I will never forget one candidate—a Sussex County native and military veteran with biker-style facial hair and a prominent country accent—who spoke at a Democratic Club luncheon, all about his family and not one issue mentioned. It was around the time that a national scandal arose about the handling of corpses of deceased troops at Dover Airforce Base. In one case the mortician sawed an arm off a marine's corpse, so he could jam the body into a casket, and workers routinely threw pieces of human flesh in the garbage—all of which I found totally appalling and a violation of my religious beliefs about the treatment of the dead. Sitting next to the candidate at lunch with not much to say, I broached the subject of the scandal. "As a vet, you must be really upset about what's been going on at Dover Airforce Base." He just stared at me, so I said, "They threw human flesh in the trash." The man replied, "Just scraps."

In my view the Sussex County custom of running on family connections and biography instead of issues poses a problem for democracy because it makes it harder for voters to understand which policies a candidate will support, if elected. Even worse, it bolsters a problematic quasi-feudal mentality—the belief that those with family roots in the county have some sort of rightful entitlement to control the political process or that the views of the longtime residents (the "from-here's") somehow count for more than those of who recently joined the community (the "come-here's"). I came to learn that in Sussex County many people believe a certain set of "good ole boys," and their anointed designees, should be in charge of the county, as they always have been, an issue discussed at length in the next chapter. To be clear, in the Delaware context, I define "good ole boys" as the bipartisan, fraternity-like network of white men with family roots in the state, who valorize masculinity, particularly in its working-class form, as evidenced by the particular esteem they show for police officers, firefighters, corrections officers, and veterans.

It also surprised me to learn that party identification does not operate in formerly rural Sussex County the way it does in national politics. Many people seemed to view party identification as part of their family heritage, not an indicator of their actual political beliefs, so they never realigned. Consequently, many Democrats did not support the current party agenda. We called them "Dixiecrats." For example, the first day I announced my run, I got this message on Facebook from a prominent local man: "As a Dem, I will not support anyone that runs on the progressive radicals or anyone supports the lgbt and trys [sic] to take my rights away for a small group of people. Why don't you try working for all the people?" His wife, also a registered Democrat, would repeatedly gay-bash me on talk radio and was a huge fan of my Republican opponent. And then she had the nerve to complain that I didn't knock on her door to ask for her vote!

At the same time, some Republicans had also not realigned. One of my supporters said she registered as a Republican back in the 1970s because she considered the Democrats in Sussex County the "redneck party," and she never switched. Another had registered Republican because she used to live in a Republican-dominated area, and even though she claimed to support the Democratic Party platform, she inexplicably refused to change her registration. Apparently, many people view party identification as a statement of their identity, rather than a commitment to a set of policies or a tactical decision. That must be the reason so many Democrats express outrage that Bernie Sanders is "not a Democrat," even though he ran on that party line—a criticism I find absurd.

While I talked with community members about local issues in homes and on doorsteps all over the district, Senator Lopez had no platform and virtually no field game. Instead, he generated a constant stream of pictures of himself with his beautiful, blonde wife and two young daughters. He even put a picture of himself and his family on his campaign signs—not a standard practice—some of which measured ten feet by ten feet and, by the end of the campaign, appeared on big-developer-owned land all over the district. The only other candidate to include a family photo on his signs was the retired cop who ran the homophobic whisper campaign against Lady Farmer. I guess they do not agree with Democratic Party campaign experts, who insist, "Signs don't vote!"

I found it challenging to run against a popular man with a good-looking traditional family who had a slim legislative record and no platform, especially since I am married to another woman and have no children. In talking about education during our one debate, Lopez came right out and said, "I'm the only one on this stage that actually has children." Apparently my twenty years of teaching experience count for nothing in his mind. While he presented himself as a nice guy, and a moderate, one of his campaign emails actually said point-blank that I, Claire Snyder-Hall, am "not the kind of person" that should be elected to office. I guess his supporters got the message, since one said loudly when she saw me, "I love Senator Lopez because he's normal. He has a normal family. He's normal."

As it turns out, however, right after the election we heard from multiple, very reliable sources—who could not wait to tell me—that Senator Lopez had been cheating on his wife during his entire family values campaign against me, a story that somehow never made the local paper. His wife divorced him shortly after that, yet he remains in office, unscathed by the scandal. His alleged mistress, a dear friend of the Speaker, also survived politically and has risen in the Democratic Party ranks, so I guess both male and female candidates can now get away with adultery. Score one for liberal feminism.

MOBILIZING A GRASSROOTS CAMPAIGN

Since I have long been committed to democratic theory and practice, I saw myself as a candidate connected to the community. We wanted our platform to reflect the things people hold valuable or needed done to make their lives and the community better. In the early stages of the campaign, I talked to people on doorsteps and in living rooms all across the district. In an approach informed by the principles of deliberative democracy, I would ask them to name the issues that concerned them, and we would discuss the pros and cons of various options for addressing the problem and the ways in which government and communities might work together to make positive change. When I got home, I sent each voter with whom I spoke a personalized follow-up letter. It was a lot of work, but a progressive state senator recommended the process. He claims that door-knocking and follow-up letters played a huge role in his upset victory against the senate pro tem in the 2012 Democratic primary.

From talking with community members, I discovered that unchecked development was, without a doubt, the number one issue of concern to people in our coastal community. They were also concerned, however, about the shortage of healthcare professionals, a lack of transportation options, and the overemphasis on standardized testing in the public schools. So those issues became my platform. Focusing particularly on the needs of seniors, who constituted the vast majority of residents in the district, I made efforts to brand myself as the good daughter who would fight for them. My social media emphasized my connections to the community and the momentum of our campaign.

Although only in office two years, Senator Lopez, like most elected officials, enjoyed a strong incumbency advantage. As a sitting state senator, he got invited to everything, and when he showed up somewhere—like a nursing home, for example—it was news, a human-interest story, covered in the local newspaper. In contrast, when I showed up at an event, it was considered political, not news, and not worthy of coverage. In addition, I was not welcome everywhere, especially not nursing homes, where administrators apparently think it is their place to deny residents (who are still voters) access to candidates. Why can't the residents decide for themselves? Indeed, one time I was invited by a resident to do a meet and greet at a nursing home, and the attendees loved it. One gentleman put my sticker on his walker to help the campaign.

Moreover, the owner of the very influential biweekly local newspaper that everybody read supported my opponent financially, which does not in itself constitute bias. However, one of his editorial board members openly made fun of me on Facebook, after I called his wife, a registered Democrat, to ask for her vote. How ridiculous that I thought a registered Democrat might vote for me! The editor and his cronies predicted I would lose with only 20 percent of the vote. I saw the post because Senator Lopez shared it on his page. After that, the paper suddenly stopped publishing the photos and press releases I sent them.

Despite these challenges, we ran a grassroots shoe-leather campaign that mobilized hundreds of volunteers and small donors. We were gratified that people regularly invited us into their homes to meet their friends and neighbors. I would spend about ten minutes telling my personal story, highlighting community issues, and asking for their help. I generally saw people nodding when I talked about our platform, since the issues we prioritized were in fact those that people cared most about, and we inevitably got volunteers, some of whom took me out door-knocking every single week. People were excited to join our democratic community!

One question emerged over and over: How would I deal with the partisan polarization of American politics? My response arose directly from my knowledge of deliberative democracy. I said the people are not really as polarized as the media wants us to think, which is still true, even in the age of Trump.[7] When it comes to issues, we all struggle internally with conflicting imperatives. To use a current example, in thinking about responses to the coronavirus pandemic, most people care about public health, economic viability, and civil liberties, but there are tensions among those values and we weigh them differently. While it is easy to demonize others, if you resist that urge, there is often a way to find common ground across difference or at least mutual respect.

At the time I believed that people could converse about political issues with goodwill and a shared respect for democratic process, although that seems to be less the case since the 2016 election, with people now at each other's throats. Indeed, since I ran, partisan polarization has made its way from Washington, DC, into state capitols all over the country, not only because of President Trump's divisiveness but also because of the Koch brothers–funded American Legislative Exchange Council (ALEC) and its agenda.[8] In other words, the current polarization did not arise naturally but has been deliberately stoked by vested interests that benefit by keeping the people divided, particularly working people. In response, I do not give up on the possibility of democracy but believe we need to reframe political issues in terms of class struggle—the 1% versus the 99%—rather than hot-button cultural issues that ignite battles over identity.

Given it was our first campaign, Mikki and I took a lot of advice from "political experts," incorporating the so-called "best practices" of contemporary campaigning where we could. We refused, however, to create a top-down organization with a campaign manager calling the shots, despite pressure to do so from experts. We had no paid staff. During the first months, Mikki led our team—her first of many campaigns—but we ran by committee. Mikki gave anyone who volunteered more than once a title and an assignment—a strategy called "ladders of empowerment" that she learned from "The Wellstone Guide."[9] As election day got closer, we asked a retired friend with a lot of political expertise to serve as campaign manager on a volunteer basis, and she graciously accepted.

I definitely did not enjoy fundraising, but I did call-time anyway. The first time I phoned someone to ask for money, I felt physically ill. In the end, however, I ended up raising more money than any other candidate not running statewide, which allowed us to pay for ten professionally produced mailers. Most contributions came from small donors, although I did take money from organizations I supported, such as labor unions, Planned Parenthood, and Emily's List, but not big developers. We also convened fundraising events at a variety of price points—from a pass-the-hat social hour to a $40 wine-tasting to a $100 VIP reception at a horse farm, hosted by a generous, well-to-do man, whom my mother called "Mr. Money Bags," and his lovely wife. I learned that there are two types of donors: the ones who say, "I will write you a check, but please do not make me attend an event" and those who expect to be feted. Personally, I am the latter type. The running joke is that before I write a check, I need a glass of wine and a mini-quiche!

OUR FIELD GAME: DOOR-KNOCKS AND PHONE CALLS

During the campaign, I was known for my door-knocking, at first by myself and then later with others. I'll never forget knocking on my one-thousandth door, in a manufactured housing community, and hoping someone would be home so I could post about it on Facebook. It never occurred to me to fake it. Luckily, a ninety-six-year-old man with a walker opened the door, and after I introduced myself, he said, "I hope you like World War II veterans!" I replied, "Are you kidding? I love World War II veterans!" So, he invited me in, and I had the opportunity to spend some time with him, his eighty-nine-year-old wife, who had Alzheimer's, and their daughter, a sixty-something senior who took care of them every day. We took some pictures, and they promised me their votes. Since my campaign focused on seniors, it felt like a sign. Sadly, the man passed away, shortly after Election Day, and of course, we sent a card.

On weekends in 2014, we would gather about a dozen volunteers to go door-to-door in neighborhoods across the district, culminating in a tailgate party with beer, wine, and cheese. Mikki and I strongly believe that building relationships—social capital—forms the foundation for successful organizing, and we found that breaking bread together really helped build the campaign. We know it deepened our relationships with the volunteers, many of whom became personal friends. I later recruited about half a dozen of them to join the 14RD committee that I still chaired. I did not feel I could resign, because then Lady Progressive would have become chair in my district, and she was already doing enough damage without that added power.

Due to both our philosophy and a lack of funds, Mikki and I ran the campaign out of our home—another no-no according to the experts—and we view that as key to generating support. We used to phone-bank every Tuesday during 2014 at our place. At the first one, I asked my former student to provide a training, like the ones he did for the marriage equality campaign. Whenever he ran a phone bank, he would push volunteers to staff the phones for close to four hours and then order pizza, around 9:30 or 10:00, after the debrief. That did not work well with my crowd of older folks. At the first event, we served pizza, albeit before rather than after call time. The second evening, however, people showed up with takeout salads in hand. Taking the hint, we implemented a new policy: Our people eat real food at 6:00 p.m., then we make phone calls for two hours only, followed by dessert during debrief. That worked very well. It was not too onerous, so it kept people wanting to come back. Originally, I cooked dinner for everyone, but soon one of our most dedicated team leaders took charge of the food, and we transitioned to a potluck format. I had the opportunity to write about those gatherings—mimicking the style of *The Things They Carried*—for my creative writing class.

CREATIVE INTERLUDE III:
THE CALLS THEY MADE AND THE FOOD THEY COOKED

They didn't believe those who said she was too inexperienced to run for state senate, that she was too new, too gay, too progressive for the district. They pointed out that her opponent had little experience when he first ran, two years prior, but since he was a man it didn't matter, that he was not from the county either, and too conservative for the district. They told her she was a great candidate, authentic, the real deal, a rising star, the next state senator, the future governor, someone who could be counted on to fight for them. They liked that she didn't take money from big developers. They believed in her.

They gave her advice on how to meet voters, at farmers' markets, grocery stores, and festivals, like Shrimp Feast, Boast the Coast, Horseshoe Crab Fest, Sea Witch, Apple Scrapple, Punkin Chunkin, and the annual chicken dinner at the fairgrounds, everywhere people gathered, even if they weren't all voters. They introduced her to friends and neighbors, family, and coworkers. They followed her on Facebook, liking all the photos she posted of herself at community fundraisers, parades, meet and greets, with friends and family, elected officials, volunteers, and voters. They donated money—a maximum donation, a monthly check, as much as they could afford, the price of an event. They volunteered their time. They lifted her up.

They gathered weekly at her home to make phone calls for the campaign, using iPhones, Androids, and old-fashioned flip phones. They sat on sofas and loveseats, on dining room chairs, folding chairs, and lawn chairs. They found space in closets, bathrooms, and cars, on the staircase, in the laundry room, and on the porch.

Before dialing, they helped themselves to food she made in Pyrex casseroles, filled with lasagnas, with rich cream sauce, earthy mushrooms, and flowery artichokes; with piquant red sauce and savory spinach; with nothing but fresh mozzarella and a tomato sauce that included orange juice as a secret ingredient; pasta layers sliding around on the plate because they didn't have time to set; or enchiladas with tortillas rolled strangely around pineapple and extra sharp cheddar or inauthentically around spinach and mushrooms; or the surprisingly delicious chicken, brown rice, and Swiss cheese casserole she made after she stopped keeping kosher.

When she got too busy to cook, they brought food from their own homes to share, special homemade meatballs, plump and oozing juice, in authentic Italian gravy; gluten-free pasta with symmetrical chunks of chicken, bright green broccoli florets, and almond-colored Alfredo sauce by Ragu; bowls of unseasoned risotto and chowder with enough for leftovers. They poured themselves goblets of the Essential Red, a good value at the local wine store. They grabbed bottles of Fat Tire from the fridge, wet with dew, drank tall glasses of cold filtered water, downed diet soda from black and silver cans, cold in their hands, and threw back the occasional glass of Maker's Mark on ice.

After dialing, they ate ice cream cake dessert from her Pyrex casseroles, made with Cool Whip and Jell-O pudding because she was rushed, or ice cream scooped from containers that are no longer half a gallon.

They brought cookies from home that they passed around on paper plates, peanut butter bars they claimed were gluten free, even though they weren't.

When they said their goodbyes, they went home to newly built homes, townhouses, and manufactured housing, spread throughout the district off roadways that were increasingly gridlocked with ritzy sedans, sexy convertibles, sporty Jeeps, and practical SUVs from Maryland, Virginia, DC, Pennsylvania, New Jersey, and New York.

They all wanted her to do something about the traffic.

PARTICIPATORY CAMPAIGN

Trying to run a grassroots campaign in a way that actualizes participatory democracy presents a challenge because that vision runs directly counter to the way professional campaign experts think about campaigns. For example, as I mentioned earlier, before I ran for state senate, I briefly considered a run for school board, having been recruited just months after moving to Rehoboth by Lady Staffer, who volunteered to serve as my campaign manager. Drawing on my work with the Kettering Foundation, I told her that I wanted to frame the campaign in terms of empowering the public to work with the public schools.[10] In response she told me, in no uncertain terms, that the average voter has a sixth grade mentality and will not understand my argument. I think she meant to say that she did not understand my argument because it was outside her bandwidth. Lady Staffer insisted that the only role for the public is paying taxes, and that we certainly do not want parents involved in the schools because all they do is cause problems. The public schools should be run by experts, she insisted. Shortly thereafter, I decided not to run, partly because of that, partly because my dad broke his hip, and partly because the Speaker enlisted Lady Progressive to get me out of the race, so his friend's wife, a supporter of Focus on the Family, could run instead, as mentioned earlier.

In contrast to that experience, during the state senate campaign, I made my argument about the need for community members to get more involved in politics directly to the people, not to my professional advisors, and the people had no problem understanding the concept of participatory democracy. While Lady Progressive told me that "nobody cares" about problems of democracy, like the distorting impact Big Money has on the political process, my supporters understood immediately the significance of my opponent's acceptance of funding from big developers: It meant he would put the economic interests of donors before the public good. They grasped my meaning right away when I said community members had been shut out of the democratic process, because they had gone to County Council meetings to voice their concerns and been dismissed because they were "not experts" on land use. Sadly, some responded that they used to be experts before they retired, instead of challenging the premise and invoking popular sovereignty and the accountability of elected officials to the people.

Personally, I wore lack of electoral experience as a badge of honor. My website read, "Claire is not a career politician, and we think that is a good thing." I tried not to be annoyed that people criticized my lack of experience holding office, while no one mentioned that my opponent had never held elective office before he ran. When I spoke, I argued that no one can predict every issue that might come up in the future, so it is most important to elect someone who shares your values, someone you can trust to do the right thing, to stand up, and speak truth to power. That message really resonated with people, and we picked up volunteers every time I gave a talk.

DR. JILL BIDEN COMES TO SUSSEX!

One of the most exciting moments of the campaign began with an idea Mikki had at a Democratic Party picnic: Maybe Dr. Jill Biden, who is from Delaware and taught English and Writing at Delaware Technical and Community College, would do a fundraiser to celebrate the fact that five women were running for office in Sussex County, a historic first. To me it sounded unlikely, but Mikki was on a mission. My wife is gregarious, to say the least; she loves talking to people, and she naturally works every room she enters. At the picnic she became fast friends with the man who ran the fundraising apparatus for Biden's son, Beau Biden, the Delaware Attorney General. Mikki asked the fundraiser to pitch the idea, and he agreed. "Give me some dates," he said.

I was at a Kettering Foundation meeting when Mikki got the email: "Does September 28th work?" It was not one of the dates provided, but Mikki replied, "Yes, that works!" We would make it work. Given the tension between our campaign and Lady Farmer's, we decided to enlist the Sussex County Women's Democrat Club to organize the event, instead of us. The planning committee included people from all five campaigns, and they dealt with a lot of micromanaging from the White House. The committee decided to hold the event at an outdoor venue on the water with a ticket price affordable for working families. Initially, Mikki had been insistent that since she made the event happen, I should get to introduce Dr. Biden, but the committee decided that the Western Sussex Candidate should have that honor, since the event would take place in her district, which made sense. However, it was specifically negotiated that she and I would together greet "Dr. B" when she arrived and escort her to the stage.

On the day of the event, as the bright sun beat down upon us, I was glad to be wearing a sleeveless turquoise dress and sandals, instead of the dark jacketed pantsuits worn by some of my colleagues. As we awaited the arrival of the guest of honor, we noticed some boats just off shore with armed guards, hovering in the surrounding waters. Feeling a little anxious, I located the Western Sussex Candidate, so we could get ready to greet Dr. Biden. "You do not need to do anything," she told me. "I will let you know as soon as I get the call. Don't worry." About a half hour later, Mikki came running up to me and said, "Claire, Dr. B is here! You need to get up there!" And let me tell you, I literally sprinted to the entry gate. Elbowing my way through the crowd, I made it to the front, just in time to see the Western Sussex Candidate escorting the Second Lady into the venue, practically arm-in-arm. Luckily, I made it just in time to get a handshake, as Dr. Biden walked by, reed thin and radiant in her blue shift dress and fuchsia suede high heels.

The rest of the event went swimmingly. All five candidates sat on stage with Dr. Biden, who gave a smart, interesting talk. The audience turned out to be filled with mostly my older, retired supporters, no working families in sight. I got to give a rah-rah speech that revved up the crowd, and we took some great photos with the guest of honor, who graciously endured selfies with everyone. It was a day to remember. Afterward, the Western Sussex Candidate reportedly went around telling everyone that the entire event was her idea. Sisterhood is powerful!

THE PEOPLE VS. BIG DEVELOPERS

As Election Day approached, our campaign came out against the plans of an out-of-state builder to construct a gigantic mall on environmentally sensitive land, right on the side of a super-congested highway. As I went door-to-door introducing myself to people, I told them about the mall, and not a single person supported it. In fact, people were outraged. When we found out about the nonpublicized, public hearing County Council had scheduled to discuss approval, we decided to let everyone know about it, as we canvassed. To our surprise, the developer suddenly decided to pull the project because it "had become a campaign issue"!

That success got me invited onto a local talk-radio show. The host claimed to support me, but as soon as we went on the air, she depicted me as a crazy radical. "You distributed flyers," she exclaimed. "Tell us what you said on those flyers and why you did it." The flyers just let people know that County Council was holding a public hearing, I told her—and the phones lit up. The first caller, whom I could identify by voice and first name, accused me of having "a degree in lesbian studies," a field that did not yet exist when I was in school. The second caller, whom I also recognized, criticized me for not knocking on her door, even though she strongly supported Lopez and had previously gay-bashed me on talk radio. The third caller insisted I had moved to the state in 2012, not 2011, apparently a significant difference in his mind. Not surprisingly, I was accused of being "against jobs," mostly by white working-class male callers, including a man the host referred to as "the right-wing blogger." I had met said man at the state fair and knew he did not even live in my district. A few supporters also called in to praise me. Believe it or not, I had a great time. I discovered I love doing talk radio—particularly the part where I always get the last word.

MEETING IN THE PARKING LOT

Right on the heels of the radio interview, I attended a candidate forum at the American Legion. As I stood outside the venue waiting for my veteran friend, a young man standing next to me said, "You don't know me, but I know you. I'm the president of the local Libertarian Party. You really got killed on the radio yesterday." I replied, "Really? All my friends said I did great. And by the way, I don't know why you're supporting Lopez. He is neither a social nor an economic libertarian. At least I support personal liberty, so I'm a half a libertarian." He was not convinced, but then again, we lived in a county where the libertarian candidates had government jobs.

After the forum, as I strode alone across the long, dark parking lot, I noticed three men leaning against my car, including the libertarian president, the right-wing blogger, and some other guy. Uh oh. "Good evening, gentleman. Are you waiting for me or is this just a coincidence?" They claimed it was just a coincidence, as it turned out, but I ended up having a great conversation with the blogger. He said he supported the Gigantic Town Center because it would create jobs. I pointed out that the developers were from out of state and would probably bring their own workers, so no local jobs. Plus, it would put the outlet mall out of business, so again, no additional jobs. We actually had a great conversation not only about jobs in Sussex but also about unions, which he opposed. My arguments did not change his opinions, but we both left the conversation respecting each other more. He even said he'd be happy to post an essay by me on his blog. He said he found me "fascinating."

UNION BUGS AND INDEPENDENT EXPENDITURES

I strongly support unions because without them workers have no way to stand up to their much more powerful employers. In Delaware, labor unions still have a lot of clout, and I hoped to get their endorsements, beginning with the AFL-CIO. Way back in 2013, before I announced, I asked a couple of friends, who own a small printing business in Rehoboth, to produce some business cards for me. They were not a union shop, and in fact only had one employee besides themselves. Once I learned that all campaign materials had to have a union bug on them, I stopped doing business with them. When I went to the AFL-CIO interview, however—a lengthy process with a large committee of inquisitors—I gave them one of my cards, not realizing business cards also needed bugs, and they called me out, which was quite embarrassing. I also had to justify the reason I drove a Subaru Forester, rather than a union-made American car. My dad gave his beloved car to me when he forgot how to drive, I told them. It was a little stressful, but they ultimately endorsed me, as did AFSCME and subsequently the UAW. Given that experience, whenever I work with candidates, I always stress the importance of having union bugs on all campaign material and swag.

I also aspired to get endorsed by the Service Employees International Union (SEIU). Sometime during her days working in DC, Mikki knew someone who knew someone who organized for SEIU, so she decided to reach out. We figured it was a long shot, and I did not think much about it. Then one night, well after 10 p.m., the phone rang. I could not imagine who would call so late. When I picked up the phone, the voice on the other end identified himself as Victor, the SEIU organizer for the area. He said he did not think he could do much for me, but he wanted to meet anyway. So, the next day, I drove to Dover to meet him for lunch, and we really hit it off. Victor was a top-notch guy on every level, an ABD who loved union work, so much so that he decided not to finish his PhD and became a full-time organizer. By the end of our meeting, he told me he would ask SEIU to endorse me and support my campaign with an "independent expenditure."[11] I was ecstatic!

In order to get an official endorsement, I had to be interviewed. During that session, Victor asked if there was anything in my past that my opponent could use against me. I mentioned my long list of publications on a range of topics—from wifely submission to Marxism. Victor and his colleague argued about whether Lopez and his cronies would use my publications against me. Victor said, "Beer-bet he doesn't look at them," and as it turns out, he was correct! None of my academic work was used against me. SEIU endorsed me, gave me a maximum donation, and did a very generous, independent expenditure that paid for mailers, professional canvassers, and a poll—none of which we knew about beforehand because we were legally prohibited from coordinating. Getting endorsed by SEIU was one of my proudest accomplishments, and we had great times hanging out with Victor during the campaign.

Independent expenditures can be great, but they also introduce an uncontrollable element into a campaign, as exemplified by the negative mailers sent by the Victory Fund that hurt the Protégé's campaign. One day, I went door-knocking in a relatively conservative neighborhood in my district. When I introduced myself on the first doorstep, the woman said, "There were people here from your campaign just yesterday." At first, I had no idea what she was talking about. "Are you sure they were for me, Claire Snyder-Hall?" She said she was positive. So, I called Mikki to find out whether any volunteers had been assigned to the neighborhood. She said, "No . . . it must be SEIU!" Wow, I thought, that's exciting. They are actually sending out canvassers to support my campaign! Gotta love Victor!

The man at the second house also informed me that someone from our campaign had been by, but he said he was not sure he could support me. He thought I was a little too radical, based on the things that were said about me the day before. When I pressed him for more information, he said, "Here. This is the information they left with me." He handed me a piece of paper with information about me, which highlighted that I was a Jewish lesbian PhD from Washington, DC. I was a little flummoxed to see those materials, but I had to laugh. Wow, it sure is too bad we cannot coordinate with the SEIU folks because the information that they think is important from my bio is not reflective of the points I would have emphasized, especially in this neighborhood! Oh well, there's nothing I can do about it, since coordination is illegal.

I told that story with a resigned chuckle for years, but when I shared it with a political theory friend a couple years later, he just looked at me and said, "Claire. You know that wasn't SEIU." What? "It was the other side," he informed me. "People do stuff like that all the time." I am embarrassed to say I was a little stunned—me and my stubbornly naïve heart—but it must be true. Certainly, SEIU canvassers would not think for a minute that "Jewish lesbian PhD from Washington, DC" should be emphasized on the doorsteps, and I've always wondered about the reason the guy handed me pieces of paper instead of one of the beautiful palm cards SEIU produced for my campaign.

Who would do such a thing? While I cannot know for sure, I suspect it was the Christian Right's Delaware Family Policy Council. They did a homophobic voter guide in 2012 against the Protégé and Lady Farmer, and I was surprised they did nothing against me. After a little investigation, I discovered that the Family Council probably did not attack me publicly because if they had, they would have been required by a new law, passed in 2013, to disclose their donors. During my 2014 campaign, the council was actively contesting the law in court, and in 2016 the Delaware Supreme Court upheld the law. So, they most likely did it, but did Lopez know about it? He's such a "nice guy." Surely, he would never do such a thing!

When SEIU did canvass, they did not leave random sheets of paper behind, but they did cause a bit of a stir in one conservative neighborhood when they asked voters to sign pledge cards. More specifically, they would ask voters to sign a card, promising to vote for me, and then right before the election, they would mail the cards back to the voters, reminding them of their pledge—a very cutting-edge technique shown to significantly increase turnout. For some reason, this tactic offended at least one white male loudmouth, who complained about it on Facebook and, for some reason, to the Speaker of the House, who shared with me his disapproval. Strangely, the tactic became controversial only in my campaign, not in the campaign of US senator Chris Coons, which also used pledge cards. As far as I know, he got no pushback. Then again, maybe it was not the pledge cards that agitated the loudmouth but the fact that the canvassers were young, hip-looking people of color, which I discovered when I had a chance to meet them after the election and thank them for their hard work.

YOU CAN'T FIGHT THE ZEITGEIST

Overall, running for state senate was a great experience. On one hand, it was an incredible ego trip to have thousands of people support me, many very enthusiastically, tell me I'm "the real deal" and should run for governor. On the other hand, it was daunting to consider that people really believed they could count on me to speak truth to power and never sell out. I will never forget the manufactured homeowner who looked me straight in the eye and said, "I know I can trust you to fight for us, Claire. We are counting on you." The gravity of that obligation weighed on me, and I literally prayed daily for strength.

As November 2014 approached, people seemed to be coming out of the woodwork to support us. The night before the election, we had well over a hundred people through our house, picking up campaign day materials, including Senator Coons. I was embarrassed that I had no food to offer him, but he arrived late and the buffet had been decimated! The crazy Republican lady down the street—who would later kill a neighbor's dog—stood out in front of her house yelling, "Don't park here. Senator Lopez is coming by any minute. Any minute!" Not surprisingly, Lopez was a no-show.

When Election Day arrived, Mikki got a text first thing in the morning from a friend, telling her about "the long line of old white guys, waiting to vote against Claire." At that moment, Mikki knew we would lose, but she did not tell me about the text until much later. We had also seen the results of a poll conducted several weeks prior that said we would lose, which helped us prepare emotionally for the inevitable. We shed tears of disbelief when we first saw it, but by Election Day, we had adjusted to the thought, and I spent the day going from polling place to polling place, greeting voters. For some reason, I felt absolutely exhausted all day—to the point of actually taking a nap in my car—but I had to look alive for our big volunteer party that night. We had a large turnout, good food and drink, and I went around thanking people and prepping them for the loss. "I don't know. I'm not sure we will win," I told them.

Shortly after the polls closed, Mikki pulled me aside and showed me the preliminary results. "Honey, you need to call Lopez," and the county chair nodded. But not all precincts have reported yet! I replied. They both looked at me with sad but firm faces. "Claire you need to make the call." But . . . ! "Claire." Believe me, it was a hard call to make. Lopez picked up on the first ring, and I said, "Congratulations Senator, and thank you for a good campaign." He thanked me then eagerly asked, "Are you going to Returns Day?" Returns Day, a Sussex County tradition that requires winning and losing candidates to ride to the county seat together in a carriage and then watch as political party leaders literally bury the hatchet—not literally, as in "my head literally exploded," but literally, as in an actual hatchet actually buried in a box of sand. "Yes, I will be there."

After getting off the phone, I strode to the microphone and broke the news to the crowd. As some wiped away tears, I thanked them again and ended with some kind of upbeat message. I lost that night, but I was not alone, which definitely cushioned the blow. Lady Farmer fared worse than in 2012, and in the end, not a single Democrat who had an opponent won in Sussex County that night, not even Senator Coons who won statewide. We all got swept away by the national "Red Tsunami" that presaged the Trump win in 2016. The Democrats lost control of the US Senate that day and lost more US House seats than any party since 1929. I am sure that being a "come-here" transplant hurt me at the polls, but it is also hard to buck national trends. Not surprisingly, however, there is more to the story.

CHAPTER 4

GOOD OLE BOYS VS. NASTY WOMEN
CULTURAL POLARIZATION IN US POLITICS

The year I ran for the Delaware State Senate was truly a pre-Trump year, a time when the forces that would propel Trump to victory two years later were gathering, but few yet realized it. Unbeknownst to me, I was campaigning in a district dominated by "good ole boys," whose culture I did not understand, or even fully recognize at the time.[1] Contrary to my belief back then, I was not simply a well-qualified woman running for office as a Democrat on the basis of issues but rather the bearer of an urban, cosmopolitan, professional class worldview that embraces equal rights for all, higher education, and a robust public sector—a worldview vehemently opposed by the provincially minded good ole boys who unofficially ran state and county, Democrats as well as Republicans.

When my opponent said I was "not the kind of person" who should be elected, I thought, at the time, he was referring only to my lesbian sexual orientation, since homophobia had been an issue in the 2012 election. In hindsight, however, I believe he was referring to my entire way of being. That is to say, in the minds of the good ole boys, I am, like Hillary Clinton, part the group that Steve Bannon maligns as a "bunch of dykes that come from the Seven Sisters schools up in New England"—a phrase that expresses animus not just toward lesbian community but also toward elite colleges, situated outside of the local community, where women learn to think of themselves as equals to men. Like Hillary, I am a "nasty woman"—a term used by Trump that has, since colonial days, denoted a woman who acts as a man's equal and refuses to defer to male authority.[2] Clearly, I had to be stopped.

DEMOCRATIC CULTURE MATTERS

Cultural issues played a big role in my campaign, and the culture I encountered was far from democratic. That poses a problem because democratic self-rule requires a democratic culture to support it. As Jean-Jacques Rousseau explained long ago, a self-governing republic needs citizens who have an internalized commitment to democratic values in their hearts, instilled through habits of democratic participation. Ben Franklin made the same point in a different way when he famously quipped that the Framers had given us "a republic if we can keep it." Our democratic republic was founded in a moment, but to maintain it, We the People must continually resist the many forces that potentially undermine political equality, popular sovereignty, and the rule of law applied impartially to all. To create and maintain a republic, an internalized commitment to an egalitarian and participatory democratic culture must replace old-school habits of powermongering and deference within civil society. People must become accustomed to standing up, rather than bowing down.

Writing on the heels of Trump's 2016 election, Rob Goodman describes the state of political culture in the United States this way:

> It's tempting to . . . point to all of the ways in which the behavior of Trump and his Republican enablers endangers democratic values. But I think that's overintellectualizing things. . . . When a system of norms is healthy, you don't follow them because you can reconstruct compelling, first-principles arguments for them. Of course, it's good that those arguments exist, so that we can step back from time to time and reflect critically on our rules for political conduct. But on a day-to-day level, the "correct" answer to a question like "Should you threaten to jail your opponent?" is not "No, and here are five reasons why." It's "*Are you crazy?*"
>
> When a system of norms is healthy, "*Are you crazy?*" works in practice because it draws on the force of habit—your own habits, and the collective habits that solidify as precedent and

custom. At their strongest, norms are ways of rendering certain uses of power nearly unthinkable and unspeakable. You don't threaten to jail your opponent because, well, you just don't.[3]

Goodman argues that Trump did not actually destroy democratic norms; he simply put his fist through the thin veneer of our so-called democracy and into the rotten, empty core where our democratic culture should be but possibly never was.

We need a democratic culture, but did we ever have one? Clearly racial and gender hierarchies have long given the lie to "American democracy," but even articulated in ideal terms, our system of representative government has allowed elites to rule in place of the people.[4] Goodman argues that when leaders get away with violating norms, it indicates that the context that gave rise to those norms has eroded. In his view, Trump's well-publicized norm-breaking has not actually undermined our democracy. It has simply revealed its weaknesses.

Yet Goodman fails to note a couple of things. First, Trump has not violated democratic norms with impunity; he has in fact angered people of all ideological persuasions (from Bill Kristol to Bernie Sanders), and many have taken to the streets in outrage. Indeed, Trump's blatant norm-breaking alienated people and arguably contributed to his loss in 2020. Moreover, in reaction to him, a democratic socialist movement has gained momentum. The Left is on the rise once again, and that arguably would not have been the case if Hillary Clinton had won. For the most part, only those who remain in the Republican Party applaud Trump's violations.

Second, when it comes to the violation of norms, we need to recognize that Trump's supporters are also outraged about norm-breaking. While they rejoice at his violation of *democratic* norms, they support him because he articulates their rage at the violation of traditional norms supporting male privilege, white privilege, and heterosexual privilege. They scream in rage when women, minorities, or LGBTQ people refuse to defer to their authority. For example, consider the approving way many white people have historically responded when a video shows police officers humiliating, beating, or even killing a Black person who did not instantaneously grovel before their power. That response was the norm for years, until things suddenly changed with the murder of George Floyd.

In the past I have found that even among white working-class liberals, criticizing the police can evoke outrage and defensiveness. Over time I have posted about a lot of controversial subjects on my Facebook page, and probably none has elicited more pushback than my criticisms of the police—and none of my friends support Trump. A lot of them, mostly women, have family members who are cops, or they worked in law enforcement themselves. Indeed, jobs in the police department are some of the few decent blue-collar jobs that remain, and a lot of people view cops as the good guys. They take criticisms of the police very personally.

In addition, a lot of white working-class men feel particularly aggrieved in this age of widening income inequality. They observe all around them the reality of white male supremacy; white men still control our political, economic, and military institutions, and according to the Christian Right ought to head the heterosexual-only family as well. Yet despite this societal dominance, many white working-class men do not feel very privileged and indeed many are, in fact, struggling. For example, 80 percent of jobs lost during the Great Recession were "male" jobs, and they have not been replaced. Moreover, during the coronavirus pandemic more women (33%) than men (28%) held jobs considered essential.[5] Sadly, working-class whites of both genders between ages forty-five and fifty-four are dying "deaths of despair"—because of drugs, alcohol, and suicide, as well as from an array of health problems. That phenomenon contributes to the larger demographic shift that will soon render white people a minority in the United States.[6]

That said, it is also important to note that while white working people face tough times, Black and brown working people also experience economic immiseration, and on top of that they have to deal with societal racism, including the government-sponsored cruelties of police violence, mass incarceration, and deportation, all exemplars of an authoritarian state. Put differently, working people of all races and genders, as well as the entire 99%, suffer under right-wing rule. "In the US, the so-called recovery since the 2008 crash has restored profits for financiers and big business many times over, but the poorest 90% of US residents are still worse off than they were in 2007."[7] The fallout of the coronavirus pandemic will no doubt exacerbate that inequality.

Despite shared immiseration, white working-class men, focusing exclusively on their own deteriorating plight, are increasingly fearful, anxious, or angry, and so are the women who are connected to them economically, culturally, or romantically.[8] White discomfort partially arises from changing demographics that are eroding their historically privileged place in the working-class hierarchy. Many feel resentful toward those they imagine are benefiting at their expense—less qualified women and

minorities, Black welfare recipients, and Latinx immigrants. They feel that
they have been waiting patiently, while those groups are "cutting in line."[9]

In addition, a lot of white working people feel they are treated with
disrespect by so-called "coastal elites," educated professionals who live on
the East or West Coast. While "many of the [so-called] 'coastal elites' are
just ordinary people conducting undramatic lives, with no outsize influence
or authority in their city or country," according to right-wing pundits, "they
fall into the same category as Wall Street executives."[10] Right-wing operatives
depict coastal elites as the class enemy of real hard-working Americans, and
in that way they keep the 99% divided. With class understood in cultural
rather than structural terms, Trump, a wealthy one-percenter, can invoke
working-class tropes to present himself as the anti-intellectual mouthpiece
of white working-class rage, among other things. He says with impunity
the unspeakable things they wish they could say.[11]

TRUMP VOTERS AND THE VALORIZATION OF PROVINCIALISM

Returning to my campaign for state senate, when you drill down to the
local level, I believe my campaign turned out to be a referendum on the
issues of culture and identity that would roil the country in 2016 and
beyond. While I doubt any Democrat could have won in Sussex in 2014,
I was not particularly well suited to run in that district, since I personally
epitomize the stereotypical "coastal elite" more than some other candidates
might have, which probably limited my appeal to people unlike myself.
Just by virtue of the type of person I am, I represent the very things that
irk Trump voters—a highly educated professional with a cosmopolitan
outlook who supports sexual freedom and nondeferential women. While
as a matter of principle, I do not look down my nose at anyone, I am
exactly the type of woman that Trump voters scorn. During the campaign,
however, I did not fully recognize the cultural divide in the district that
Trump has foregrounded so effectively.

As discussed in the previous chapter, in Sussex County, a lot of
people embrace the idea that being born and raised in the county gives
you some kind of special status in politics. That status is further enhanced
if your ancestors also came from Sussex and never left. The running joke
was that even if you lived in Sussex for eighty years, if you were not
born there, you were still a "come-here," never a "from-here"—a position
I find preposterous. Local pride is not just a Delaware thing. I know it

is a phenomenon in Florida as well, and I imagine all over the country, because so many Americans never move away from home. According to a 2008 Pew study, 57 percent of Americans have never lived outside their home state, and 37 percent never move out of their hometown, largely because of family ties. During the campaign, I learned that a lot of Sussex County parents do not want their children to leave the county, but the lack of affordable housing and decent-paying jobs pushes them away.

While I can imagine the appeal of having your children live nearby, my parents had a completely opposite set of aspirations for my brother and me. They wanted us to attend college in another state, away from our high school friends, and despite their modest means, they made sure we both had the chance to travel internationally as part of our education. They expected my brother and I would relocate to wherever our jobs—or, in my case, marriage—took us. That is the trajectory they both followed, and my brother and I did the same, although he ended up taking a professional job in Sarasota after college and has remained there. Honestly, I never expected to move back to Florida after I left in 1988, but I did return thirty years later, in order to spend time with my mother in her last years. After she passed, however, Mikki and I moved back to Rehoboth.

Over time, I have come to better appreciate the appeal of localism. It makes sense to believe that someone from your hometown will be more like you and thus better able to represent your interests in the legislature. Certainly, local knowledge can be very important. Yet, I would not take that position too far. I still believe that a person does not have to live somewhere for twenty years to understand local problems and play a role in fixing them, and certainly having ancestors who lived in an area for generations seems irrelevant as a job qualification. Political issues in Delaware, Florida, or any other state are really just particular versions of common US problems, which becomes evident when you read about controversies in other places.

CLASS IDENTITY AND CULTURE

Over time, I have come to understand the ways in which my worldview, as just described, is a product of my class status and the professional identity that shapes my self-conception, even when I am unemployed or underemployed. Joan Williams, who writes about "white working class" culture, explains this class-based difference of perspective as follows.

"Americans who graduate from college typically live very different lives than those who don't."[12] College graduates generally become professionals with " 'entrepreneurial networks': broad national networks of acquaintances who help them get jobs and do deals. For college-educated professionals, "families often live far apart, and their ties are chiefly emotional rather than economic."[13] Or, as in my case, you barely know most of your relatives.

In contrast, "non-elites," Williams tells us, "typically live their lives in tight, rooted 'clique networks' of people who have known each other forever and help each other out with everything from babysitting to house repairs. Family ties are different too. Family ties often remain central in the lives of adult children of those outside the elite."[14] They need each other to survive. Consequently, "Americans in different class locations live deeply different lives—in bubbles that rarely intersect," which contributes to political polarization, as evidenced in the 2016 election.[15]

Williams explains that when professional and working-class whites do interact—her study focuses exclusively on white people—the former often inadvertently offend the latter. "So much of what the professional elite identifies as normal life the white working class sees as a display of class privilege."[16] At social gatherings, professional class people normally ask, "What do you do?" as an icebreaker. That makes sense for those who are proud of their jobs, but most working-class jobs are nothing to brag about. Indeed, I will never forget a man who worked at the local hair salon angrily ranting at length about a time when one of his clients introduced him to her friends as "my hair stylist." He found that possessive term deeply offensive.

According to Williams, honor accrues only to a "few [jobs] in the working class—to firefighters, police, soldiers."[17] Indeed, she suggests that "patriotism . . . remains robust in working-class circles" because "being American is one of the only high-status categories they belong to."[18] I would add that patriotism is also strong because working-class people are more likely to have done military service, due to the so-called economic draft, and people tend to be proud of their accomplishments, particularly when they are challenging. Military training seems to profoundly affect the way people see themselves and the world.

In addition to the *cultural* differences highlighted by Williams, however, class conflict also involves *material* differences—which in my opinion ought to be more of the focus in discussions of class. We cannot overlook the fact that members of the professional class generally have more disposable income than working-class people—although not always—and some purchase second homes in quaint small towns in the mountains or on the coast, consequently changing the traditional way of life in those places, much to the chagrin of locals. That is exactly the transformation that was taking place in Rehoboth Beach and the surrounding communities during the time I lived there. People from large urban areas, such as myself and Mikki, moved to Sussex County, including many lesbians and gay men. Consequently, the cost of living increased, low-paying service jobs predominated, and traffic snarled.

Those changes fueled the battle between the "from-here's" and the "come-here's" or as David Goodhart calls them, the "somewheres," whose lifeworld is rooted in a particular place—like the Iowa farmer and the West Virginia coal miner—and the professional class of "anywheres," who can (and sometimes have to) relocate to advance their careers.[19] When anywheres choose to move to a small town, or "summer" there, they generally bring urban expectations and problems with them. That explains why small resort communities all over the country face vicious conflicts over noise, congestion, vacation rentals, and the pace of change—just like in Sussex.

According to a study by Katherine Cramer, people from small towns and rural communities often have a distinctive mindset, and one that does not necessarily track along party lines—especially in states where voters have not fully realigned. Her study of Republican Scott Walker's political rise in traditionally Democratic Wisconsin frames polarization in terms of urban versus rural consciousness. A lot of Walker supporters she interviewed—including some Democrats—had a "rural consciousness," a mindset that identifies with "rural people and rural places and denotes a multifaceted resentment against cities"—and no doubt against everything associated with cities, including Black people, the LGBTQ community, and independent ("nasty") women who live outside of patriarchal control and refuse to assume a deferential posture.[20] Unsurprisingly, she found that this resentment extends to people affiliated with universities as well.

In terms of politics, Cramer discovers that the rural-identified prefer to elect "people like themselves."[21] They ask "not how closely does this person's stances match my own, but instead, is this person like me?"[22] Cramer argues that it is the underlying group identity that shapes their choices, rather than party identification per se. In other words, they vote Republican not because of ideology but because Republicans articulate the grievances of rural folks better than Democrats do. That is the reason even a lot of rural Democrats supported Governor Walker and President Trump—and why a lot of Sussex County Democrats did not vote for me. Identity matters. In fact, when you look at public opinion, a lot of common ground actually exists on issues across the partisan divide. As Liliana Mason argues, partisan polarization has more to do with social identity than it does substantive issues.[23] For example, Republicans loved Romneycare, but when Obama proposed the same plan, they hated it. It is no longer the force of the better argument that matters, but rather the force of personality or party ID that determines political opinion.

DOES GENDER MATTER?

A lot of people ask about my experience running for office as a woman. Surprisingly, I encountered only a little explicit sexism during the race; the homophobia was worse. In terms of sexism, it irked me that my male opponent routinely showed up with his two young daughters in tow. It rankled because I am old enough to remember when, not too long ago, having school-aged children would disqualify a woman from being able to run for office. In fact, that might still be the case. As one congressional candidate tweeted in 2019, "As a mom of 3, I often get asked how my candidacy affects my kids. Dads aren't asked that. The question only feeds the stigma that moms shouldn't run."[24] During my campaign, my opponent got mostly applause for dragging his little girls all over the district.

I also encountered double standards. The most obvious example would be the constant echo that I was not experienced enough to run for office, a critique I never heard leveled against my male opponent, who had not held elective office when he first ran and who was ten years my junior, not even forty years old. Surprisingly, that line of criticism came mostly from women in their late sixties and older. For example, as recounted previously, Lady Farmer told me to run for school board first, before entering the race for state senate—a strange suggestion since she ran for state house without running for school board first. An eighty-something woman, a former city council member, complained behind my back—reportedly "like a rabid dog"—that I did not get "permission" to run, from whom she did not specify. In addition, a sixty-something county council woman—the only female Dem to hold office in Sussex—told me in an email to "try not to think you are better than other people," a criticism I found *deeply offensive*, which I told her, thus, no doubt, confirming my arrogance. These older female politicos apparently considered themselves gatekeepers. They did not like my ambition and resented the fact that I refused to defer to their imagined authority—even though I made a point of kissing all their rings before running.

In thinking about the ways in which gender mattered, however, we must consider intersectionality.[25] "Using intersectionality as an analytic lens highlights the multiple nature of individual identities and how varying combinations of class, gender, race, sexuality, and citizenship categories differently position each individual."[26] In other words, people are not simply women and men; they are women and men modified. Individuals are constituted, not only by gender but also by race, class, sexuality, and a host of other factors. Thus, I am not simply a woman in general but a white, professional-class lesbian in particular. In analyzing my campaign in this book, however, I focus mostly on the intersections of gender and class and not so much on race, since almost every player in this narrative is white. Indeed, my district was the second whitest in Delaware. While I fully recognize that the worldview of every white person in this story is *profoundly shaped by race*, I hold that factor constant for the purposes of this analysis.

In terms of the 2016 campaign, we know from empirical studies that appeals to masculinity and a sexist agenda both played a large role in the election of Donald Trump.[27] This should not be surprising. Studies show that "especially during times of social unrest, presidents have performed hypermasculinity to appeal to voters who feel unsure about their place in the social order."[28] In a historic first, however, the Republican primary candidates in 2016 actually engaged in thinly veiled conversations about the size of their penises, and the eventual winner survived public revelations that he feels entitled to grab women by their genitals. Toxic masculinity was clearly on display, not only among candidates but also among voters, as exemplified by popular T-shirts reading "Trump that bitch" or "Hillary sucks but not like Monica." Despite such unchristian behavior and rhetoric, conservative evangelicals strongly supported Trump because he vowed to advance their political agenda of strengthening patriarchy by packing the courts and empowering theocrats.

Many people believe Hillary Clinton lost the election because of sexism. Indeed, how else do you explain the reason those who voted twice for Barack Obama would prefer Donald Trump to her? It cannot be denied that sexism and misogyny played a role in the way people—women as well as men—perceived and treated Madam Secretary.[29] At the same time, however, many progressives did not like her record—her support for mass incarceration as First Lady, her vote for the Iraq War as a senator, her advocacy for regime-change in Libya as secretary of state, and her overall establishment worldview, to name just a few of the issues that matter to me. Not every vote against Clinton resulted from sexism. People disliked her for a range of reasons.

At the same time, however, we cannot overlook the fact that much of the animus against Secretary Clinton originated from her early violations of patriarchal norms.[30] First, she outraged the Arkansas masses by refusing to take her husband's name and having her own career despite being a politician's wife. Then, she offended traditional sensibilities in a number of other ways, from belittling the cookie-baking of stay-at-home moms to working on policy during her husband's administration, instead of just planning dinner parties like a traditional wife. For example, consider Pat Buchanan's words during his 1992 presidential campaign against Hillary's husband: "Elect me, and you get two for the price of one, Mr. Clinton says of his lawyer-spouse. . . . Hillary has compared marriage and the family as institutions to slavery. . . . This, my friends, is radical feminism. The agenda that Clinton & Clinton would impose on America . . . is not the kind of change America needs. It is not the kind of change . . . we can abide in a nation that we still call God's country."[31] Hillary had been a polarizing figure for decades, partly because she violated traditional gender norms before it was cool.

Recent academic literature on women and politics by Danny Hayes and Jennifer Lawless argues that gender no longer matters in elections.[32] Contrary to popular misconceptions, they argue, "female candidates do just as well as men" when they decide to run. "In federal and state races, [female candidates] raise just as much money, garner just as many votes, and are just as likely to win."[33] Current research "finds little evidence of bias, sexism, or disadvantages arising from gender stereotypes, especially when we look beyond presidential politics—granted a huge exception."[34] That is, "today, male and female candidates have few reasons to campaign differently, the media have little incentive to cover them differently, and voters have no reason to evaluate them differently. As a result, candidate sex plays a minimal role in the vast majority of US elections."[35] Moreover, "although previous research has often found that assessments of candidates are shaped by gender stereotypes, we find that voters' attitudes have little to do with whether candidates are men or women and everything to do with whether they are Republicans and Democrats."[36]

Hayes and Lawless correctly emphasize the importance of party identification in determining recent elections, but they fail to understand that gender also plays a role in elections because the parties themselves are gendered. In short, the masculinist GOP supports traditional white heteropatriarchy, and the feminized Democratic Party does not. Back in 2004, George Lakoff highlighted the gendered nature of the parties when he referred to the GOP as the party of the "strict father," in contrast with the more feminine Democrats who are "nurturing parents."[37] Or, as former MSNBC host Chris Matthews put it, they are the "Daddy Party" and the "Mommy Party."[38]

The strict father framework combines two important forces, patriarchy and authoritarianism, and that culturally powerful trope fuses together a range of issues from domestic relations to foreign policy. Consider, for example, this comment made by a voter during the Bush-Kerry campaign: "I really think [George Bush] is the man for the job to face down our enemy. He won't just give [Osama bin Laden] a time out. He'll smack him in the mouth."[39] Far from being just a bizarre comment, empirical studies show a very strong correlation between support for corporal punishment of children and a vote for Bush in 2004.[40] Under Trump, the Republican Party continues to support that authoritarian and patriarchal worldview. Many imagine the president as Big Daddy, the ultimate heavy, the bully who protects us from bullying and punishes those who get out of line.

President Trump's 2018 State of the Union address provides a good example of the way Republicans glorify patriarchal gender norms and valorize masculinity:

> We are a people whose heroes live not only in the past, but all around us, defending hope, pride, and defending the American way. They work in every trade, they sacrifice to raise a family. They care for our children at home. They defend our flag abroad. And they are strong moms and brave kids. They are firefighters and police officers and border agents, medics, and marines. But above all else, they are Americans. And this capital, this city, this nation, belongs entirely to them. Our task is to respect them, to listen to them, to serve them, to protect them and to always be worthy of them.[41]

In this passage about American identity, Trump invokes a series of traditionally manly jobs—tradesmen, soldiers, firefighters, police, border patrol agents, first responders, marines—and although those occupations are now-adays pursued by some women, they remain male-dominated and culturally coded as masculine. His mention of traditionally feminine roles includes only mothers; he does not mention nurses, teachers, or social workers.

The 2016 election pitted the liberal feminist vision of Hillary Clinton against Donald Trump's incitement of white male grievance, among other things. Indeed, white racial resentment played a large role in the 2016 election, more so than economic grievance, with a majority of whites in every demographic category voting for Trump, not for his Democratic opponent, with particularly strong support coming from white working-class men (72%), although women in that demographic category supported Trump almost as strongly (62%).[42]

Since losing, Clinton has made it clear that she believes sexism played a huge role in her loss, and she particularly notes her lack of support among white women (45%).[43] She says this during an interview on National Public Radio:

> In the book [*What Happened*] . . . I talk about a conversation I had with Sheryl Sandberg [author of *Lean In*]. . . . And she said, look, the research is absolutely definitive. The more professionally successful a man is, the more likable he is; the more professionally successful a woman is, the less likable she is. And that when women are serving on behalf of someone else, as I was when I was Secretary of State, for example, they are seen favorably. But when they step into the arena and say, wait a minute I think I could do the job, I would like to have that opportunity, their favorabilities goes [*sic*] down. And Sheryl ended this really sobering conversation by saying that women will have no empathy for you, because they will be under tremendous pressure—and I'm talking principally about white women—they will be under tremendous pressure from fathers and husbands and boyfriends and male employers not to vote for "the girl." And we saw a lot of that during the primaries from Sanders supporters, really quite vile attacks online against women who spoke out for me.[44]

Clinton makes an important point here, but unfortunately clouds it by alleging that Republican women cannot think for themselves and demonizing the supporters of Bernie Sanders.

While I do not deny that some so-called "Bernie bros" attacked Clinton supporters online, I can personally attest to being attacked online by male supporters of Hillary. A lot of my Delaware allies expressed surprise and outrage upon discovering that I favored Sanders over Clinton—obviously, not knowing me very well—and multiple male Facebook friends were particularly aggressive about it online. Indeed, one elderly man denounced me on Facebook on Easter morning for not being a good feminist because I refused to defer to his political agenda. This suggests to me that the problem is male bullies in general, not Bernie supporters in particular. In fact, one study reveals fewer sexists among Sanders supporters (16.3%) than among Clinton supporters (19.5%), most likely a product of age.[45] Apparently, a lot of men cannot stand it when a woman persists with her own political views despite male disapproval.

When I first heard Clinton's comments on NPR about women being pressured by men to not support "the girl," it brought to mind a number of other condescending comments disrespectful of women's political choices. For example, Gloria Steinem said that young women supported Sanders over Clinton because "when you're young, you're thinking, . . . 'Where are the boys?' The boys are with Bernie."[46] Likewise, Madeleine Albright commented, "There's a special place in hell for women who don't help each other," in reference to female supporters of Sanders.[47] Finally, after the election, Michelle Obama said, "Any woman who voted against Hillary Clinton voted against their own voice. . . . What does it mean for us as women that we look at those two candidates, as women, and many of us said, that guy, he's better for me, his voice is more true to me? . . . Well, to me that just says you don't like your voice. You like the thing you're told to like."[48] Personally, I do not vote based on identity, just as I do not vote for someone because they are from my state or county. I vote on issues and values. I supported Sanders, not because I seek the attention of men or fear their wrath, and not because I dislike my own voice, but because he shares my values, values I have held my entire life, and we agree on the issues. And I trust I am not going to hell for it.

More white women voted for Trump than for Clinton, but I do not believe that choice resulted simply from capitulation to explicit male pressure, although that might have happened to some extent. Instead, the decision of women to support Trump likely resulted from two factors. First, I would suggest, contra Michelle Obama, that white working-class women probably share more in common with their husbands, boyfriends, and brothers than they do with wealthy professional class women, particularly a one-percenter like Hillary Clinton. Remember intersectionality: race and class matter, as much as gender. Second, a lot of women probably voted for Trump because they live in a good ole boy culture that glorifies white masculinity, and the norms of that culture shape their consciousness. That's how hegemony works: you consent to the power structure regardless of whether it serves your material interests.

It is important to note here that Trump Republicans do not scorn all women in politics, just the so-called "nasty women" who refuse to defer to male authority. As Steve Bannon put it, it is fine to have right-wing women "lead this country [who] would be pro-family, they would have husbands, they would love their children." Remember Sarah Palin, the darling of the Tea Party? Bannon is fine with women leaders as long as they are not "a bunch of dykes that came from the Seven Sisters schools up in New England."[49] Again, we must consider intersectionality. It is not all women that are the problem. It is a particular kind of woman—the kind of woman Hillary Clinton is (Wellesley College 1969), and the kind of woman I am (Smith College 1986). People did not oppose me because I am a woman per se, but rather because of the particular type of woman I am. As my opponent put it, I am not "the kind of [woman]" who should be elected. I am a nasty woman.

GOOD OLE BOY CULTURE IN SUSSEX COUNTY

The recent literature on the 2016 election and the benefit of several years of hindsight have made me aware that I never fully appreciated the power of the good ole boys in my district. During my campaign, a kindly retired state senator made this comment: "In Delaware, there are Democrats, Republicans, and Fire Companies." While his comment initially confounded me, I now understand his meaning: In Delaware, there exists a bipartisan group of good ole boys who unofficially rule state and county. If you want to get elected, you must be good ole boy approved.

My opponent, Ernie Lopez, though Hispanic, was good ole boy approved, probably because he married into one of the old Sussex families. He certainly valorized good ole boy culture. For example, consider his tweet from Christmas Day 2016: "Blessings this Christmas & join me in prayers of thanks for our military, police, fire & emergency medical personnel."[50] It goes without saying that only a rare person would not wish those folks well, but why are those particular occupations singled out for special praise, over and over again? Why do politicians thank military personnel for their service but not teachers? Why mention fire and emergency personnel and not nurses? Why does a Sussex County convenience store give free coffee to cops and not to social workers? Again, while some women occupy positions within those categories, their presence does not alter the masculine nature of those sectors.

The good ole boy culture I encountered during my run dovetails with the culture of grievance that would catapult Trump to victory two years later. Indeed, Sussex County Republicans voted 70 percent for Trump in the primary, and Trump won almost every district in the county in the general election (although the state as a whole went for Clinton, thanks to the large population of African Americans in Wilmington, the state's one large city). In 2014, only two Democrats held elective office in Sussex County—a female county council member who endorsed Trump and started tweeting daily about right-wing conspiracies, and the Speaker of the House, a retired police captain who was born and raised in Sussex County. When the Speaker first decided to run for office in 2002, he said he did not know which party to register with, so he choose the majority party, the Democrats. Based on his legislative record, he should have registered Republican.

The good ole boys did not support my campaign for state senate. One of them, a registered Democrat who voted for Trump in 2016 and a close friend of the Speaker, wrote a letter to the editor against me:

> I have had the opportunity to meet Ernie's opponent and came away troubled, as it was obvious she lacks knowledge of local issues. Instead as she makes clear in recent writings on her blog where she calls a local state representative a "homophobic good ole boy," and espouses a need for the "equivalent of a left-wing Tea Party." Ernie's opponent, who only recently moved to the Cape Region from the Washington, D.C. area, brings extreme partisanship to her first campaign for office which makes me and many others suspicious of her reasons for running. I am a strong believer that voting for the right person is so much more important than which party they are from. I am a Democrat who believes all politics should be local.[51]

Clearly, I am not from there; I'm from the City.

For the record, I never had a single conversation with that man about anything, and my campaign focused almost exclusively on mostly nonpartisan, local issues—overdevelopment, the shortage of doctors, lack of transportation, and the overemphasis on high-stakes testing in the public schools—not on extremely partisan issues. In fact, in hindsight, I believe a left-wing platform might have helped my campaign. I did, however, call "a local state rep" a "homophobic good ole boy" in a 2012 blog post, after the man—a retired cop, born and raised in Sussex County, and formerly a Democrat—conducted a homophobic whisper campaign against Lady Farmer when she ran for state house in 2012 (as discussed in chapter 3).

I would not say that good ole boy culture includes good ole girls, but I would say it includes the good ole boys' girls. In other words, women have standing only when they are good ole boy approved. A motorcycle-riding, butch lesbian friend of mine once commented, "When I first came here, I had a lot of problems with the good ole boys. Now I am a good ole boy." It's a funny line, and while it could possibly be true for her, it could never be true for me. I am just not the kind of woman who blends in with the good ole boys, not because I scorn them, but because my life experiences are about as far from that lifeworld as can be, and I do not mean because I am gay. Indeed, the openly gay man elected Clerk of the Peace, mentioned in chapter 3, was definitely good ole boy approved.

Just to be clear, my campaign did not target local good ole boys. In accordance with best practices, we ran a "targeted campaign" that focused specifically on Democrats, particularly liberal ones, most of whom came from nearby cities—DC, Baltimore, Philadelphia—and the surrounding areas, and on Democratic-leaning Independents. In other words, I was not under the illusion that I would receive a groundswell of support from longtime locals. That said, if I had understood more clearly the extent to which good ole boy culture permeated the district and the Democratic Party and the importance of informal networks, I might have developed a strategy to better counteract those forces.

"DEMOCRATS, REPUBLICANS, AND FIRE COMPANIES"

When that kindly, retired state senator informed me that "there are Democrats, Republicans, and Fire Companies," I asked him for some strategies for contending with the power of the Fire Companies, given my gender, and he kindly suggested that I join the "Ladies Auxiliary." I actually considered it. For the record, however, Rehoboth Beach dropped the "ladies" modifier a while ago, although as of 2020, all active auxiliary members were, in fact, women. The actual Fire Company, on the other hand, is only 90 percent men, better than the national average of 93 percent.[52]

To get more information about the auxiliary, I asked a friend about her experiences as a new member, and she recounted that the auxiliary was populated by a lot of older women who were very unwelcoming at first but over time became more civil. Yet the ladies continued, she noted, to be resistant to change and seemed very vested in male dominance, repeating the mantra, "The men say we can do this, and we can't do that," which my friend found frustrating. Given that the purpose of auxiliaries is to support fire companies, perhaps that attitude makes sense, yet it seems you could do that work without assuming a submissive posture.

According to some accounts, firefighting remains one of the most misogynistic fields in the country. An article in the *Washington Post*—about a heterosexual female firefighter who hanged herself (one of Mikki's former coworkers) after being relentlessly bullied by the men in her unit—notes that firefighter culture remains very masculinist and misogynistic.[53] "William R. Metcalf, the former president of the International Association of Fire Chiefs, called firefighting a 'white guys club.' He said too few departments have made a substantial effort to welcome women."[54] Indeed, nearly 85 percent of professional firefighters are white and 95 percent are male.[55] The problem, however, according to Metcalf, is not just that firefighting has traditionally been done by white men, and so they remain dominant. It is much worse than that. As Metcalf explained in an open letter to his organization's membership in 2014, "In a surprisingly large number of fire departments . . . it's OK to harass and physically assault women and minorities—even rape women—in our fire stations."[56]

Unionized firefighters have traditionally supported Democrats, but they did not support Clinton in 2016. That is, union leadership chose not to endorse Clinton—although they did not endorse Trump either—but more importantly their membership supported Trump. That is, a poll of the International Association of Fire Fighters membership after the 2016 election indicated that only 27 percent voted for Clinton, whereas 50 percent voted for Trump.[57] They "had a much more favorable view of Bernie Sanders than Clinton," but "Trump surpassed them both."[58] Even down ballot, "in 2016 support for Democrats among fire fighters cratered."[59] It is important to note, however, that the poll queried unionized firefighters only. In Delaware fire companies are not unionized but rather volunteer brigades, as is the case for 70 percent of fire companies nationally, which probably makes them even less Democratic.

GOOD, OLD-FASHIONED, SEX-SEGREGATED FUN

The highly gendered world of firefighting manifested itself in Sussex County in a pair of sex-segregated annual fundraisers held simultaneously: Oyster Eat for men and Shrimp Feast for women. I decided to attend Shrimp Feast at the urging of two "from-here" supporters of mine, who emphatically insisted that I absolutely had to attend Shrimp Feast, if I wanted to get elected. The first kind of chuckled when he suggested it. The second expressed doubt that I would be able to "handle it." I could not imagine. Feeling intrigued rather than scared, I asked a heterosexual female friend, a former firefighter, to go with me. She too was leery about my attendance. "I don't know, Claire." When I asked her why everyone was so worried about me going to Shrimp Feast, she asked, "Have you ever partied with redneck women before?" "Actually . . . ," I told her, "I have not." Well, apparently, it can get kind of rough.

When we arrived at the firehall, the place was packed and the beer was flowing. It was exactly as one might imagine a stereotypical girls' night out—lots of women being loud and drunk and dancing around, gesturing to raise the roof. Would you be surprised to learn that the DJ was playing Bon Jovi? The crowd appeared to be almost exclusively straight, white women—no doubt the mothers, wives, and girlfriends of the Oyster Eat boys—except for a few women who appeared to be firefighters or cops themselves. Long tables surrounded the dance floor, and on each placemat sat a red, plastic fire helmet. And while at that point in the campaign, I had become accustomed to working a room, I felt out of place. I did not feel that the attendees would be interested in meeting a candidate that evening, especially not a stranger like me. You would have to be part of that social network to benefit politically by attending.

So instead of going around the room shaking hands, I ate my fill of shrimp, did some authentic moonshine shots with my friend, took a few selfies, and left around 9:00 p.m., before any fights started. On the way out the door, we bought T-shirts and snapped a few photos of me standing next to a fire truck, which immediately went up on my Facebook page. Needless to say, my Republican opponent was at Oyster Eat with the

Democratic Speaker, Lady Farmer's Republican opponent, their friends, and probably every fireman, male cop, politician, and good ole boy in the county. Despite the gender segregation of Oyster Eat, I did notice in the paper the next morning that the one female Republican house member in the county had been allowed in, at least to get a photo. I guess she was good ole boy approved.

I have often told the tale of my experience at Shrimp Feast—and I still wear the really nice black and pink T-shirt that reads "Got Shrimp?"—but the story of Oyster Eat, an event attended by every powerful man in the county yet closed to women, is the one that really needs telling. Oyster Eat was founded in 1933, and it took almost fifty years until some women started Shrimp Feast in 1991 because they decided excluding women "wasn't fair."[60] The 2017 event chair denies that women are barred from attending the Eat. "We say 'stag.' We don't turn women away." However, "they very rarely make it through the door. . . . I've been in the fire company 21 years, and I've been chairing this thing for 12 years and I think I've seen two or maybe three women try to come in."[61] A fire chief says, "What we do do is not encourage them to attend."[62]

Every year, Oyster Eat attracts a thousand or more men. A video of the event in 2018 features crowds of men—many with beards and ball caps—standing around eating oysters and drinking beer, a bluegrass band, and a knife and gun raffle.[63] "The Oyster Eat was recognized by the United States Congress for its 'historical and cultural significance' during U.S. Rep. Michael Castle's tenure in Washington. Its immense notoriety also landed a feature spread in the *New York Times* in 1992."[64] That article described the cross-class group of good ole boys who showed up for the stag event:

> The firehouse floor was two inches deep in sawdust, to absorb the tobacco juice and beer that flowed freely during the Eat. . . . Sussex County, sometimes referred to as the "northernmost county in Mississippi," is 100 miles south of the Mason-Dixon Line and is reflective of Southern social mores, even though officially it remained loyal to the Union. Every other pickup truck in southern Delaware seemed to be parked on the streets around the red-brick firehouse, along with a smattering of up-market foreign-built sedans. . . . [An insurance salesman] surveyed the mob in the firehouse, many dressed in down vests, plaid shirts, baseball caps and denims, and noted that "the Eat is getting bigger and bigger each year,

and the different groups are getting all mixed up because their clothes are so much alike."[65]

In 1991, the Republican governor "stopped by and was asked if he felt comfortable among enrolled Democrats bearing oyster knives. 'I don't fear for my safety,' he answered, 'but I do hope no one asks me to dance.' "[66]

Oyster Eat functions as a way to bring young men into the good ole boy fold. A newspaper article from 1986 recounts, " 'Everybody comes here. It's just one of those things.' It has been 'one of those things' and more for 49 years. For adolescent boys, who can't wait to be allowed to attend, it is the forbidden fruit; for young men, who come for the first time, a rite of passage into adulthood, and for adult men, who bring their sons, it is a tie to the past."[67] A 2016 article echoes that point: "When they walk in the door, they'll say, 'This is his first Oyster Eat.' They'll just make it a tradition after that."[68] Senator Lopez agrees: "I try not to miss it. I always attend with my father. It has become somewhat of a tradition."[69]

Many women have no problem with the men-only event. A local woman notes that Oyster Eat is "passed from generation to generation to generation," sharing that her "father attended for many years—leaving her at home, of course. . . . 'It's the type of thing that builds character within a town,' she said. 'It's part of the folklore for Sussex.' " The article notes that the county is "one of those places where 'good ol' boy' is a title not just of affection but also of distinction. Of course, many natives have left town. But it is nearly an article of faith that they will return each February to catch up on local happenings and renew their roots."[70]

THE HIDDEN ROLE OF UNOFFICIAL NETWORKS

Interestingly, I know the woman quoted in the 1986 *New York Times* article just cited. She was an active member of the Sussex County Women's Democrat Club when I was a member in 2014, and also a proud member of the Degree of Pocahontas, serving as the "Grand Pocahontas" in 2012.[71] That organization is the women's auxiliary for the Improved Order of Red Men, both founded in the early 1800s for whites only. Apparently, the groups base their costumes and rituals on the ways white people of that era imagined Native Americans to dress and behave, and they maintain a very hierarchical structure. "The order has historically opposed federal welfare programs, waste in government and Communism," while the auxiliary "provided financial support to fight communism."[72] The organizations now say they want "to inspire a greater love for the United States of America and the principles of American liberty" and "support various charitable, youth, and educational programs."[73]

I will admit to knowing nothing about the Improved Order of Red Men or the Degree of Pocahontas until writing this chapter. When the very white-looking Great Pocahontas mentioned the organizations in conversation a few years ago, the names startled me—Why are you in a group for red men? And who uses the term "red men"?—and so I took note. I will admit that I have no context for understanding the ways in which such hierarchical and secretive societies function, just as I had no context for understanding the rituals and customs I encountered at American Legion events, when I attended them during the campaign. The ranks, the marches, the flags all made me feel like an alien from another planet. Those types of organizations stand completely outside my life experience, and I have no doubt that my ignorance of such local customs—my total outsiderness—hurt my chances of getting elected. Yet, even if I had waited a few years before running, I expect the situation would have remained the same. I could probably never blend in, nor would I want to. My only hope would be the continuation of demographic change, until there were more people like me in the district, and less like them.

In fact, my one attempt to blend into a conservative Christian event failed miserably. Back in 2012, during Lady Farmer's campaign, I heard that the Delaware Family Policy Council had called a meeting to discuss electoral politics. So, I put on clothing that I imagined a soccer mom might wear and drove to the church to attend the meeting. Although I expected a large crowd, only a dozen and a half folks showed up, and my presence immediately struck the leader as questionable. Was it my Chanel eye glasses? "Hi! What church do you go to?" Not expecting the question, which I have never before been asked, I said, "Uh . . . well I have been church shopping." Then, she asked, "Are you liberal or conservative?" Trying to pass myself off as one of the mythical undecided voters, I responded, "Uh . . . I am not really sure." So, she pulled out a book with a list of issues and asked where I stood on them. As I hemmed and hawed, she asked about my discovery of the group and its meeting. When I said I friend told me about it, she said, "This is a private meeting. You need to leave." So much for blending.

These anecdotes illustrate a number of things, including the importance of informal networks for campaigns. It is hard to break into an informal network if you are not already a member. For example, my opponent did a lot of campaigning at high school football games, and some of my supporters suggested that I start attending. I did not do so, however, because I had no connection to the high school at all, whereas my opponent had two children in public school and knew everyone. I did not think I could make much progress on his home turf. Trying to infiltrate that venue would be like Lopez attending the women's dance on Friday night at The Pond Bar and Grill or the gay cocktail hour at the Blue Moon. That was my home turf. Besides, accessing informal networks is even harder when you do not even see them.

When I lost the election, I did not understand the reasons people opposed me so strongly. Indeed, even a significant number of registered Democrats voted against me. A lot of first-time candidates have trouble with name recognition, but as Mikki frequently jokes, "They definitely knew your name, and every good ole boy in the district came out to vote against you." In light of all I have learned about cultural polarization since the election of Trump, however, I have a better sense of factors that contributed to my defeat, and one factor was this: I was not good ole boy approved, and there were more "good ole boy" supporters in the county than there were people like me.

CHAPTER 5

THE ROYALIST MINDSET

During my run for state senate, I learned a whole lot about campaigns, but the following year, I received a crash course on power politics. When I was a professor, I studied the "allure of authoritarianism," mostly on the political right, and while being dominated can meet certain needs for some, I never imagined that Democratic activists and self-proclaimed progressives would do anything other than stand opposed to coercion in all its guises.[1] Sadly, I have learned from the legendary school of hard knocks that despite living in the so-called greatest democracy in the world, a lot of people do not have a strong internalized commitment to democratic values or the democratic courage to defend them. I learned that lesson over the course of 2015, when I was subjected to a bullying campaign by the Democratic Speaker of the House because I pressed him on a number of progressive issues, and instead of standing with me, or even defending my right to express my views, almost all of my friends in the Democratic Party essentially abandoned me.

Far from being simply a sad commentary on a particular group of people, I believe the events that occurred illustrate a larger problem that threatens the future of our democratic republic—the willingness of people to tolerate or condone authoritarian practices. It is my contention that deferring to powermongers, rather than having the courage to stand up for democratic values, reveals a mentality better suited to a royalist regime than to a self-governing republic of free and equal citizens. Democratic courage does not come naturally. It needs to be developed. Unfortunately, however, few opportunities exist in our society for people to engage in practices that instill or reinforce democratic values, so people too easily fall prey to a dynamic of powermongering and deference, and the spread of that mentality puts our republic on a perilous path.

IS THIS OUR "MACHIAVELLIAN MOMENT"?

While it was a long time coming, the election of Donald Trump brought us face-to-face with the situation that J. G. A. Pocock calls the "Machiavellian moment," when a republic begins its inevitable demise, as people lose commitment to the values and principles necessary to sustain a system of self-rule and allow tyrants to take control. As mentioned in the introduction, in *How Democracies Die*, Steven Levitsky and Daniel Ziblatt identify "four behavioral warning signs that can help us know an authoritarian when we see one. We should worry when a politician 1) rejects, in words or action, the democratic rules of the game, 2) denies the legitimacy of opponents, 3) tolerates or encourages violence, or 4) indicates a willingness to curtail the civil liberties of opponents, including the media."[2] Those who follow the news know that Trump has done all those things, repeatedly. Consequently, many pundits and scholars consistently argued, over the course of his four-year term, that he posed a serious threat to our republic, and that turned out to be the case, as exemplified by the postelection debacle. The fear of threats to our republic are nothing new. Indeed, the Founders recognized the possibility that monarchy might be restored or a tyrant take power in the new republic, and so they implemented a number of safeguards to protect the demos from would-be oppressors, including institutional checks and balances and the ability of citizens to hold representatives accountable—both of which assume people will have the democratic courage to stand up, not bow down.[3] Will we be able to fight off the perennial allure of tribalism, hierarchy, and powermongering, or will we capitulate to creeping authoritarianism?

Maintaining a republican form of government requires citizens who actively engage. I spent my entire academic career educating students about strong democracy and encouraging them to engage politically because only an engaged citizenry committed to democratic values can prevent demagoguery. I often assigned Jean-Jacques Rousseau, who put it this way: "As soon as public *service* ceases to be the main business of the citizens, and they prefer to serve with their pocketbooks rather than with their persons, the State is already close to ruin. Is it necessary to *march to battle?* They pay troops and stay home. Is it necessary to *attend council?* They name deputies and stay home. By dint of laziness and money, they finally have soldiers to enslave the country and representatives to sell it."[4]

Taking our hands off the wheel and looking the other way, while others drive governmental decision making on our behalf, risks political wreckage. At a minimum, citizens must communicate their views to elected officials and vote on Election Day. More than that, however, people need to exercise their right to use public discourse to persuade their representatives of the justness of their cause. And if the force of the better argument does not work, people need to organize social movements and wage primary challenges to make elected officials do the right thing. As Franklin Delano Roosevelt once said to a group of activists, "You've convinced me. Now go out and make me do it."[5]

Being inattentive toward government creates the opportunity for tyranny to develop, but so does a deferential mentality. In his book about Silvio Berlusconi—the right-wing media tycoon elected to four terms as Italian prime minister—Maurizio Viroli describes the emergence of a problematic Prince-courtier dynamic. That dynamic entails a powerful alpha male who attracts servile flatterers "who depend on him to gain and preserve wealth, status, and reputation." That hierarchical dynamic stands directly opposed to the republican ideals of political equality and freedom from domination, yet some people willingly capitulate to power in order to gain wealth and status. We saw this every day in the Trump administration. How many formerly respected political leaders will end their careers bowing and scraping before a wannabe tyrant?

Ingratiating yourself to a powermonger for personal gain makes sense, but I also observed, during my forays into Delaware politics, another dynamic, in which those assuming a deferential posture gained nothing tangible, just the pleasure of basking in power's glow. Having been educated to be an independent thinker, who lives in accordance with my own professed principles, and who has developed the democratic courage to defend them, I could not comprehend the willingness of so many ostensibly autonomous, mostly retired people to kowtow to the Speaker of the House, no matter what he did. He had no power over them, yet still they kissed his ring. I wanted to say, "You do not work for him; you are not married to him; he's not your dad. Why won't you stand up to him?" Because I can see no material basis for their obsequiousness, they do not quite fit Viroli's definition of courtiers. Hence, I refer to them as *minions.* And here is the key point: Both courtiers and minions assume a submissive posture toward their rulers, more appropriate to a royalist regime than to a democratic republic.

PRINCE OF THE GOOD OLE BOYS

While Donald Trump blatantly reveled in claiming absolute power, he is far from the only elected official to behave like a wannabe monarch or feudal lord, accountable to no one on earth. Indeed, mini-Trumps can be seen all over the country, most often on the Republican side of the aisle—but not always. For example, the Delaware Speaker of the House (2013–present) has that same authoritarian mentality, even though he is a Democrat. A former police captain, holding office since 2002, essentially unopposed, the Speaker acts like he is entitled to rule—as if he's a prince. The man, henceforth called Prince Speaker, considers himself the boss-man and expects people to fall in line, and for the most part they do. Prince Speaker seems to view not only his district but all of Sussex County as his personal fiefdom, and many share his view. Indeed, when Vice President Joe Biden attended our Democratic Party picnic, he quipped, "I need a passport from [Prince Speaker] just to set foot in this county." Everybody laughed, but I did not find it funny because it was so close to true.

Prince Speaker fully embraces the significant power of the Speakership. Considering himself the decider, he alone determines whether a bill makes it to the floor for a vote, and he controls the committees—who is on them and to which committee bills get assigned. With no referendum process available for citizens to work around him, he maintains virtually unchecked power. Moreover, he reportedly behaves in an authoritarian manner toward his colleagues at Legislative Hall—or "Leg Hall" to use local parlance—wreaking vengeance on those who dare to oppose him instead of respecting their right to dissent. While his behavior is not atypical for Speakers in general, his modus operandi stood in marked contrast to the respectful and democratic way his counterpart in the state senate reportedly behaved toward her colleagues.

Prince Speaker has no discernible agenda besides maintaining power and supporting his "brothers in blue," as he calls them, and other donors. While he prides himself on controlling the legislative agenda, when it comes to the police, he defers. For example, in the wake of the Black Lives Matter uprising in 2020, Prince Speaker said that a law requiring police to wear body cameras would never pass because it does not have "the approval of law enforcement officers, I'm going to tell you that right now."[6] Apparently, they have veto power. Moreover, Prince Speaker does not believe that the police should be accountable to civilian oversight: "As a cop, we don't go in to tell somebody how to operate on somebody because we don't know anything about it," he said. "It's very difficult to ask people that don't know anything about policing, who've never been a cop, how they should fix policing."[7] The people, he believes, must defer to the police, like he does. This should put him in an awkward position, since the Delaware police endorsed Trump (despite Biden hailing from the First State), and Prince Speaker leads the Democrats, but that has not been publicly raised.[8]

Although he supported marriage equality in the years right before the US Supreme Court legalized it nationally—which makes sense given the demographics of his district—Prince Speaker functions as a one-man barrier to progressive change in the state, opposing death penalty repeal, a living wage, progressive taxation, and cannabis legalization, as well as reforms designed to protect the democratic rules of the game, like increasing transparency, getting money out of politics, and putting an end to gerrymandering. In fact, Prince Speaker strongly supports the right of the majority party to gerrymander because, as he told me point-blank, "I will not be the one to give up power." Sadly, his support for marriage equality has earned him the blind loyalty of many in the LGBTQ community; he can do no wrong in their eyes. While many lesbians and gay men are not politically progressive, even the self-proclaimed progressive ones still pledge allegiance to Prince Speaker.

Every morning, Prince Speaker held court over breakfast with his clan of close male cronies at one of two local restaurants. He called their unofficial meetings "Leg Hall South," presumably because political decisions got made there. His friends literally laughed at my wife, when she ventured into their meeting place in search of some coffee, during my campaign. And while Prince Speaker said he supported my campaign, a friend told me that his cronies used to sit around bashing me over their sausage and eggs, with no objection from the Prince. "I can't change their views," he reportedly said when confronted about it.

At least two of Prince Speaker's close friends are registered Democrats who openly supported Trump and opposed Obama, Clinton, Pelosi, and Biden. One of them has a Facebook page that has, over the years, included plenty of pro-cop, pro-gun, pro-flag, pro-Bible, pro-spanking, and anti-immigrant memes, all indicators of an authoritarian mindset, as well as, more recently, antimasker and QAnon talking points.[9] Another has a similar Facebook page, as well as several DUIs and a criminal record for multiple counts of domestic violence, with charges ranging from harassment to felony strangulation, yet he always had the gall to give me a dirty look whenever he saw me.

The good ole boys of Sussex wanted someone like themselves, who understands their views, to represent them in Dover and they got exactly that with Prince Speaker. He even sympathizes with the white racial resentment so common to Trump voters who believe people of color are getting ahead unfairly. That is to say, in the wake of the Black Lives Matter protests in 2020, Prince Speaker claimed that he was subjected to reverse discrimination in the police department: "They bypassed me twice to promote a person of color," he said. "I worked hard for the promotion."[10] He says that over time he has come to understand the need for affirmative action: "When I got done feeling sorry for myself and feeling bad and thinking I was treated unfairly, I also understood" the need for people of color in leadership. Prince Speaker argues that the experience of reverse discrimination makes him more sensitive to racism, but then he says, "It's time for the people of color to quit feeling like they're less of a person than we are," as if Black and brown people are somehow to blame for their own subordination.[11] In addition, like many on the Right, he denies the existence of systemic racism in police departments, says peaceful protesters should be held accountable if any violence occurs, and believes some of the protesters are paid.[12]

LADIES-IN-WAITING FOR THE PRINCE

Prince Speaker's male cronies are not the only ones who pledge allegiance to him. Lady Progressive, Lady Staffer, and Lady Farmer (discussed in chapter 3) also kowtow, and for no discernible reason. Their behavior illustrates that a royalist mindset of hierarchy and deference can develop, even within a democratic republic. That is the reason I append the aristocratic title of "Lady" to their nicknames. For example, Lady Progressive, known throughout Delaware as a progressive firebrand, always acted like a woman in love when it came to Prince Speaker. When she and I used to hang out, she always wanted to drive by his house, which made me laugh to myself because in high school my friends and I used to do exactly that when we liked a boy. Maybe he will be standing outside the house!

One time, Lady Progressive actually said she would "do *anything*" for Prince Speaker, and that was not just an idle exclamation. After Trump's election, she reoriented the entire agenda of Progressive Democrats of Sussex County to focus only on opposing Trump, instead of continuing to address issues in the state legislature, where Prince Speaker worked to block every progressive bill introduced.

While Lady Progressive's devotion to Prince Speaker might result from infatuation, what explains the fealty of Lady Farmer and Lady Staffer? Indeed, after the 2012 election, Prince Speaker went all over the county blaming Lady Farmer for his Protégé's loss, specifically for inspiring the homophobic email that supposedly hurt both candidates, yet she continued to support him. At first that made sense, since she needed his support during her second campaign in 2014. After losing a second time, however, she continued to pay homage. Lady Staffer, on the other hand, had no reason at all to support Prince Speaker. Indeed, she frequently said she could not stand him, yet during the 2016 primary election, when Prince Speaker faced a truly *progressive* opponent for the first time ever, an openly gay man, Lady Staffer put an oversized Prince Speaker sign in her front yard.

Why did the three Ladies bow down to Prince Speaker like they did? Personally, I could never bring myself to fawn on him, which no doubt hurt my political career. Truth be told, I never felt comfortable around Prince Speaker, a large rough-looking man with a ruddy complexion and oversized hands. A lot of people seemed to find him alluring, but I always tried to avoid him, while still seeming friendly, because once he started talking it was hard to escape. Having been through graduate school and working in academia, I have a lot of experience feigning interest and flattering egos, but I had a visceral inability to do those things with Prince Speaker. I had no interest in flirting with him, like the female majority leader always did, and I know I did not come across as sufficiently deferential, which I am sure did not help my political career any. In fact, it might have contributed to his decision to badmouth me behind my back during my campaign, despite his promise to support me. After all, if I refused to kiss up to him during my first campaign, how would I act once elected?

As mentioned previously, when I first considered running, I called Prince Speaker to ask for his support, and to my surprise, he said, "If you run, I'll support you." I actually did not believe him, but the county chair, who had asked me to run, told me not to worry. He considered himself the person in charge of recruiting candidates in Sussex and insisted the

Speaker would respect his prerogative. I remained skeptical, however, because I knew my patron had a very inflated view of his own stature. He seemed to fancy himself some kind of Cromwellian manipulator, a valued advisor to Prince Speaker and others. After we met with Prince Speaker, the county chair insisted I had his full support, yet he also mentioned that as soon as I went to the restroom, Prince Speaker said, "You don't support *her*, do you?" The county chair replied, "Yes, I do," and, in his mind, that settled it: Prince Speaker was on board.

But of course, he wasn't really on board, and, in fact, after my defeat, Prince Speaker told a local blogger that the Dems lost because "none of the candidates were worth getting off the couch for." Gee thanks! When I met him for lunch to debrief, he complained that one of my supporters had criticized him on Facebook for always hanging out with my opponent and not doing more for me, and I knew his wife spent the entire election day hanging with Lopez and crew. Plus, friends told me Prince Speaker went around telling everybody, "She can't win." Obviously, he was correct in that prediction, as it turns out. Yet while I am sure his lack of support did not help my cause any, I believe I would have lost anyway. Consequently, at the end of 2014, I honestly bore no particular animus toward him.

THE "GIRL" WHO REFUSED TO DEFER

The truly malevolent nature of Prince Speaker became clear to me, however, the year after I lost. As the legislative session opened in 2015, he began his second term as Speaker by removing his most progressive colleague, Rep. Lefty—a blustery man with a Bernie Sanders–style hairdo, and the same kind of backbone, who enjoyed rock-solid support in his district—from a coveted committee as payback for not supporting the governor's educational "reform" and probusiness agenda. As should have been anticipated, Rep. Lefty went ballistic, expressing his outrage to every reporter, radio host, and blogger who would listen, blasting Prince Speaker for being petty and vindictive. Progressive Democrats in our district, and all over the state, were outraged.

When Mikki and I drove to Wilmington to attend a Progressive Democrats for Delaware meeting for the first time—to thank them for supporting my campaign from afar and also to expand our organizing reach—as soon as we walked in, they said, "Nice to meet you Claire. You need to primary [Prince Speaker]." I just laughed and said, "I couldn't even beat Lopez." To a person, they were angry about the attack on their beloved leader, Lefty. They could not stand Prince Speaker, whom they considered a complete DINO, and they were quite vocal about it on their high-profile blog, Delaware Liberal, that every politico in the state reads. It was a major dustup.

In response to the blowback, Prince Speaker made no public statements at all but instead launched a whisper campaign, maligning Lefty behind his back. Progressives in our district were very upset about the way Lefty was treated by Prince Speaker, and since I was party chair of his district at the time, I had to listen to all their complaints. When their outrage did not dissipate, the county chair persuaded Prince Speaker to tell his side of the story to the small group of party leaders who sat on the county executive committee. As soon as the meeting started, Prince Speaker went on the offensive. "Somebody had to do something," he told us. "[Lefty] is out of control. He's crazy and off his meds. Believe me, people were relieved to have him off the committee. He's a pain in the ass." Prince Speaker clearly viewed himself as man enough to do whatever it takes to maintain order and was appalled that Lefty, an elected official, would act "like an activist" and talk to the press about House Democratic Caucus matters.

I found Prince Speaker's position disturbing on a number of levels. Yet his tirade somehow had most of the other party leaders nodding in awe of his backroom bravado, as if thinking to themselves, "What else could you do? Glad you put him in his place." A couple of executive committee members literally pledged allegiance to Prince Speaker, including a man who called himself a socialist, saying something like, "I stand with you. We've got your back." So, I sat there a few minutes, hesitating, wondering about the reactions that a dissenting view might provoke, but I knew in my heart that I had to say something. When I ran for state senate, I presented myself as a leader, as a would-be peer of the Speaker. I could not just sit there, condoning his actions with my silence. Plus, as a progressive leader and party chair in his district, I needed to share the positions I had been hearing about the incident. People were really disappointed, even some of his strongest supporters.

So, in as mild a way as I could manage, I said, "When you removed [Rep. Lefty] from the committee, didn't you expect blowback? You see this as a personal matter, about [Lefty] in particular, but for the progressive wing of the party, it's political. They don't support you for ideological reasons, and by purging their leader you played right into their hands. You gave them a reason to demonize you. If you want to smooth things over, perhaps you should throw them a bone." Like supporting death penalty repeal, I thought to myself. In response, Prince Speaker said simply, "I will not reward bad behavior," as if he were Big Daddy, responsible for doling out rewards and punishments. He did not get visibly angry at the time, but Mikki believes he turned against me in that moment, when I—a person he reportedly refers to as "that girl"—dared to speak to him as an equal in front of others.

At that same meeting, the county chair—who regularly touted his progressive bona fides—began to reveal his authoritarian colors as well. He told us that as committee people we were not allowed to criticize Prince Speaker. In his view, taking on a leadership position in the Democratic Party justifies the curtailment of our right to speak freely and hold our representatives accountable, necessary prerequisites for a fully functioning democracy. And as if that were not bad enough, he also told us to make sure our spouses remained silent as well—as if that could ever happen. Have you met my wife?

Moreover, although he claimed Lefty and his spouse as personal friends, he announced in front of the entire executive committee that Lefty's wife had asked him, confidentially, to find someone to primary Prince Speaker, visibly shocking the latter. The county chair—henceforth referred to in this narrative as "Lord County Chair"—said he would "do anything" to support Prince Speaker, whom he took to calling "my incumbent." I guess after every single Democrat with an opponent lost under his watch in 2014, he felt a sense of urgency about retaining that last remaining seat, even if an authoritarian DINO occupied it—exhibiting a kind of royalist fealty inappropriate in a republic.

PROTECTING THE RULES OF THE DEMOCRATIC GAME

In the middle of this party crisis, I accepted a position as director and lobbyist for the state chapter of Common Cause, a national, nonpartisan organization that focuses on issues like voting rights, reversing *Citizens United*, decreasing the influence of money in politics, putting an end to gerrymandering, and increasing transparency in government.[13] Consequently, I resigned as local party chair but remained on the 14RD committee. As I considered ways to advance the Common Cause agenda, I came to realize that Prince Speaker would block my organization's entire agenda at every turn. For example, in previous years, he had single-handedly blocked redistricting reform, which had angered my state board of directors. In addition, Prince Speaker also opposed the entire progressive agenda. How could we move the state in a positive direction with him as Speaker?

I did not articulate my thoughts to anyone other than Mikki, but the topic of Prince Speaker came up in conversation at a meeting of the Rachel Maddow Social Club, a group Mikki and I started in an attempt to organize the bar women, liberal lesbians who were not politically active. As it turns out, however, the bar women simply wanted to drink, not talk about politics, so "Rachel," as we called the group, became a social meeting for progressive activists. One of those activists sat on the Common Cause state board, and she was angry at Prince Speaker both for blocking redistricting reform and also for attacking Rep. Lefty. She suggested that someone should primary the Speaker. Several people agreed. I did not say much, and no concrete plan was hatched. The discussion remained at the level of wishful thinking, and I quickly forgot about it.

A few days later, at a New Jim Crow meeting about criminal justice reform, a friend and fellow committee member approached me, very upset. "I hear you guys are talking about primarying [Prince Speaker]," he said. At first, I was flummoxed. "What are you talking about?" I had no idea. As it turns out, his husband had been at Rachel and had recounted to him our brief conversation. I was actually surprised to hear the distress my friend expressed about the prospect of a primary, since he was one of the progressives who had complained to me about Lefty's treatment. Plus, how could my friend, who claimed to have spent his entire adult life—over fifty years—working for progressive change, support the person blocking the entire progressive agenda in the state? Apparently, Prince Speaker's vote for marriage equality had won his undying loyalty.

That conversation with my soon-to-be former friend, henceforth named "Lord Minion," got me thinking. Perhaps I should primary Prince Speaker! Indeed, we still had an intact campaign apparatus, thousands of grassroots supporters who wanted me to run again, and leftover money in the bank. Part of me really wanted to do it, but I was excited about my new job with Common Cause, and I had assured them I would not be running for anything, so I ruled it out very quickly, and I told no one except Mikki that I had even considered it.

THE BATTLE ROYALE BEGINS

Around this same time, the anti–death penalty campaign in Delaware started really gearing up, with organizers from several national organizations descending upon the state. The repeal bill had passed the senate, but Prince Speaker had it bottled up in a house committee that he knew would not release it. When Lady Progressive and I lobbied him about repeal in the past, he promised us he wouldn't block the bill. He said he would "take a walk" when the bill came up for a vote and would let his caucus members know they could vote their conscience. I guess he expected they would fall in line behind him, unless granted permission to do otherwise. When the time came, however, he actively blocked it.

Prince Speaker said that if we added an amendment retaining the death penalty for killing a cop, he might support it, but repeal advocates found that unacceptable. Besides being morally questionable—are police lives worth more than other lives?—leaving a small loophole would most likely lead to its expansion. Why not expand the exception for killers of children, of the elderly, of more than one person? If you leave the death penalty apparatus intact, state actors will most certainly find reason to use it.

When the call went out from repeal organizers for letters to the editor, one of our local Democratic Party committee members pushed for our committee to issue a proclamation. After all, Prince Speaker represented our district, so we should let him know our views. I had just stepped down as chair, so the "New Committee Chair," a retired academic and ostensibly strong progressive, revised the proclamation we had issued two years prior, calling on Prince Speaker to support repeal, and the entire committee (minus one) voted to approve it. The New Chair sent it to all members of the legislature and to the press.

In addition to that, I personally wrote a letter to the editor, as an individual citizen, asking Prince Speaker to bring repeal to the floor for a vote. This letter had nothing to do with my new position with Common Cause; it was simply an expression of my personal opinion as a citizen and constituent. It went as follows:

> We know from the news that our nation's criminal justice system is riddled with errors, from mundane mistakes to gross injustices. A few recent examples: we have evidence tampering in Delaware, evidence planting in South Carolina, and evidence falsification by the FBI.
>
> In addition, the racism throughout our criminal justice system is so pervasive that it has rightly been called the "new Jim Crow." Consequently, an irreversible punishment like the death penalty should never be used. In Delaware the death

penalty is not reserved for the worst of the worst. You can get death for driving a getaway car, even if you killed no one. Delaware ranks third in the number of executions per capita. And in Delaware, a unanimous jury decision is not required in capital cases.

Why would law enforcement oppose repeal? Certainly, they know better than anyone the problems with our system. Capital punishment takes precious resources away from crime fighting, and it is not a deterrent. Moreover, in death penalty states, police and correctional officers are more likely to be killed.

We must repeal the death penalty. Please ask your representative to do the right thing. My representative is [the Speaker of the House], one of the most powerful men in the state. If he wants the bill to come to a vote, it will.

So, I am making a public plea to the Speaker: Please do the right thing on this critically important life-or-death issue and get the bill to the floor for a vote!

My letter to the editor made the state newspaper, and I didn't think much about it.

A few days later, I went to Leg Hall to begin the lobbying portion of my new job. I had a meeting scheduled with the state senate pro tempore, an aloof yet collegial woman who had strongly supported my campaign, and who reportedly ran her caucus in a democratic manner. I shared the Common Cause agenda with her, and we discussed bills that might be passable. At the end of the meeting she said, "Can I ask you a question?" Sure. "Are you planning to primary [Prince Speaker]?" What? I was gobsmacked by the question. No, of course not, I replied. "Well he thinks you are." What? "I hear things are a little frosty." Frosty? I was puzzled, and then it dawned on me: Maybe he is upset about my letter to the editor asking him to support death penalty repeal. Bingo!

Our meeting had run long, and I was late for my next appointment with a house member. In the stairwell, I ran into a key leader of the repeal effort, who served on the Common Cause board, and she said, "Prince Speaker is furious about your letter. I wish you would have consulted with me before you sent it. Now he is even more opposed to repeal than he was before." At first, I found her comment quite unsettling, but then I had to wonder: How could he be more opposed to something he already totally opposed?

A short while later, an activist from the League of Women Voters accosted me in the basement: "You crossed the line, Claire. You never should have mentioned his name. Lady Progressive says Prince Speaker is really mad." What? I can't say his name? Finally, a little stunned, I went to my scheduled meeting with the progressive senator who sponsored the repeal bill, Prince Speaker's archenemy. When I mentioned that Prince Speaker was upset about the letter, she said, "I know. He accused me of writing it." I guess he thinks I'm illiterate. "Don't worry about it," she said, and then she grinned.

While I knew I had done nothing wrong, still, I found the situation disconcerting. When I got home, I texted Prince Speaker, his preferred form of communication: "I understand you are upset about my letter to the editor. Should we talk?" He never responded. Instead, he began a smear campaign against me, telling every single state legislator that I was planning to primary him. One of the Common Cause Delaware board members, who frequented Leg Hall, texted me about Prince Speaker's angry rampage, which made me nervous for my job. Then, a senate staffer told me that his boss did not want to be seen talking to me because I upset Prince Speaker. Would this end my lobbying career, before it even got started? It felt to me like everyone in the building was frantically whispering about me: "Oh my God. Have you heard what Claire did?"

Shortly thereafter, Mikki and I ran into our district's New Committee Chair, who was a dear friend at the time, and he told us Prince Speaker was livid about the proclamation that our Democratic committee had issued, calling for him to support death penalty repeal. Our friend was visibly shaken and full of remorse. Apparently, he had gotten an ear full. We told him that he did nothing wrong, but we could not soothe him. He just kept shaking his head with regret.

At the next Democratic committee meeting, a heated discussion broke out. Learning of Prince Speaker's rage about the committee's proclamation, several people started backpedaling, including Lord County Chair, who disingenuously claimed he did not understand the contents of the procla-mation when he voted for it. Lord County Chair, his husband, and Lord Minion all told the committee, "We have to support [Prince Speaker] no matter what because he is the incumbent. You don't have to agree with him on every issue, but you have to support him."

Honestly, I was dumbfounded by their position for two reasons. First, I found their dismissiveness about Prince Speaker's support for the death penalty, one of the most pressing moral issues of our time, deeply disturbing. The death penalty is not just some trivial issue upon which people disagree. It is an immoral, barbaric, and racist practice, both cruel and unusual, and the epitome of authoritarian government. Second, they apparently had no understanding of the basic premise of democratic government. As I put my hand up, Mikki leaned over and whispered, "Don't sound angry!" When called on, I stood up and made a rousing speech about popular sovereignty and accountability. "[Prince Speaker] is accountable to us," I told them, "not vice versa! And it's our job as citizens to tell him what we want him to do and then evaluate his job performance come election day. He answers to us. We don't answer to him!" It gratified me to see about half the committee nodding vigorously.

I WAS WARNED, YET I PERSISTED

As a former democratic theory professor and free citizen of the United States, I believe very strongly in the accountability of elected representatives to the people and in the right of the people to express dissenting views. I will not allow the Democratic Party or any entity to curtail my civil liberties. Moreover, I refuse to capitulate to bullying. Consequently, I felt that I had to keep speaking out because otherwise it would look like I had been cowed, and I had no intention of trying to make nice, smooth things over, assume a deferential posture. Hence Prince Speaker and I were locked in battle.

Two months later, when another important issue came up, I spoke out again, with these two posts on Facebook:

> Post 1: What a surprise! Ernie Lopez—a man who got an award from the Charter School Network and who said . . . that he's "open to vouchers"—supports overriding the Governor's veto of the popular Opt-Out bill [allowing parents to opt their children out of high-stakes testing], whereas [Prince Speaker] opposes it!!

> Post 2: The people have spoken. They want HB50 [the Opt-Out bill]. I hope [Prince Speaker] comes around on this.

Believe it or not, I did not aim to antagonize Prince Speaker with those posts, which in my opinion were extremely mild, but I was hoping to influence his position. I had no expectation of blowback as I flew to Ohio the next day for a meeting at the Kettering Foundation on deliberative democracy.

Thus, it came as a complete surprise, when I got this message from the house majority leader in my Facebook Messenger inbox:

> Hello Claire, as a women and democrat I'm very concerned about why you continue to call out the only political official in Sussex County, [Prince Speaker]. I just don't understand why a fellow democrat would go after another democrat. I think if you would call [Prince Speaker] and have a conversation you would have a better understanding of what really goes on in Leg Hall and not formulate an opinion or comment until you get all the facts. [Prince Speaker] is a good person and always thinks things through. I wish you would get to know him and talk to him before making statements. It hurts our party, especially in Sussex County. If you would like to chat sometime I would really welcome the opportunity. [Majority Leader]

I was flabbergasted. The Majority Leader had essentially told me to keep my mouth shut—and over the mildest of posts on Facebook. The fact that this happened while I sat at a meeting about deliberative democracy made it all the more surreal. I am sure Prince Speaker put her up to it because her message includes two things he always says: 1) He's the only one who knows "what's really going on," and 2) he's a "good guy" who is doing "a good job."

Here is my response:

> Hi [Majority Leader], How surprising to get your message. You mention you are contacting me as a woman. Are you also contacting the men who posted about [Prince Speaker] not supporting a veto override on HB50 or is it just me? I have to say that I do not see how two posts about [Prince Speaker] opposing the veto override—one saying I was surprised, the other saying I hope he changes his mind—constitute me "going after" him. As a citizen and a constituent in his district, I have the right and the responsibility to let him know my views on the issues, and I also seek to inform others so they can get engaged as well. That's part of the democratic process. Newspapers and social media are full of people voicing their views on the issues and asking their representatives to do the right thing.

> Additionally, I don't believe I need to hear about what is "really going on" in Leg Hall in order to have a position on

the issues. My political positions are based on my values and have nothing to do with whether or not [Prince Speaker] is a good person. My concern is public policy and law. Having an open discussion of the issues and how our elected representatives—who are accountable to the people—vote is an essential part of the democratic process, and people, even Democrats, are not going to agree on every issue. If the Democratic Party feels the need to silence dissenting voices, then we have serious problems.

She responded with this:

Hi Claire. Thanks for the return response. I guess I see people in my [district] are big supporters of me and help me continue to stay in office. My members usually call me if they don't understand a vote or stance and we walk through so I can better serve them. They usually don't go on social media and air out their ideas and dismay against me. [Prince Speaker] is in a district that could swing republican if our own democrats don't have his back. We don't always agree as democrats but we should always have each other's back. I'm a democrat and I have been frustrated with our party and other politicians but I handle it one on one. Everyone I guess has a different style.

Then I said:

[Majority Leader], I think [Prince Speaker] needs to get more in touch with his constituents. I don't think he has the strong relationship with them that you do with yours. He is scheduled to come to [his district's Democratic Party] meeting in August, which is a start.

That ended our exchange.

Meanwhile, our supposedly dear friend, the New Committee Chair, was suddenly busy every time we proposed getting together for dinner with him and his wife. We were starting to feel social, as well as political, pressure.

On a more positive note, the public pressure campaign for repeal worked. The house committee unexpectedly released the repeal bill, but then Prince Speaker scheduled the vote for the one day that Rep. Lefty had to leave town for family reasons. And although Prince Speaker told Lady Progressive and me long ago that he would not vote against repeal, he did not "take a walk" as promised. Sadly, the bill did not pass the house; however, the Delaware Supreme Court subsequently ruled the state's death penalty law unconstitutional because it did not require a unanimous jury decision. So, we won in the end.

PRINCE SPEAKER VS. THE PROGRESSIVE DEMS

On the last day of June, the legislative session ended with Prince Speaker making a backroom budget deal with the Republicans, cutting short negotiations with his progressive colleagues. The budget rewarded state police and charter schools, while gutting social programs for the most vulnerable. Prince Speaker refused to bring two progressive taxation bills to the floor for a vote. Instead, he raised revenue by commandeering one-time settlement money that was supposed to help homeowners defrauded by Bank of America. The progressive representatives, the so-called "Big Six," voted no on the budget and their leader wrote an op-ed in the state newspaper explaining why.

In response, Prince Speaker refused to engage his colleagues but instead gave a series of talks in Sussex County, during which he bashed the "Big Six," essentially calling them traitors and liars. I heard his mono- logue twice. The first time, I just listened silently. The second time, at a Democratic Club luncheon, when I saw every head nodding in agreement and a few people muttering in disgust—"How could Democrats act that way?"—I knew I had to speak out because I am not one to say nothing, while friends and allies are maligned.

When Lord Minion called on me, I thanked Prince Speaker for coming and said I wanted to give him a chance to respond to the specific points raised by the Big Six, which I summarized. In response, Prince Speaker became visibly angry—literally red in the face—and simply reit- erated that the Big Six were "liars and traitors" and that none of us know "what's really going on." He also gestured to the reporters in the back of the room, indicating he did not want to say too much, which, of course, guaranteed his comments would be reported. And indeed, the next day, the entire exchange, including his gesturing, made the state newspaper. That is the point at which I learned that due to my status as a former candidate, every time I spoke about politics at a public forum, it would get published—which actually helped my organizing overall.

As a former academic, I am accustomed to asking questions at public forums. That is part of the job we do. When I was in graduate school, one of my professors explicitly told us that whenever we attend a talk, we need to ask the presenter a "devastating, career-advancing question." When I questioned Prince Speaker, however, my intention was not to devastate him or advance my career. Believe it or not, I genuinely wanted to hear his response to the particular points made by the Big Six, and I felt I had the right to ask. Indeed, wasn't he there to discuss the conflict? In addition, however, I wanted to ask him publicly in a way that conveyed to people the other side of the story. Isn't that the kind of thing that should happen at a public forum, a conversation where all sides get their due? The crucial point that I failed to remember, however, are the words of my mentor, Steve Bronner: "Politics is not a graduate seminar."

No one criticized me to my face after the meeting—although Prince Speaker and his minions formed a whispering circle in the hallway—but when the newspaper article came out, a man who served with me on the local Democratic committee sent this email to all committee members plus Prince Speaker:

> Attached is an article which is very troubling to me. A member and past Chairman [sic] of our Democratic Committee, Claire Snyder Hall, is attacking [Prince Speaker] every chance she gets and her comments, including at the Eastern Sussex Democratic Club meeting recently held, in my view, are not consistent with my views as well as many members of the [District] Committee. I am not sure whether she is doing this as a paid lobbyist for Common Cause, but she should acknowledge that these views are not the views of the 14RD Democratic Committee of which she is a member, without a vote within the committee. [Prince Speaker] is the only Democrat elected member of the Delaware Legislature from Sussex County and is Speaker of the House of Representatives. This clearly planned attack embarrasses [Prince Speaker], the 14RD committee and affects the view of many citizens of the county of our committee.

When I saw the email, I was livid, especially because the author mentioned my job, which I feared might be in jeopardy because of my conflict with Prince Speaker, and while I loved my job, I refused to be cowed. I responded like this:

I strongly object to your mischaracterization of my intentions and dragging my job into it. How dare you!

I have a lifelong commitment to advancing progressive issues and encouraging civic engagement. [Prince Speaker] is a public official who spoke at a public forum about the public's business and as a citizen in this district and a constituent of his, I have every right to ask a question, which is what I did. Indeed, it is my constitutionally protected right. Several people asked questions, but the press chose to focus on me because I'm a public figure [having run for office].

I have no idea why you would say I am attacking [Prince Speaker] every chance I get. Like when? I did NOT ATTACK [Prince Speaker] at the . . . meeting. I asked him a question. I wanted his response to what his 6 colleagues are saying.

I certainly hope you are not including my letter to the editor about death penalty repeal as an attack on [Prince Speaker]. I wrote that with good intentions and believe me had NO IDEA what reaction it would cause. Having an elected official go around Leg Hall and tell everyone he sees how furious he is about a constituent's letter to the editor is so far outside the box of anything I could ever imagine happening, that I am still shocked by it.

My only purpose was to pressure [Prince Speaker] to support repeal. I did nothing wrong. I simply exercised my constitutional right to request that the person representing me vote the way I want. It's normal practice to write such letters. The letter was very respectful. Frankly, I am the one who has been attacked.

What else you are referring to, I can't imagine.

My intention is NOT to embarrass [Prince Speaker], and my activism as a citizen in my private life has NOTHING to do with Common Cause.

Mikki and a couple of my friends defended me, but then Lord Minion jumped in and accused me of publicly "berating" Prince Speaker. Apparently, he subscribes to Lord County Chair's idea that since we as committee members have "access" to elected officials, we must remain silent in public.

The next Saturday morning, Mikki was checking the state blogs on her phone, like she always does, and she said one of them referenced our district committee. I laughingly asked, "Does it mention my name?" She just stared at me wide-eyed for a moment, and then passed me the phone. The "right-wing blogger" (from chapter 3) had posted the entire email exchange on his high-profile website, Delaware Right!

When I notified Lord County Chair, he said he thought I was the culprit—the logic of which alludes me. Why would I send a private email exchange to a right-wing blog? What kind of strategery would that be? During our conversation, however, I caught him in a lie, so I know he was involved somehow. I actually called the right-wing blogger—I still remembered our great conversation after the American Legion event, and he seemed strangely intrigued by me—but he refused to tell me who sent him the emails. "You know I can't tell you that, Claire. But if you ever want to do a guest column, I will post it on my site!" The New Committee Chair demanded that the culprit confess, but of course no one did, and nothing more was done. What more could be done?

The next week I got an email from a state senator friend, whom I was supporting for Congress, telling me that because of the conflict between me and Prince Speaker, he was going to steer clear of me in public. I considered the email gratuitous and odd because Prince Speaker strongly supported my friend's opponent, so besides hurting my feelings, the purpose of the email was unclear. When I mentioned the email to one of my young activist friends from upstate, he asked with a smirk, "Was that before or after you did the big fundraiser for him?" After. Of course.

Meanwhile, an ally of ours, who staffed the state chapter of a democracy reform organization, had started a satellite group in Sussex County. Mikki and I suggested that the group invite the Big Six down to tell their side of the story. When we pitched the idea at the meeting, Lord Minion literally started shouting at the top of his lungs, "I can't believe you!" Needless to say, I was temporarily dumbstruck by the outburst. In my experience, people don't start screaming at other people in the middle of meetings. After a pause, I suggested we finish the meeting, and then he could tell me the reason he was so angry at me. I knew it had something to do with Prince Speaker, but what exactly? At first, he just kept shrieking, "You know what you did! You know what you did!" Then, he bellowed out, "We wouldn't have marriage equality without Prince Speaker! He supported you!" Finally, he dramatically stormed out of the room. For the record, this occurred after the Supreme Court legalized same-sex marriage across the country, so neither claim was true.

That was the first of three meetings where Lord Minion literally screamed in my face. At times, I worried that he might have a heart attack. The last time was almost comical. The staffer and I walked into the meeting and said hi to Lord Minion, who after giving the former a hug, put his face less than six inches from mine and loudly barked, "Not you!" Was I going to have to take out a restraining order? A few minutes later I accused Lord Minion of leaking my emails, at which point he stormed off in a huff, and the group permanently disbanded.

Again, since I refuse to capitulate to bullying, I felt compelled to continue with our plan to convene a forum. The staffer did not want to do it under his umbrella, however, because "that would close off the possibility of reconciliation" with Lord Minion, a longtime member, a sentiment I considered admirable. So, Mikki and I, along with some friends, formed an ad hoc group to organize a budget forum for the community that was open to the public. We invited the Big Six, but only the group's leader and Lefty could make it. The night of the event, we were gratified that people began arriving in droves, including a lot of new faces. Then, all of a sudden, in walks Prince Speaker—followed by every Republican representative in the county! Their arrival was quite unexpected. The Big Six leader and Lefty appeared startled but quickly regrouped. The forum yielded a great deliberative conversation among community members and the panelists, but Prince Speaker just sat there, silently sulking, and playing with his phone.

"I DON'T KNOW WHY THAT GIRL DOESN'T LIKE ME"

Near the end of September, a story broke in the state newspaper: In a year in which state workers got no raises at all, Prince Speaker secretly gave his personal staff raises of up to 16.6 percent, and when the other legislative leaders found out about it, they secretly gave their personal staffs comparable raises. The state newspaper said, "The raises cost taxpayers about $140,000—not enough to solve Delaware's budget problems. But the increases are striking considering that lawmakers, in 2014 and 2015 budget negotiations, reduced or eliminated across-the-board pay increases for state employees, while heaping hefty pay increases on their closest political advisers."[14]

As director of a statewide organization that supports transparency and opposes cronyism, I emailed my state board chair and the Common

Cause office in DC, asking, "Is this something we should comment on?" The vice president of communications in DC said, "Absolutely," and my state board chair agreed. Working with the two of them, we issued a press release and wrote an op-ed, which ran in the next day's paper. The press release said, "At a time when many . . . families are feeling pinched economically it is a grotesque abuse of power that political leaders in both parties would ensure raises for their staff, while ignoring the hard-working women and men who keep Delaware safe, who nurse our sick, who pave our roads, and do the many other jobs necessary to make Delaware the special place it is." An op-ed quickly followed, and it really hit a nerve; I kid you not: several people literally came up to me on the street to shake my hand and thank me for my commentary.

Prince Speaker, however, was not pleased. As soon as the press release hit, he sent Lord County Chair and the New Committee Chair an email saying, "Thought you might want to see this latest from Claire. Again, she has not reached out to me to find out what happened before she attacks." In retaliation, he accelerated the smear campaign, cornering my friends at events and calling my political allies on the phone to malign me at length. "I don't know why that girl doesn't like me," he reportedly said. "We used to be such good friends."

Then he tried to get me fired. More specifically, one day, after a work meeting, my board chair pulled me aside to inform me that Prince Speaker called one of our most influential board members and complained about me "for forty-five minutes." I was stunned. He reportedly went on and on about the death penalty and some imagined conspiracy between me and his senate archenemy (whom I barely knew at the time) to take him out as Speaker. Believe me, it is very unsettling to have your boss inform you that one of the most powerful men in the state has a problem with you, and I feared for my job, which I loved. I did not say much in response but was greatly relieved when my board chair said he supported me. In fact, he even volunteered to talk to Prince Speaker man-to-man, even though he did not know him, a gracious offer that I quickly declined.

Trying to get people fired for their political views is increasingly common, and journalist Liza Featherstone calls it one of the "creepiest and most authoritarian" recent trends in American politics.[15] The day after it happened, I emailed Lord County Chair: "FYI, [Prince Speaker] is now calling my board members, presumably to get me fired. At what point does his behavior become unacceptable?" His reply: "I am sorry to hear that. I doubt you will lose the support and confidence of your board." So, as long as my board supports me, it's OK?

That exchange forms a great example of the ways in which Democratic Party operatives differ from everyday people. When I tell people outside the party that Prince Speaker tried to get me fired from my job, they are aghast and outraged, but when I tell insiders, they generally just shrug. It is hard to describe the feeling of being subjected to an angry vendetta by one of the most powerful men in the state, but it makes me feel like I know a little bit—just a little bit—about the way Megyn Kelly and Katie Tur must have felt, getting relentlessly attacked by Donald Trump. Luckily, no angry Twitter mob went after me—Prince Speaker does not use Twitter—but I did feel threatened. I am not trying to be hyperbolic, but I honestly felt like if I lived in a different country, he might have had me killed. Mikki and I made double sure to follow all traffic laws, lest one of his brothers in blue pull us over, and Mikki stopped telling people where she worked and alerted her bosses about the situation, just in case. Luckily, her bosses are not right-wingers, and they value her work. Otherwise, we could have been destroyed.

COLLAPSE OF THE PROGRESSIVE CONTINGENT

Personally, I found Prince Speaker's authoritarian mentality and bullying tactics totally unacceptable, but at least I could understand them. It is no surprise that a powermonger wants power. Less comprehensible to me was the willingness of my fellow committee members to appease him, including many self-proclaimed progressives and several close personal friends, one of whom actually blamed me for the conflict. While studies show that 62 percent of the American people score high on measures of authoritarianism, indicating that a lot of people probably fall in line because of a submissive disposition, it surprised me tremendously to see *Democratic Party leaders and progressive activists* tolerate or defend Prince Speaker's behavior.[16]

Consequently, after many long conversations, Mikki and I finally decided to resign from the district committee, after five years of service, right after a very successful October townhall meeting—an outreach project that was summarily terminated. We decided to exit for several reasons. First, we were disappointed that many of our friends on the committee took Prince Speaker's side against me. Second, we could no longer trust our fellow committee members, not knowing who leaked the emails.

Third, we did not want to raise money to help reelect Prince Speaker. Fourth, although we realized we were ceding control to Lord County Chair and the minions, we were tired of the emotional roller-coaster. I felt strongly that staying on the committee meant seeking out negativity. So, after weeks of deliberation, we decided that instead of working inside the party, we would continue building progressive community outside the party, supporting progressive candidates, pushing a left agenda statewide, and convening the monthly Rachel meetings in our home to build the progressive network.

In the end, after all Prince Speaker had done—wreaking vengeance on Democratic colleagues in the legislature, blocking progressive issues, capitulating to the Republicans on a terrible budget deal, bullying me, and trying to get me fired—can you believe my former committee voted to endorse him for reelection? Two of my closest friends on the committee, who had served on my campaign inner team and who knew every detail of Prince Speaker's attacks against me, voted for endorsement, even though one of them ran the death penalty repeal campaign for the county. Another older friend who worked on my campaign, who organized the weekly phone-bank potlucks, also endorsed him; she said she loves Prince Speaker because he was a cop, "just like my daddy." Another dear friend who had instigated the committee's resolution for death penalty repeal also voted for endorsement. He called me afterward and said, "Claire, if you are still speaking to me, I want to apologize. I don't know what happened; I got caught up in the moment and forgot about all the terrible things he did to you. Can you ever forgive me?" Of course, I can!

Interestingly, all these folks were retirees. Prince Speaker had nothing on any of them, and they gained nothing from him. I believe they are mostly good people who mean well, yet they dropped to their knees when power pushed back. They seemed to be hoodwinked by Lord County Chair's rhetoric about having to "support the incumbent no matter what" and about the importance of having a Speaker who lives in Sussex County. Got to support the home team! Their collapse exemplifies the Prince-minion dynamic.

In contrast, another friend, who had worked on my campaign, repeatedly called Prince Speaker "an embarrassment," and spoke openly with us about ways to curtail his power, including through a primary challenge, also voted for endorsement. In that case, she did so because she had decided to run for office herself. After she lost, Lord County Chair got her a state job. That woman had something to gain by capitulating, which illustrates the Prince-courtier dynamic described by Viroli.

The Democratic Party committee, under the direction of Lord County Chair, endorsed Prince Speaker, even though it actually had a longstanding policy against endorsing candidates in a primary, a policy designed specifically to prevent nasty splits. Lord County Chair persuaded everyone to ignore precedent and endorse Prince Speaker in early January 2016. He thought that would dissuade possible primary opponents, who would consequently be denied access to any party resources, such as Votebuilder, the vitally important Democratic Party database. He hoped to portray any opponents to Prince Speaker as essentially illegitimate.

And, just as anticipated by committees past, the endorsement caused a split. All the minions just described, minus one, ended up resigning from the committee, shortly after the vote. Perhaps they regretted bowing and scraping before Power. Two other progressives also resigned—my dear friend who was not present for the vote and the one person who did not vote yes on endorsement. Consequently, the committee was decimated, but that just gave Lord County Chair a chance to pack it with courtiers and minions to better support his incumbent, Prince Speaker.

It is hard to understand why progressive activists—most of whom I brought into the party after my campaign—would collapse like they did, but three factors possibly played a role. First, despite our claim to be a great democratic republic, the culture of party politics in our country seems to transform even people of goodwill into either powermongers or submissives, which is one reason so many members of the public hate the political parties. As Morris Fiorina argues, "There is a disconnect between the world of contemporary Americans and the political order that purports to represent them. Citizens see . . . a political order dominated by a political class whose behavior and operating style would be unacceptable outside of politics. Citizens can hardly be blamed if they increasingly regard government as . . . something best kept at a distance."[17] Based on my experiences, I agree that the realm of partisan politics is populated by politicians and party operatives who behave in ways no normal person would recognize as decent. Those who collapsed simply got co-opted by the dominant party culture of incumbent protection, authoritarian badgering, and habits of deference to power.

Second, it takes a lot of courage to stand up to a bully, and in our society, not many opportunities exist for people to develop *democratic courage*, defined as the fortitude to stand up for democratic principles. In Delaware, politics operates largely through cronyism and backroom deals. The state has no tradition of civic engagement, elections are generally noncompetitive, and no referendum option exists to allow people to work

around the legislature. Blocked from participation, people become habituated into passivity. The political culture imbues deference not democratic
courage. I mean, you could stand up for democracy, but why bother when
faced with a closed system? Prince Speaker would have gotten reelected
anyway, so why bother resisting? It's easier to go along to get along.

Third, and most importantly, I have learned from my political forays
that a lot of people need strong leaders to follow; without strong leaders
they either get confused or lose their nerve. It is hard to go against the
crowd, particularly when the crowd includes bullies who will scream
in your face, malign you behind your back, or make you feel socially
isolated or threatened. It is easier to have democratic courage when you
have someone to lead you into battle. So, when Mikki and I quit the
committee, no one remained who could articulate a vision of strong
popular sovereignty and accountability to inspire people, so most of our
progressive allies lost focus and collapsed when power pushed back. Sadly,
our exit ceded power to Lord County Chair, a master manipulator, who
successfully convinced members that as party committee members they
"must support the incumbent no matter what." That framing probably
affected people's understanding of actions they might take. We knew we
were ceding power when we quit, but at that point, I felt the need to
prioritize my own mental health.

This disappointing story actually has an interesting denouement. The
one man who did not endorse Prince Speaker became so outraged about
the course of events, and about the death penalty debacle, that he decided
to challenge Prince Speaker in the primary. Months earlier, when Prince
Speaker tried to get me fired, Mikki was determined to find someone
to primary him, and she targeted that lone man, who was a dear friend
who worked on my campaign. "I'll give you a field plan and a maximum
donation," she told him. Nothing she said could convince him, but that
endorsement vote did it. When our friend saw Lord County Chair and
the minions maneuvering to prevent the possibility of a competitive
primary, he decided to run. Consequently, for the first time ever, Prince
Speaker had a primary opponent, and as luck would have it, he also had
a Republican opponent, which had not been the case in 2014. Mikki ran
our friend's insurgent campaign, dealing payback to Prince Speaker for
attacking me. While our friend did not win, he caused Prince Speaker
some anxiety and extra work.

As I have shared this very personal story with people, I have learned
that it is far from uncommon. People are battling demagogic little princes—
mini-Trumps—in political positions all over the country. But "battling the

Prince" is not only about individual people; it is also about the perennial allure of power and the habits of deference—the royalist mindset—that people develop to make their lives easier, which undermine their ability to govern themselves as dignified equals. They allow the metaphorical Prince to live rent free inside their heads and command their deference. In light of all this, one thing is clear: We can never take our hands off the democratic wheel. Only an engaged populace, with a commitment to democratic values, and the courage to defend them, can keep the authoritarian threat at bay and allow us to keep our republic.

CHAPTER 6

SOFT AUTHORITARIANISM
IN THE DEMOCRATIC PARTY

I have always been ambivalent about the Democratic Party (DP), ever since I became politically active as a teen, and my experiences in Delaware and Florida have reinforced those feelings. While the DP's agenda better accords with my values than does the agenda of the Republican Party (GOP)—historically standing for social welfare programs and currently for social equality—when it comes to militarism, immigration, and the prison-industrial complex, the Democrats have not distinguished themselves as champions of justice. Thus, although it stands to the left of the GOP, the DP stands to the right of where I situate myself on the ideological spectrum. Consequently, for most of my life the Democratic Party did not excite me, so I basically ignored it, although I did vote party line on Election Day.

Then, in 2007, my wife Mikki and I started lobbying for marriage equality in the Maryland General Assembly. We had a very positive experience, particularly because our representatives led the state on equality issues. Consequently, when we moved to Delaware in 2011, we decided to increase our level of engagement with electoral politics by getting involved with the Democratic Party. For the following eight years, I occupied a variety of leadership roles inside the party—in Delaware, serving as party chair, county executive committee member, state senate candidate, state convention delegate, and regular committee person; in Florida, serving as a precinct captain, county steering committee member, county executive committee member, local progressive caucus president, state progressive caucus board member, and state convention delegate—and in the realm of electoral politics, I also interacted with Democrats in my work as a registered lobbyist, campaign communications director, and political consultant.

Seeing the party and electoral politics from the inside broadened my understanding of the situation we face in the United States. While I always knew that the DP fell short on policy—chasing the Republican Party as it moved to the right, failing to put forward an agenda for working people; not doing enough to address social inequality; supporting mass incarceration, deportation, militarism, and a foreign policy that is often antidemocratic, even criminal—my experiences in the party trenches reveal that things are worse than I thought. Not only does the policy agenda of the DP need radical change, but the culture does as well because right now powermongering, toxic partisanship, and an authoritarian mentality increasingly permeate party culture.

THE POLITICAL CONTEXT

In the months before the 2020 election, the political situation looked grim to me—reminiscent of the way I viewed things as I entered graduate school right before the 1988 election. In both years, a malevolent Republican president occupied the White House, willing to do whatever it took to advance his right-wing agenda and push the world closer to annihilation, even if it meant breaking the law, and Congress refused to stop him. Moreover, reminiscent of today, a visionary progressive leader had emerged who sought the Democratic nomination but lost to a lackluster establishment candidate, thanks partly to the machinations of Democratic Party elites.[1] Finally, in both years, the Republican candidate tried to win by manipulating racist fears. Although Democrat Joe Biden ended up winning the presidential election in 2020, I do not expect that to alter the underlying conditions that led millions of people to elect Trump in 2016, to vote for him again in 2020, and to support his efforts to remain in power despite losing. While things looked bleak in '88, monumental positive change would soon come to pass, seemingly all of a sudden but actually after years of organizing, including the fall of authoritarian regimes in the USSR, eastern and central Europe, and South Africa, which gave people hope. Who knows what unexpected changes await us in 2021 and beyond?

Despite Biden's win, we still need to address the problems that led to Trump's rise and the acceleration of antidemocratic trends within the Republican Party and recognize that the threats we face come not from one toxic individual but from the entirety of one political party with the complicity of the other. While Trump might fancy himself a world-historical figure, transforming society, he is really just a right-wing tool. Although some view him as unique with his belligerent violations of political norms, inflammatory bombast, relentless narcissism, and inability to empathize, his agenda actually included nothing original. He has not "fundamentally altered" the overarching trajectory of US politics nor offered any type of "Trump Doctrine" in any area of public life.[2] He merely ripped the disingenuous veil of civility off the long-standing agenda of right-wing Republicans—shredding the safety net, cutting taxes for the wealthy, rewarding cronies, manipulating racial resentment, deporting Hispanics, packing the Supreme Court, empowering conservative Christians, funding the military, meddling in the politics of other countries, and so on.

How could anyone support such a man? If we fail to understand the underlying reasons that people voted for Trump in 2016 over a well-qualified establishment Democrat, we are destined to see more authoritarian demagogues take power in the future, and if the next one is more disciplined, intelligent, and strategic than Trump, we are in deep trouble. People voted for Trump because they were unhappy with the status quo. After forty years of neoliberal policies, more and more people see an economic future that looks bleak and those elected to address public problems, in both parties, have done little to make conditions better for working- and middle-class people—and given that 90 percent of incumbents get reelected, it is hard to hold them accountable. In 2016, Trump took down two political dynasties, the Bushes and the Clintons, because people wanted change so badly. His authoritarian style made people think he was in control and would actually get things done, and his continuing popularity among the Republican base has allowed him to dominate the GOP—although that might change because of blowback from the insurrection and his pending legal and financial problems. Only time will tell.

In any event, we cannot simply move on from Trump and return to "normal," as Biden suggested during the primary.[3] In order to move forward in a positive direction, we must address the deteriorating economic situation that makes people amenable to right-wing authoritarianism, offer a progressive vision to address those problems, and advocate a more participatory democracy, so people get used to ruling themselves democratically rather than submitting to the authority of elites. The DP does not offer any of that. Moreover, its culture essentially says, "Fall in line, defer to power, or suffer the consequences," which undermines the goal of fostering democratic courage and critical thinking and so does not help move people away from authoritarianism. Indeed, if it had not been for Trump's botched response to the coronavirus pandemic and the subsequent crash of the economy, he might well have gotten reelected.

WE NEED PARTICIPATION NOT INCUMBENT PROTECTION

When I was growing up, voting was considered a nonpartisan, democratic value, something every citizen should consider an obligation. That was not always the case. Universal suffrage used to be a radical left-wing idea, opposed by property owners who feared the masses. Women's suffrage did not pass until 1920, and racists prevented Blacks from voting until 1965. What would happen if everyone could vote? As it turns out, not as much as people feared or hoped, since so many people do not bother to exercise that hard-won right. Even in presidential elections, until 2020 turnout had not reached 60 percent since 1968, usually hanging around 55 percent or less.[4] Nevertheless, it should not be controversial to enable every eligible person in the United States to vote on election day. As supporters of republicanism have argued since Roman antiquity, "What affects all must be decided by all."[5]

Sadly, voting has become a polarizing issue with Republicans claiming widespread voter fraud, despite evidence to the contrary. The GOP now advocates voter suppression of multiple types because the party fears it cannot win fair elections. For example, Donald Trump actually said out loud that "if voting were made easier, 'You'd never have a Republican elected in this country again.'"[6] Not a new insight, Trump's proclamation echoes American Legislative Exchange Council (ALEC) cofounder Paul Weyrich's declaration in 1980: "I don't want everybody to vote. . . . Our leverage, quite candidly, goes up as the voting populace goes down."[7]

Democrats should support policies that enable people to vote for both principled and strategic reasons, but that is not always the case. Serving as a lobbyist for Common Cause in a state in which Democrats controlled all branches of government, I learned that Democrats in power can be just as self-serving and unprincipled as Republicans. I already recounted that Prince Speaker refused to support independent redistricting reform, saying, "I will not be the one to give up power." Knowing him, that did not surprise me, but having a highly respected, progressive leader in the Delaware State Senate refuse to support same-day voter registration (SDR) because she claimed it would lead to fraud shocked me.

At first, I could not understand it, but then I learned that some Democratic incumbents opposed SDR because it would "destabilize the voter universe"—meaning, it would put a wild card into their carefully calibrated game plan for reelection. While no legislator or staffer ever explicitly said this to me, several of my organizational allies informed me that some incumbents feared that the Black churches would do a "souls to the polls" effort and send busloads of previously unregistered African Americans to vote on Election Day—people that were not in the voter file and so had not been contacted by the incumbent's machine. Who knows what might happen when busloads of Black people show up at the polls unannounced? I did not expect Democrats to take that position, especially not progressive ones, and it really tarnished my view of the Democratic Party and its elected officials.

During both legislative sessions during my two years lobbying for Common Cause (2015 and 2016), I fought repeated attempts by Democrats to pass bills raising the amount of money that could be donated to candidates. Larger donations increase the influence of wealthier entities and usually help incumbents add to their war chests. One of my progressive allies in the house wanted the bill to pass badly, but because Common Cause opposes money in politics as part of its core mission, I considered the issue nonnegotiable. I really appreciated that he acknowledged my position as valid, even though he held a different view. "I understand," he said. "It's your brand." But of course, he still kept trying.

Every morning during session, I would immediately check the Leg Hall website to see the bills that had been filed. Whenever I saw a bill to raise contribution limits, I would spring into action—emailing all the legislators, activating our membership, and taking the fight to social media and the state newspapers, which reliably published my editorials. "We need to stop the 'More Money in Delaware Politics Bill,'" read one op-ed:

> Last week we observed the six-year anniversary of the *Citizens United* decision that unleashed Big Money into our political system, and all across the country, people are rising up in protest. Indeed, Fighting Big Money has become a major issue in the 2016 election. And not only that, voters also reject the

power of political parties, supporting insurgent candidates on both the Left and the Right. Yet on the eve of that anniversary, politicians and party operatives in Dover put forward a bill (HB 247) that would *increase* the amount of money in Delaware politics and the power of party insiders.[8]

Together with allies and organizational members, we stopped multiple versions of the "more money in politics bill."

My biggest Common Cause moment of glory was getting the legislature to rescind its circa 1970s call for an Article V constitutional convention. Then and now, right-wing behemoth ALEC, funded by the Koch brothers, is trying to get enough states to call for a convention, so they can get a balanced budget amendment added to the US Constitution. A federal balanced budget amendment would be a disaster from both a democratic and a Democratic perspective. It would inevitably curtail spending on programs that help people and limit the ability of the government to respond during a crisis, such as the coronavirus pandemic, even if the public wanted government help.[9] Some groups on the left, such as Wolf PAC, also want a constitutional convention, so they could pass an amendment overturning *Citizens United*. While Common Cause definitely wants *Citizens United* overturned, it does not believe convening a constitutional convention is a good strategy because once convened, the convention could arguably amend or rewrite the Constitution however it wants—repealing birth-right citizenship or outlawing abortion, for example. A convention would not be a fantastic example of strong democracy in action, as much as I wish it could be, because delegates would be chosen by those currently in power.

Back in 2016, Delaware was one of only two states with a Democratic legislature (along with Maryland) that had a live call for a constitutional convention on the books, and Common Cause wanted to get those calls rescinded. To approach the task, I convened a coalition of state activist organizations to lobby for rescission. Unfortunately, my very poor relationship with Prince Speaker, as discussed in chapter 5, complicated the situation because he refused to attend any meeting that included me. Yes, he can do that!

Consequently, the coalition decided that I would work the senate side and another person would work the house side. Leadership in both chambers said they would support rescission, but Prince Speaker kept stalling. I feared he might sabotage the effort just to deny me a win—he was petty like that—but my allies assured me that he was on board, and I, in turn, told my colleagues in DC not to worry. To help move things along, however, the national Common Cause team collaborated with several national unions to enlist Delaware's only congressmember, John Carney, to give Prince Speaker a call. Smart move! Even the Prince could not say no to the presumed future governor. It seemed to take forever, but when the vote finally got scheduled, I spent the entire day at Leg Hall, anxiously awaiting the roll call vote. I had the DC team on standby, ready to send out my press release, as soon as I texted them. Then, finally, we won! It felt great to finally see success in the Democratic-dominated legislature. I had initially expected better.

I learned a lot during my time lobbying in the Delaware legislature, and after the 2016 session, I shared some insights on the blog I used to maintain, called *Moments of Clarity*. I did not realize at the time that it would be my final year with Common Cause, but in October, Mikki and I decided to move to Florida to spend time with my ninety-year-old mother, whose health was declining. Here's the post.

CREATIVE INTERLUDE IV: *MOMENTS OF CLARITY* BLOG POST

Yesterday, I drafted an email to Common Cause Delaware members about our legislative accomplishments during the 2016 session. We did have some big wins. We helped pass a number of bills—rescission of all calls for a constitutional convention, removing financial barriers to the restoration of voting rights to people returning from prison, reducing the waiting period for municipal voting, and a couple relatively minor transparency bills. And we beat back two more attempts to increase the amount of money in Delaware politics. (Add that to the two similar bills we killed in 2015.)

What stood out most clearly, however, were all the bills we were unable to get passed—bills to increase disclosure, allow same-day voter registration and no-excuse absentee voting, prevent conflicts of interest in the legislative branch, majorly increase transparency, end partisan gerrymandering, ban gifts from lobbyists to lawmakers, establish equal protection, and create a system of small donor public financing that would eliminate barriers to running for office. And to be clear, *politicians in both parties opposed our agenda.*

What will it take to move a democracy reform agenda forward in Delaware?

The first thing people say when someone complains about the political situation is "you need to vote!" Voting is important, but it is hardly a panacea. Consider this: In 58 percent of general election legislative races this year in Delaware, the candidate has no opponent from the other major party. So, in 58 percent of legislative races, whether people vote or not will not affect the outcome.

In addition, however, only nine legislative districts will have primaries (17%). And since Delaware is a Democrat-dominated state with gerrymandered districts, primaries can be more determinative than the general election. For example, we know whoever wins the Democratic congressional primary is our next representative.

Clearly, we need to recruit people to run who will support the democracy reform agenda. We need to elect courageous, principled people who will stand up for reform, do the right thing, even when it does not advance their career or maintain their power. Obviously, this is a tall order.

Even if you can find such individuals to run, the realities of our current system work against political courage. Once you start focusing on raising money and getting votes, it can make principles seem like self-defeating purism. "Well," you tell yourself, "I won't be able to do any good, if I don't get elected. So maybe it's OK to compromise in this case." Next thing you know, you are on the proverbial slippery slope.

Partly it's a character issue; candidates should have backbones. When I was running for state senate, I examined educational funding and discovered that here in Sussex County, we are obviously in need of a property tax reassessment. We haven't had one since 1974! "Oh no," one of my advisors told me, "you can't propose a property tax reassessment. You won't get elected! Wait until you're in office. Then you can propose it."

Yeah right. A person too timid to propose something while running for office is definitely going to grow a spine once elected!

We all know that politicians can lack courage—which is why we need strong social movements. As FDR reportedly once said, "OK, you've convinced me. Now make me do it!" And that is where issue-based organizations come in.

Problematically, however, many supposedly independent organizations seem to be more concerned about stroking incumbents than endorsing candidates who support their agenda. In a way that makes sense. Many politicians are petty and vindictive—indeed the culture seems to encourage it—and so organizations are scared to alienate incumbents who (on average) have a 90 percent chance of getting reelected.

For example, during my campaign, I sought the endorsement of the Delaware State Education Association (DSEA). I have twenty-five years of classroom teaching experience and came out 100 percent in support of the DSEA agenda, yet they decided to endorse my opponent, who strongly supports charter schools and is "open" to considering vouchers. Some might say they made the right choice. I did lose, after all, but how much did their decision hurt me?

In my opinion, issue groups should remain neutral when there are multiple candidates running who support their agenda. Otherwise, what are they basing their endorsement on, the personal preferences of the leadership?

That is why I am disappointed in the recent endorsement decisions by the Barbara Gittings Delaware Stonewall Democrats. Why would they endorse [a sitting state senator running for lieutenant governor] over [her primary opponents] who support equality just as strongly, if not more strongly, than she? Why wouldn't they remain neutral?

Even more perplexing, why would Stonewall endorse [Prince Speaker] over [his primary opponent], who is running for the house as an openly gay man—a first? Both men fully support the LGBT agenda, and with legal equality firmly established in Delaware, it seems like electing more openly LGBT people to office would be a priority for Stonewall.

Stonewall says they "endorsed [incumbents who] supported [their] efforts at non-discrimination, marriage equality and transgender rights." Yes, those incumbents did—but they only had the opportunity to do so because they were actually in office! (Many primary challengers would have supported the LGBT agenda . . . Why weigh in?)

I find the pro-incumbent policy of many issue-based organizations unfair and politically problematic. It simply augments the tremendous advantage incumbents already have. It's hard to run against an incumbent. Their names are known. Their activities are considered newsworthy. The party apparatus favors them. Their districts are gerrymandered. They hardly need stroking from "independent" groups.

I am glad to be a part of an organization that does not put its hand on the scale but simply calls on all candidates to support the democracy reform agenda. Common Cause works to let voters know where candidates stand, we work with elected officials to pass legislation, and we call people out when necessary. It's all about the issues.

Given the political terrain, it's tough work to move a reform agenda forward. People with power do not want to give up power. And people who think they have "access" to power want to keep it.

But all is not lost because the real power in this state and country is the power of the people. We still have the right to speak out, to organize, to mobilize, to pressure our elected officials to implement our will, to recruit good candidates to run for office, and support them when they do.

What will it take to move the democracy agenda forward in Delaware? An engaged citizenry. Let's get to work.

WE THE PEOPLE SHOULD DECIDE, NOT PARTY OPERATIVES

The Democratic Party uses a primary and caucus system, through which voters decide which candidate wins, not party bosses in a smoke-filled room. During the 2016 primary, however, the public learned that high-level Democratic Party operatives who supported Hillary Clinton and resented Bernie Sanders for daring to challenge her "coronation," as some called it, put their thumbs on the scale in a number of ways to predetermine her nomination.[10] Exposure of that rigged system, the contentious primary battle, and Sanders's eventual loss created bitter feelings among Bernie's supporters, matched by equivalent levels of resentment among Hillary's supporters, that continue to this day, but some significant positive changes also came out of the primary process. The Bernie movement helped make the party platform more progressive, changed party rules to curtail the unfair power of superdelegates, and brought many left-wing activists into the party all over the country.

Furthermore, the Bernie campaign moved the Overton Window, so that bold ideas like Medicare for All, a $15 minimum wage, and the Green New Deal now animate public discourse. Indeed, almost every major Democratic primary candidate in 2020 claimed to embrace some combination of those ideas in some form, even if watered down. Moreover, democratic socialism is back on the public agenda. Just to illustrate the fast pace at which things have changed, when I ran for state senate in 2014, I got pushback for advocating $10.10 an hour, which seemed like a reach at the time. Indeed, Lady Farmer, a self-proclaimed "progressive," told me I was "crazy" to think I could run on raising the minimum wage that high. As an aside, polling data in my district revealed raising the minimum wage as the one issue that really made people more likely to vote for me. Sadly, I did not find that out early enough, or I would have prioritized it more.

When the Sanders campaign came to red Sussex County, right before the state's presidential primary in April 2016, Mikki and I felt elated. Mikki had wanted to serve as a Bernie delegate, but because she was running the insurgent campaign against Prince Speaker at the time, the state party chair reportedly blackballed her. We were told that he would start screaming every time her name came up. She and I let the campaign know that we had a guest room available to house a campaign worker. We frequently joke that we do not feel right unless there's a twenty-something organizer sleeping upstairs. We did not hear back from the campaign, but then late one afternoon, we got a call from a twenty-year-old, official Bernie staffer. He was just touching base, but when I told him we had a spare room, he got excited. When he finally arrived around 10:00 p.m., he took one look at our house and said, "Hey, can we use your place as the campaign headquarters?" For some reason, Mikki and I looked at each other and said "OK," even though we both work from home.

For the next two weeks, the Official Berner and two self-funded young volunteers ran canvasses and phone banks out of our house, setting up shop in the large three-season room we had just built on the back. Every day at 10:00 a.m., the Official Berner would roll out of bed and start making calls, joined by the other two who slept elsewhere. "Good morning! It's a great day to work for Bernie Sanders," he would proclaim. I told them some fun places for lunch and dinner, but the Official Berner seemed uninterested in allowing anyone to take breaks, so I stocked the fridge with food. When they shut down the phones each night at 9:00 p.m., the Official Berner regaled the others with Bernie videos on his computer. This man was hard core.

My almost claim to fame was being asked to introduce Bernie when he came to Delaware. Although extremely honored, as state director for Common Cause, a nonpartisan organization, I did not feel I could take a high-profile role in a partisan event. Besides, it was Mikki's birthday weekend, and I had secured front row tickets to Alison Bechdel's *Fun Home* on Broadway in New York City, made dinner reservations at I Sodi, a West Village hotspot, and booked a room at a boutique hotel in Chelsea. When I told Mikki about the ask, she said, "Can we cancel the birthday trip?" We did not, but the running joke was "#WorstBirthdayEver"—although we actually had a great time. Dinner was particularly fantastic. We sat at the bar, sharing food with fellow diners—"Here, put your fork in this!"—and the young woman sitting next to me said, "My husband just started reading a new journal called *Jacobin*. Have you heard of it?" Yes, indeed, I have a subscription!

Meanwhile, back in Delaware, Bernie gave a rousing speech to an overflowing crowd. The Official Berner did not attend, however; he knocked on doors that day—solo. The next Tuesday was primary day, and we offered to host a party for volunteers. It was Mikki's actual birthday that day, so we went out for a nice dinner at the Blue Moon and came home to a party already under way. After polishing off the spicy corn dip with Fritos and devouring the cake, which was decorated with a Twitter bird, the young folks went out carousing. The next morning, as we observed pillows and blankets everywhere, Mikki said, "I wonder how many babies were made last night?" And we laughed.

At that point, after two weeks of excitement, we really wanted our house back, but it would not be so easy. The Official Berner got pink-slipped by Jeff Weaver via Skype the night Bernie lost the primary, but the next day, I overheard him on the phone with a friend. "Yeah, I think I'm going to hang here for a few days and then head back to college for graduation." Hang here? What? I went outside and accosted Mikki, who was mowing the lawn. "They are not going to leave! What should we do?" I did not want to kick them out and end on a sour note. So, I went back inside and said, "Hey guys, let's go out for a goodbye dinner tonight! A goodbye dinner!" I guess they did not get the hint because the Official Berner and one of the volunteers stayed until Friday morning. When I told my brother about the situation, he said, "They don't know when to call it quits . . . just like the boss."

WE NEED THE PARTY TO REMEMBER
THAT THE PEOPLE ARE SOVEREIGN

In both a democracy and a republic, the people are sovereign, not political elites, yet within the DP, leaders often seem to think that they know better than everyday folks. At the national level, Thomas Frank has criticized the fact that the vast majority of Obama cabinet members held Ivy League degrees because that type of homogeneity, in terms of educational background and class status, leads to groupthink. It also helps explain the reasons many party leaders view more education as the solution to every problem. Can't make ends meet? Go get more education, but definitely do not blame free trade agreements that ship jobs overseas or tax policies that create income inequality. Indeed, the DP has become the party of the professional class, and that brand does not appeal to the white working people who voted for Trump in large numbers, a topic discussed at length in chapter 4.[11]

In "Brand New Dems?" Joseph O'Neill suggests that the DP needs to rebrand itself as the grassroots party of the people. "The Democratic Party, at its strongest," he argues, "has stood for ordinary people. . . . If the Democratic Party wants to be viewed as the party of ordinary Americans, it must embody that vision. The DNC website currently proclaims, 'The Democratic Party elects leaders who fight for equality, justice, and opportunity for all.' That should read, 'Democrats are Americans who fight for equality, justice, and opportunity for all. The Democratic Party exists to give them power.'"[12] A change like that would empower the people and, consequently, disempower party elites.

Like elites everywhere, Democratic Party leaders do not want to give up power. In my experience, a lot of people who volunteer to serve on DP committees fancy themselves little deciders and believe it is their place to substitute their own judgment for that of the voters. Because they attend meetings, they believe they have a superior view and need to function as gatekeepers. For example, when I served as president of the Sarasota-Charlotte Democratic Progressive Caucus, an authorized subsidiary of the Florida Democratic Party (FDP), the caucus decided to convene a townhall meeting to discuss Medicare for All (M4A). We aspired to reach out to both establishment Dems within the party, many of whom kept telling us they had questions about M4A, and also to community folks, not currently engaged. Consequently, I asked all the precinct captains to send an email to Democrats in their precincts, letting them know about the event. I consider that a reasonable request, yet some of them angrily refused to cooperate because they personally did not support M4A and therefore wanted to prevent voters in their precincts from even knowing about the event.

Upper echelon party leaders also maintain power by being exclusionary or not allowing rank and file members to participate in a meaningful way. While they claim they want to attract folks from underrepresented groups to the party, in actuality, they do not want to include anyone new who might change their agenda or challenge the power structure. For example, in both Sarasota and Sussex counties, I heard party elites complain regularly about the lack of young people on their committees, which were comprised of mostly retired people. When young Democrats offer suggestions for attracting millennials, however, their ideas generally fall on deaf ears. Leaders only want young members if they do not have to change anything. Similarly, Democratic candidates generally offer nothing to young people, but then the party demands that they "vote blue no matter who." But why should a young person vote for a candidate who says, "The younger generation now tells me how tough things are—give me a break. . . . I have no empathy for it, give me a break"?[13]

The lack of genuine interest in recruiting young people to the DP became obvious to me in Sussex County during the Bernie campaign. When Mikki and I attended the campaign's kickoff event at Grotto Pizza on Route 1, there were hundreds of people there, including many young people, none of whom we had ever seen before, despite years of involvement with local Democratic organizations. What a great place to recruit for the party! Yet not a single party leader attended to take names or pass out cards—not Lord County Chair, not the New Committee Chair, not Lord Minion, no one. Especially given the many times party leaders moaned about not having any young people involved locally, we found that stunning.

The desire of Lord County Chair and gang for exclusivity became crystal clear in January 2017, when party committees held caucuses in their districts to elect new members. Even though state party rules require caucuses to be advertised in the local paper, Lord County Chair and the New Committee Chair refused to do that. Instead they convened a secret caucus, so they could elect their handpicked cronies. When Mikki and I got wind of their plan, we considered organizing a progressive takeover. If we were to arrive with thirty people unannounced, we could have easily elected our own slate. We faced two problems, however. First, I could not run for chair, since Mikki and I were moving Florida, and second, we could not find anyone else willing to do so. Consequently, we dropped the idea, and so Lord County Chair got his secret caucus, and now the entire committee pledges allegiance to Prince Speaker.

WE NEED DEMOCRACY IN THE DEMOCRATIC PARTY

The nondemocratic culture of the Democratic Party became more glaring to me when I served as an at-large delegate to the Democratic Socialists of America (DSA) convention in 2019, the largest gathering of socialists in the United States since the 1920s. I have always supported DSA, since I first learned about the organization, during my early years of graduate school, when Prof. Steve Bronner took some students to a meeting, at which Barbara Ehrenreich invited us to join. I once asked one of my senior colleagues in political theory, a long-term officer in DSA, about the relationship between DSA and the DP, and he said something to this effect: "When the Democrats are not in power, they can sometimes be helpful, but when they are in power, you basically have to work around them." Having worked in blue state Delaware, I agree with his insight, totally.

Since the Bernie Sanders campaign in 2016 and the election of Donald Trump, membership in DSA has grown more than tenfold. The organization has transitioned from 5,600 mostly left-wing college professors to almost 100,000 mostly millennials. The DSA convention enacted a highly democratic process, in which over 1,000 delegates had a chance to propose, debate, and vote on resolutions and proposals, over the course of three days. While I will admit to finding the vigorous interactions frustrating at times—does it really have to take an entire day just to approve the agenda?—and some deliberations became quite contentious, I applaud the organization's commitment to participatory democracy. People learn by doing; they acquire the skills to run an organization democratically by experiencing it. Indeed, I learned more about Robert's Rules that weekend than from decades of participation in noncontentious meetings.

I appreciate DSA's commitment to democratic participation even more after having served as a delegate to the FDP Convention in 2019, at which delegates had no role at all in the decision-making process. When Mikki and I headed to Walt Disney Coronado Springs Resort for the convention, I was looking forward to voting on resolutions, but as it turns out, delegates did not actually get to debate, revise, or vote on any individual resolutions at all. Over the course of three days, delegates only had one opportunity to vote, and it was merely an up or down vote on a bundled package of nonbinding, watered-down resolutions that the Resolutions Committee put together. Although the schedule allotted 1:30–3:00 on Saturday for resolutions, party leaders filled that time with a long litany of speakers, mostly themselves and down-ballot candidates. The discussion of resolutions did not begin until 2:45. The moderator allowed only a handful of people to speak. After fifteen minutes, she cut the mic, even though only two people remained in line. Voting took place after 3:00, at which point many delegates had left for other meetings.

When it came time to vote, I was in a quandary. How do you vote when there are ten different resolutions bundled together, from a call for Puerto Rican statehood to a watered-down gun violence bill, some positive and some problematic? The only choice was up or down. Both the Progressive Caucus board, on which I served, and the Sarasota delegation (excluding leadership) found the antidemocratic process troubling and voted no, but the resolutions passed anyway, which I guess doesn't really matter, since they were simply suggestions and mostly not actionable.

I had been particularly looking forward to voting against the FDP requirement that party members must sign a loyalty oath. To join the DEC, members must sign a pledge stating, "I will not support the election of the opponent of any Democratic nominee, I will not oppose the election of any Democratic nominee, nor will I support any non-Democrat against a Democrat in any election other than in judicial races." In Sarasota County, the DEC actually makes new members read the oath aloud at the monthly meeting. As it turns out, however, the convention delegates did not get to vote on the loyalty oath. Only members of the state executive committee did, and they voted to keep it.

In terms of the content of the oath, it makes sense to expect members of the Democratic Executive Committee to support party nominees, yet having to pledge loyalty does not sit right with me. First of all, how does it apply in the case of primaries, when Democrats run against each other? Moreover, given that the party includes candidates from the neoliberal center to the democratic socialist left, should members really have to resign from the party if they decide to vote for a Green candidate instead of a DINO in a particular race? Would Democratic National Committee (DNC) members and elected officials be held to the same standard? Would they have supported Bernie Sanders, if he got the nomination? In a well-publicized interview in January 2020, Hillary Clinton suggested that she might not but then walked her comments back after a media uproar.[14] I assume she would never get kicked out of the party for disloyalty.

In addition to offending my democratic sensibilities that respect the right to dissent, the pledge seems both insulting and pointless. Why should someone who volunteers to work for the party or who serves in a leadership position be considered suspect and required to sign a loyalty oath? Plus, if I were a pro-Republican infiltrator, how would the oath stop me? The bylaws already provide a way to purge destructive individuals from the party, so what is the point of the oath? Perhaps the real goal is to create a culture of deference, where people agree to fall in line from day one.

After our disappointing experience at the FDP Convention, I had to wonder: Why did I drive all the way to Orlando, use up an entire weekend's worth of time, and spend a huge amount of money—the hotel rooms cost over $200 a night and gala tickets were $270 per person (unless you bought them at the early bird price of $180, before the speakers were announced)—when I did not get to participate in any decision making? Is it unreasonable to expect some democratic process at the Democratic Party Convention? I understand that the FDP is a large organization and so not every decision can be brought to the whole body, but if nothing is, why even have delegates? Moreover, if the important decisions are to be made by elected committee people in executive session, I believe that nonelite members need to have a chance to convey their views to their representatives. In Sarasota, that did not happen, and when I broached the idea to our state committeewoman, she just stared at me with a puzzled look on her face.

The antidemocratic machinations at the FDP Convention returned me to a question a political science colleague asked at the DSA Convention: "Claire, why are you still working with the Dems?" He was not the only one to ask that question. Indeed, after the convention, I was asked the same thing by a very nice comrade, who subsequently broke the news that I could not join his particular caucus because of my affiliation with the DP, an organization they scorn. He assured me, however, that we could still work together as part of the larger DSA.

Why was I still working with the Dems? It was a good question, and one I asked myself at least weekly, during the eight years I worked inside the party. My answer was twofold. First, the Democratic Party is often the only game in town. Neither Sarasota County, Florida, nor Sussex County, Delaware, has a DSA chapter, as of this writing. Moreover, neither county has any third-party presence and the progressive groups that do exist are comprised of left-leaning liberals, have strong links to the Democratic Party, and focus most of their energy on getting Democrats elected.

Second, I continued to work with the party because I know from experience that when progressives opt out that simply empowers centrists and anti-progressives. For example, as explained earlier, when Mikki and I ceded power to Lord County Chair, we empowered Prince Speaker, the quintessential anti-progressive DINO, and his minions. Mikki and I realized our resignations would serve the purposes of our nemeses, but honestly, I got sick of taking abuse and leaving the party improved my mental health. You have to take care of yourself before you can help others!

WE NEED LEADERS WHO HOLD DEMOCRATIC VALUES

Can the Democratic Party be reformed? In thinking through this question, it is important to note that the party is not a monolith with its own autonomous will. The decisions it makes are made by people, so leadership matters. Theoretically, if we can get the right people into positions of power, we can change the party, but that is not an easy task. It is remarkably hard to find people willing to serve in leadership positions, and then you have to make sure they are committed to a progressive agenda, will not be co-opted by the dominant party culture, and will have the democratic courage to stand up to bullying.

When I complained on the *Delaware Liberal* blog that my former committee endorsed Prince Speaker, another poster accused me of naïveté, saying something like, "Of course, the committee endorsed Prince Speaker. He's the Speaker of the House. There is no way they would not endorse him. That's how it works." But it only works that way when people in power choose to make it work that way. I guarantee you, if I had still been chair, we would not have endorsed. Indeed, the committee had a long-standing policy against endorsing in the primary, and I would have made a strong case for the merits of that position. Lady Progressive used to always make that argument, and that kept Lord County Chair in line for years, but she had also resigned because of irritation, so our mutual archenemy operated unopposed.

Consider a second example. After Mikki and I moved to Florida, the Delaware DP elected a new chair whom most people consider very progressive, and he is certainly less authoritarian than the volatile man who prevented Mikki from serving as a Bernie delegate. Subsequently, the new leader changed the endorsement policy, so now any candidate who has filed to run is allowed to purchase access to the Votebuilder database, even those challenging incumbents, which makes the rules of the game fairer. Moreover, progressive activists really started mobilizing in Delaware after the 2016 Bernie campaign, and having a progressive party chair helped that movement flourish. So, again, leadership matters.

One final example. In April 2019, the Democratic Progressive Caucus of Florida decided to issue a proclamation calling for an impeachment inquiry against Donald Trump. The proclamation argued, in short, "The United States President is not a King who is above the law. That has always been a near-sacred belief of the American people. As Thomas Paine put it long ago, 'in America the law is king,' not the President." I wrote that proclamation on behalf of the state caucus and then led efforts to have DECs all over the state ratify it. Naturally, our local caucus chapter voted unanimously to approve the document, and I asked the Sarasota County chair to put the proclamation on the DEC agenda for a vote. This took place before Speaker Pelosi got on board with impeachment, before the Ukraine call, so I did not think our moderate-leaning DEC would ratify the proclamation, but we wanted the DEC to take a vote anyway.

Despite the reasonableness of my request, the woman who serves as the Sarasota County chair stonewalled me for six weeks. Our Lady Chair did not directly refuse my request, but she insisted that the proclamation must go through a byzantine Issues Committee process before it could be placed on the agenda. The head of the Issues Committee, a high-handed older lady, gave me a seven-page document she had written that included not one but two flow charts explaining the time-consuming process for approval. The flow charts were designed to help the applicant navigate the procedural steps that included 1) completing a four-page application, explaining the ways in which the issue—in my case, impeaching a criminal president in accordance with the US Constitution—accords with "Democratic Values," 2) participating in a twenty-minute phone conversation with the committee head, henceforth called Lady Flow Chart, to discuss the application, and then 3) making an in-person presentation to the entire Issues Committee, reiterating everything already said in the paperwork and phone call. If the proclamation made it through the process, it would then go to the Steering Committee, which would consider whether to place it on the DEC agenda, with arguments for and against. I thought that as the elected president of an official caucus and a member of both the Steering Committee and the DEC, I should be able to get something on the agenda upon request. Lady Flow Chart said absolutely not; I had to go through the same process as would *any random person off the street*.

I had a significant back and forth with Lady Flow Chart because I did not believe I should have to go to such time-consuming lengths to explain the obvious, but she remained inflexible. Eventually, it became clear that she *personally* opposed the proclamation and thought that I had to convince her to support it, or else she would not release it to the Steering Committee. I argued that her personal opinion should not be grounds for blocking our proclamation. "If someone submits an issue that accords with Democratic values, on what basis can the Issues Committee not approve it? Being in agreement with the personal opinions of people on the Issues Committee should not be a legitimate part of the criteria for evaluation," I eventually argued in an email to the entire Steering Committee, after getting no satisfactory response from either Lady Flow Chart or Lady Chair, despite weeks of effort.

In response, Lady Flow Chart refused to budge. She took the position that I had to follow her instructions, or my issue would not be considered, period. I asked Lady Chair to intervene. She said she would but did nothing. In the end, my goal became to get the process changed, and I pitched the case for reform to the entire Steering Committee. While a handful of its members told me privately that they agreed with me, no one supported me publicly—which did not surprise me, given my experiences in Delaware. Apparently, they did not want to challenge authority, so Lady Chair prevented my proposal for reform—if a caucus requests that an issue be put on the DEC agenda, it should happen automatically—from even being discussed, and so my eventual successor experienced the same frustrations, trying to get a progressive issue on the DEC agenda for a vote.

In the end, Lady Chair and her minions kept the impeachment proclamation mired in unnecessary bureaucracy for six weeks, before finally relenting. Eventually, she agreed to make a special exception for me, basically because I pitched a fit, but refused to allow any discussion of changing the process.

Was all my effort worth it? Probably not; getting the DEC to endorse the proclamation did not rank as an issue of great importance. Nevertheless, Mikki and I saw the DEC vote as a chance to practice mobilizing the progressive contingent. "It will be a good fire drill," she said. So, once it made the agenda, I sent out an "all-hands-on-deck" email to the progressive contingent, worked a few reluctant allies, and showed up at the DEC meeting ready to lose.

Then, we watched as our progressive allies arrived at the meeting-house, including many who did not regularly attend meetings. It was off-season, so party officers did not expect a big turnout. Indeed, there might not even be a quorum, they probably hoped. But so many people showed up that they ran out of voting cards. Lady Chair permitted me to speak for five minutes—although she started hovering after three—and then she let DEC members make discrete comments into a microphone, but no discussion allowed. When we saw certain people stride up, we thought, "Oh no. Here comes the opposition." But to our surprise, some of the people we least expected to support the proclamation argued for an affirmative vote—some out of friendship, others for political reasons.

The proclamation passed by a margin of 3:1. One woman commented that she had been feeling dejected and hopeless, but with the proclamation she felt like we were at least doing something. Another friend told me I "should have seen the look" on Lady Flow Chart's face when we won the vote; it reportedly "crumbled." I alerted the media first thing the next morning and trumpeted the news on Facebook and Twitter. The party never said a word about it, but because of the caucus press release we made the front page of the *Sarasota Herald Tribune*'s local section.

Mikki and I were gratified by the successful fire drill, but then, the very next day, the local leader of Indivisible (a national organization that formed in opposition to Donald Trump)—another one of the Lady Chair's minions—sent out the following email:

> Sunday's [newspaper] had a lengthy piece . . . about how the Sarasota Democratic Party supports impeaching Trump. It is my understanding that the Progressive wing of the local party (as is the case statewide and nationally) spearheaded an effort to require a voice vote at the last DEC meeting and by that vote, such a motion was carried. However, I know that there is no consensus among Democrats at all levels on beginning Impeachment inquiries and it is no different in Sarasota County.
>
> But what I also know is that at the end of the day, if we fight bitterly among ourselves and ascribe motives and behaviors to each other, we only strengthen Trump and his chances at re-election. Our common ground is our belief in Democratic values and our concern for the future of our country, our people and our planet.

In other words, the vote was really not legitimate because the progressives pulled a fast one, but we all need to come together! Just like so many establishment Democrats on social media, Lady Indivisible blasts progressives, then demands unity. I had to laugh, though, because she apparently failed to realize that national Indivisible had already called for an impeachment inquiry.

In contrast to the frustrating experience I had with Sarasota's Lady Chair, when I asked the chairs of the two adjacent counties, Manatee and

Charlotte, if they would put the proclamation on the agenda for a vote, they both said, "Sure." It was that easy. Clearly, leadership matters. Again, we did not expect to win, but the proclamation passed both committees, by margins of 11:1 and 2:1, after a vigorous back and forth among members. Interestingly, the 2:1 vote came from a DEC in very conservative Charlotte County, so the margin of passage surprised us. But it just goes to show: It is a myth that Democrats in conservative districts are conservative, which seems to be the common wisdom of the DNC, and why would they be? Indeed, Bernie Sanders won the primary in every district in West Virginia.

WE MUST REJECT THE AUTHORITARIAN MANTRA, "VOTE BLUE NO MATTER WHO!"

The Democratic Party wants to maintain power by getting Democrats elected, which makes sense. Hillary Clinton's loss to Donald Trump in 2016 traumatized party members, and many of them blame Bernie Sanders and his supporters for maligning her during the primary, a standard part of the democratic process in which multiple candidates compete for votes. Given the antidemocratic, quasi-fascist, criminal behavior of the Trump administration and its cruel, hurtful policies, Democrats rightly worried that he would somehow get reelected, and they wanted to do everything they could to prevent people from staying home or voting third party, as happened in 2016. Consequently, a mantra developed among Democrats: "Vote blue no matter who." While I understand the sentiment behind that slogan, and agree about the importance of voting Republicans out of office in 2020 (and every other year), the mantra bothers me for two reasons. First, I consider it quasi-authoritarian, in that it demands unthinking loyalty, which a lot of Democratic Party leaders, official or unofficial, seem to expect from rank and file voters. For example, one party leader in Sarasota criticizes anyone who expresses reservations about a Democratic candidate by saying, "Republicans fall in line. Democrats have to fall in love. That's why we lose."

It used to annoy me that every time I posted an article on my Facebook page that criticized a Democratic primary candidate's record, someone inevitably instructed me that I must "vote blue no matter who." In fact, at a Democratic Steering Committee meeting, Lady Indivisible actually told me, point blank, that I should demand that all the members of the Progressive Caucus sign a "vote blue no matter who" pledge. I was quite taken aback at her suggestion. At first, I just stared at her across the table for a long minute, creating an awkward silence. Then, I replied that since Progressive Caucus members have chosen to join a caucus officially certified by the Florida Democratic Party, I would assume that they plan to vote for the Democratic presidential candidate in 2020 (as most Berners did in 2016, by the way).

Furthermore, I informed her, I do not consider it my place to tell caucus members what to do. My members make their own decisions. They will either work for the Democratic nominee or engage in other political activities instead, as they see fit. Indeed, the presidential race is not the only one that matters. My caucus allows room for a variety of progressive perspectives. I did not ask her: Are you also asking the president of the Black Caucus to have her members sign a pledge, given that a large percentage of African Americans did not turn out for Clinton in 2016 (as was their right)? Why are only progressives blamed?

My second problem with the mantra involves strategy. In my judgment, as long as progressives continue to support Democratic candidates no matter what, even when they fail to support progressive issues, the party will continue to ignore or marginalize us. When progressives pledge to vote for whoever wins the primary, they give up any leverage they might have over candidates. Why should a candidate move to the left on policy issues, if they know they will get all the progressive votes regardless of their positions? In terms of smart negotiating strategies, even those progressives who actually plan to "vote blue no matter who," which is most people, should not say that in advance. That makes no sense strategically. In the 1980s, the Christian Right gained power because they said they would not vote for any candidate who did not oppose abortion. Whether they followed through with that threat or not, they made their point. If the DP takes progressive votes for granted, we have no power vis-à-vis the party.

It is my strong belief that as active participants in the democratic process, each person needs to make their own judgment in each particular electoral race, after considering the trade-offs of each option. On the one hand, if the party continues to use its vast resources to push nonprogressive candidates, perhaps progressives need to deliver a message by refusing to "vote blue no matter who." On the other hand, sometimes the cost of making that point is too high. For example, given that in 2020 the DP once again acted to stop a progressive candidate from getting the nomination—piling on endorsements this time instead of using superdelegates to predetermine the outcome—some on the left argued that the party needs to learn, so progressives should refuse to vote for Biden. The trade-off, however, would have been risking Trump's reelection, and since I basically consider him evil incarnate, I decided to vote for Joe. But why should I have announced that ahead of time, instead of making him earn my vote by supporting progressive policies?

While allowing the usually horrific Republican candidate to win is often too high a price to pay, that is not always the case; unfortunately, a lot of people fail to grasp that nuance. Consider the case of the female DINO who got elected to represent our district in the Florida State House. When she first ran for the seat in a special election in 2017, she opposed Medicare for All, cannabis legalization, and a $15 minimum wage, calling $10.51 an hour a living wage. The local Our Revolution group, Progressive Sarasota, of which I was a core member for about three years, tried to pressure her into moving more to the left, but she refused to budge. Consequently, we ran a progressive candidate against her in the primary—and Mikki and I led the campaign team—but sadly our candidate lost.

In the general election, there was no compelling reason to "vote blue no matter who" because whether Rep. DINO got elected or not would make little difference, given that Republicans dominate both chambers of the Florida legislature, and Democrats are nowhere close to taking over either one. Consequently, when it came time for the general election, I did not vote for Rep. DINO. If you want my vote, you need to support my issues, and I told her that on the phone when she called asking for my money and my vote. But alas, a lot of progressives voted for her anyway. Indeed, some even worked on her campaign.

Rep. DINO won the special election with the help of an army of relentless volunteers and a huge influx of money. She was able to flip the seat largely because Republican women supported her over her very weak opponent. Rep. DINO is now a local rock star, and she is a tireless worker and an incredibly successful fundraiser. So, after serving only a partial term in the state house, she decided to run for Congress in 2020 against an entrenched Republican incumbent who completely supports the Trump agenda, while somehow fooling people into thinking he is a moderate. Rep. DINO's presence in Congress could make a difference, so Mikki and I made a small donation to her campaign to show goodwill.

Then she came out against the impeachment effort that I was leading in Florida, saying the "narrative now seems to be that no matter who is in the White House, the other party will try to impeach. . . . I oppose using the impeachment process for political gamesmanship because it deepens party divides and ultimately divides us as Americans."[15] While Democrats of goodwill had different views on the political wisdom of pursing impeachment, mostly based on projected consequences for 2020, Rep. DINO's depiction of the attempt to hold a criminal president accountable to the law as "political gamesmanship" deeply offended us. While she got a lot of pushback from Democrats for saying that, she responded by doubling down. That is to say, even after Speaker Pelosi officially began the impeachment inquiry, once Trump's quid pro quo phone call came to light, Rep. DINO continued to waffle.[16]

In my view, if Rep. DINO really remained unclear, in October 2019, about whether Trump abused power and obstructed justice, given all the evidence that had emerged by that point, I would question her judgment. I assume, however, that she was just pandering, hoping to get Republican votes by playing both sides—a strategy that rarely works. Rep. DINO assumes that Democrats will vote for her regardless of the things she says, so she can undermine the party with impunity. Sadly, she is probably correct. But if she cannot be counted on to side with the Democrats during heated battles, then why bother electing her?

On the heels of her impeachment comments, Rep. DINO proudly announced that she had been endorsed by the Blue Dog Democrats, a very conservative caucus in Congress that favors a balanced budget. Given my work with Common Cause Delaware against precisely that issue (as previously discussed), her foolish embrace of balanced budgets, straight off the ALEC/GOP wish list, really rankled me, and I was not the only upset Democrat. One of my moderate friends, an older gentleman who had worked on her campaign, called me on the phone very upset. I told him she probably figures Democrats will vote for her anyway, and she wanted to get Republicans on board. That thought outraged him, but when I mentioned that she had lost my vote, he was taken aback. "What? You have to vote for her anyway, Claire. I am going to vote for her anyway. You have to." Well, I told him, that is exactly why she doesn't care what you think. Furthermore, not only do I not have to vote for her anyway, but Mikki and I have asked for our $100 back!

Progressives cannot allow our issues to be marginalized or ignored. As I posted on Facebook, immediately after reading Rep. DINO's statement about the Blue Dogs, "We need to elect Democrats who can be counted on to side with the Democrats on contentious issues. If someone cannot be counted on, they should not get our votes." While Rep. DINO's refusal to stand with the Democrats prompted my post, I also had in mind the campaign of Amy McGrath, the establishment Democrat and former fighter pilot running against Senate Majority Leader Mitch McConnell, who said she would have voted to confirm Brett Kavanaugh to the Supreme Court.[17] If any possibility exists that a Democratic candidate would support Kavanaugh, in my opinion, we do not need them in office.

Before making such a decision on Election Day, however, each voter must also consider the costs of not voting "blue no matter who." If McGrath could beat McConnell in that senatorial election, would it be worth the compromise? Given how much damage McConnell has done to our republic, it would be worth it, in my estimation. On the other hand, if she is going to lose anyway, why compromise by voting for her? The best-case scenario would have been to nominate a better candidate during the primary, and people tried. Sadly, however, the strong progressive opponent who challenged McGrath—campaigning "from hood to holler" and receiving endorsements from Bernie Sanders, Elizabeth Warren, and Alexandria Ocasio-Cortez—did not make it through, largely thanks to the Democratic establishment, so McGrath went on to lose to McConnell on November 3, 2020, getting only 38.2 percent of the vote.

In challenging the "blue no matter who" mantra, some Democrats will no doubt accuse me of being a "purist," by which they mean a rigid and unrealistic idealist who refuses to think pragmatically. Obama has repeatedly rebuked the so-called "purists," saying, for example: "This idea of purity and you're never compromised and you're politically woke, and all that stuff—you should get over it quickly. The world is messy. There are ambiguities. People who do really good stuff have flaws."[18] Honestly, I find the accusation of purism offensive. I consider myself a person with integrity, opposed to hypocrisy, committed to living in accordance with my principles. That is the way I was raised, and that is the way I strive to live my life. With all due respect, President Obama, we know the world is messy. Some of us are just trying to use our moral compass to navigate our journey.

Having a democratic culture means respecting other people, even when they have dissenting views. I am disheartened at the frequency with which people show a lack of respect toward those whose views differ from their own, an attitude all too commonly expressed on social media, including by supporters of the Democratic Party. Support the party establishment, or prepare to be blasted! I find that position problematic because democracy entails equals governing themselves through collaborative decision making, so respecting the views of others, even when you disagree, constitutes an essential component of self-rule. Standing opposed to authoritarianism means not trying to force people to fall in line by insulting and haranguing them. People who hold dissenting views are not toddlers having temper tantrums or a basket of deplorables. Moreover, taking that position is counterproductive because arguing with and insulting people (rather than respectfully deliberating) just makes them dig in their heels.

We do need to understand the things that are possible and those that are not, but too much emphasis on pragmatism limits people to just reacting to the existing status quo, rather than formulating a plan to move society toward a more just future. Remember, "It always seems impossible until it is done." We need to generate bold ideas. A lot of people say Occupy Wall Street was a failure, even some progressives, but that movement gave us the language of the 1% and the 99%, which has completely reframed debates around income inequality. Some people say Bernie Sanders has gotten nothing done, but look at the profound changes in our public discourse since he started to share his visionary ideas for a better world. His principled articulation of democratic socialism, even when the cause seemed hopelessly marginal, opened up a space, decades later, for people like Alexandria Ocasio-Cortez, Rashida Tlaib, and Ilhan Omar to run for office, and for DSA to galvanize young people all over the country. Indeed, increasing numbers of progressive candidates, many endorsed by DSA, have recently won elections all over the country. Who would have thought that possible a few years ago? We cannot be afraid to work for the future we want, even when we cannot see it on the horizon.

At the same time, we need to refrain from putting our energy into endeavors that have little hope of success. For example, some of my progressive allies suggested that I run for chair of the Sarasota Democratic Party—I could be Comrade Chair instead of the next Lady Chair—but I do not believe that would be a good use of time. Sadly, given the registration advantage Republicans hold in the county, trying to get Democrats elected is largely a waste of time and money. Moreover, to move the Sarasota Democrats in a more progressive direction would require getting a lot of progressives onto the DEC, which has over a hundred members, many of whom are openly hostile toward progressives. Plus, even if we did that, many Democrats who claim the progressive label would no doubt defer to establishment leaders, when push came to shove, rather than fighting for progressive change, as happened in Delaware.

Moreover, even if we could execute a progressive takeover of the Sarasota DEC, it would remain a part of the Florida Democratic Party, which exemplifies the worst kind of establishment mentality. Indeed, after eighteen months of economy-killing Red Tide, with its toxic fumes and piles of dead fish—a naturally occurring phenomenon, greatly exacerbated by agricultural runoff, allowed after Republican governor Rick Scott deregulated—the FDP accepted money from Big Sugar to underwrite its Leadership Blue weekend and its state convention, both held at very expensive hotels owned by Disney, another donor. FDP also takes money from Florida Power and Light, a company that works against the transition to solar energy in the state. Moreover, not a single Democratic member of Congress from Florida supported Bernie Sanders in 2020. In fact, some, like Debbie Wasserman-Schultz and Donna Shalala, led red-baiting attacks on him because he said Castro improved literacy rates in Cuba, which happens to be true. Finally, in spring 2020, during the pandemic, the FDP took money from the Paycheck Protection Program, designed to help small businesses, even though the program explicitly prohibits political entities from applying. After the media exposed the scheme, the party returned the $780,000, but what a disgrace.[19]

In light of all these experiences, I remain ambivalent about the Democratic Party. At this point, I believe the best strategy for the progressive movement as a whole involves some people working inside the party and some outside, depending on the personal inclinations and ideological orientations of people and where they live, and both paths require long-term planning. Those working inside the party need to remember that it took right-wing leaders fifteen years to take power, after they hatched their plan in 1965 in the wake of Barry Goldwater's shellacking, because they had to shift people's consciousness. The Tea Party takeover went a lot more quickly because it built on years of ideological work. On the other hand, those who want a new party also have to think long-term, as they build a party to supplant the DP or change the laws so a third party becomes competitive. Either way, success will require cultural change. We must disrupt the neoliberal hegemony that currently exists if we are to build support for a progressive agenda—or even better, for a democratic socialist agenda. Either way, we cannot lose patience or hope.

CONCLUSION

WHAT IS TO BE LEARNED?

What have I learned from my experiences in the realm of US party politics? After articulating and analyzing my own experiences, I worry for the future of our democratic republic. We have a political context in which the Republican Party, with the help of big donors and savvy operatives, has been able to maintain power for nearly forty years, and in response the Democratic Party has moved to the right, away from the will of the people, as expressed in public opinion polls. We have an electoral process that rewards powermongering and makes it difficult for decent candidates who advocate progressive or people-centered politics to win elections or maintain their integrity once elected. We have an anemic political culture in which people have little opportunity to develop their democratic capacities, including the democratic courage required to resist power. Instead, too many assume a passive or deferential posture, better suited to a royalist regime than to a self-governing republic of equals. And we have a Democratic Party filled with operatives who are willing to jettison democratic participation and backburner, if not obstruct, an agenda for working people and the public good, even use authoritarian tactics, in order to maintain their own power.

I find the situation grim and do not believe anyone is going to save us. In fact, waiting for a savior is a part of the problem. If we are to be saved, we have to save ourselves. As the old saying goes, "We are the ones we have been waiting for."[1] We need good progressive candidates to run for office, but they need to have a clear understanding of the milieu in which they operate and a commitment to a left ideological vision that prioritizes economic as well as social justice. We need people committed to battling

185

political powermongers, the "little princes" who consider themselves entitled to rule, authoritarianism personified. We need to recognize and resist our own willingness to defer to powermongers out of laziness, fear, pleasure, or the desire for material gain—battling the metaphorical Prince inside our heads that tells us to bow down. And we need a strong, progressive, democratic party to bring people together—both left-leaning liberals and socialists—and provide a vision for positive change. Inspired by Antonio Gramsci, who called his ideal mass party the "Modern Prince," I call our new party the Modern Prince Collective to underline its plurality.

LESSON 1: WE NEED TO UNDERSTAND THE CURRENT POLITICAL MOMENT IN HISTORICAL CONTEXT

This volume began with a brief history of US politics from 1965 through the 1980s and beyond. I became an activist, as a teenager, in the early 1980s, when I joined one of the largest mobilizations of the Left in US history. After the Cold War ended in 1991, however, the Left receded from view, and Democratic president Bill Clinton pushed the Democratic Party to the right. His administration oversaw a trade agreement that arguably killed manufacturing jobs (NAFTA), the erosion of banking regulations (Glass-Steagall Act of 1932) that would eventually help produce the Great Recession of 2007, anti-LGBT legislation (Defense of Marriage Act and Don't Ask, Don't Tell) that set back the cause, the end of welfare as we knew it (Aid to Families with Dependent Children) that shredded the safety net, the failure to implement universal health care that left forty million uninsured, and the acceleration of mass incarceration that has decimated the Black community, and that is just the domestic side.

When Clinton's vice president Al Gore ran for president in 2000, Ralph Nader challenged him from the left, running on the Green Party ticket. Many people remain angry because they believe Nader cost Gore the election, which turned out to be very tight. Ryan Grim recounts that Nader was "a cranky, proto-Bernie candidate who packed stadiums across the country, filling young people with hope of a better world."[2] Personally, I had many heated discussions with leftist friends about the pros and cons of voting for Nader. Embracing the lesser of two evils approach, I voted for Gore because I feared a vote for Nader would help elect George W. Bush, whom I thought had to be stopped; in hindsight, I think I made the right choice, given the multiple catastrophes of the Bush-Cheney regime.

I bear no animus toward those who voted for Nader. However, in my view, if left-wing third-party candidates are going to act as spoilers, they need to proudly proclaim success when the Democrat loses. Nader should have said, "Do you see what happens when you ignore the Left? You can't win without us." Sadly, however, he took a defensive posture and said, "Don't blame me."[3] While I agree with his point that Gore lost because of his and his party's own inadequacies, a stronger position for the Left would be to trumpet our power to determine elections.

A similar thing happened in the wake of Hillary Clinton's loss in 2016. Many people blame Bernie Sanders for her loss, and in response we hear a lot of "don't blame Bernie." According to his defenders, Clinton did not lose because Sanders criticized her. She lost because she ran a poor campaign, had a problematic record, and offered an uninspiring agenda. I myself have made that argument many times, insisting that most Bernie supporters ended up voting for Clinton. Indeed, while empirical evidence is hard to come by, the best estimate says 74 percent of "Berners" cast ballots for Clinton, whereas 12 percent voted for Trump.[4] That latter number might seem high, but remember that Sanders had crossover appeal, so a significant number of his supporters were white, rural conservatives, a demographic that broke for Trump.[5]

Over time, however, I have come to believe that the defensive posture is wrongheaded. The Left should take credit for deciding the 2016 election. Let it be known that Bernie voters will not be taken for granted, ignored, or maligned. Indeed, if Hillary lost because Bernie supporters refused to vote for her, then the only thing that makes sense is for Democrats to nominate a candidate in 2020 that Berners will vote for.

But of course that was not the conclusion drawn by establishment Democrats, who circled the wagons to support Joe Biden in the 2020 primary. They seemed to think that finger-wagging and repeating the mantra "vote blue no matter who" would get nonsubmissive Sanders supporters to fall in line. I doubt that it would have, particularly because Biden chose Kamala Harris, an establishment candidate, as his running mate. Fortunately, however, over the course of 2020, Trump repeatedly shot himself in the foot. His disastrous response to the crises that emerged after the primary—the COVID-19 pandemic, economic collapse, and Black Lives Matter uprising—helped convince most progressives to vote for Biden in the end. Because Trump's authoritarian tendencies and racist sympathies became so blatant, many progressive leaders framed a vote for Biden as a vote against fascism, which is the way I viewed it.

Even as early as July 2020, however, a poll in six battleground states showed that 83 percent of Berners and 96 percent of Warren supporters intended to vote for Biden, with only 4 percent and 0 percent, respectively, planning to vote for Trump.[6] And for those critical of the tiny percentage of progressives who did not rally around Biden, please note that in June 2008, only 60 percent of Clinton supporters said they would vote for Obama, whereas 17 percent said they would vote for McCain, and other polls found that latter number to be even higher.[7]

Back in 2000, as Gore and Nader lost and the Bush-Cheney regime took power, the Left began to rise again. "Throughout the '90s . . . energy on the left coalesced around what came to be called the anti-globalization movement, [also known as the global justice movement], which burst into public view in Seattle in 1999 and then in Washington, DC, in April 2000" with protests against the World Trade Organization and against the International Monetary Fund and World Bank, respectively.[8] The movement planned to convene the largest protest ever seen in Washington, DC, in fall of 2001, but tragically the terrorist attack of September 11th derailed those plans, and subsequently the global justice organizers decided to focus on antiwar activism instead.[9]

When the United States invaded Iraq two years later, millions of people took to the streets, all over the world, to oppose the war.[10] In 2004, Howard Dean ran in the primary on an antiwar platform, and I strongly supported him because of that, as well as his support for universal health care and opposition to the Bush tax cuts. In his recent history of the Left, Ryan Grim comments, "For people who know Howard Dean fifteen years later as the corporate lobbyist who trolls the left on social media, it may be difficult to absorb just how path-breaking his campaign in 2003 and '04 was. He ran as an anti-war candidate and, as a doctor and governor of Vermont, made providing universal healthcare the centerpiece of his campaign."[11] His campaign was the first to emphasize small donors and utilize the internet for campaigning.[12] Four years later, I did not support Hillary because she voted for the Iraq War, voting instead for John Edwards whose campaign focused primarily on income inequality, until he dropped out amid scandal.

A lot of people have fought the good fight for progressive change over the decades, but since the election of Ronald Reagan in 1980, policies in the United States have moved significantly to the right, income and wealth inequality have skyrocketed, and the Republican Party has started attacking the very foundations of democratic republicanism. In my estimation, we are now in the middle of a class war, but most people do not understand that. One-percenters along with their courtiers and minions have moved from destroying the compromise struck between capital and labor after World War II—which resulted in an economic "golden age" during the height of the Cold War—to destroying democracy itself, as exemplified before the 2020 election by attacks on the Post Office to stop people from voting by mail and other forms of voter suppression and afterward by the refusal of most Republicans to accept the results of the election as legitimate, even after sixty court cases found no meaningful voter fraud. In the past, many capitalists supported policies that resulted in widespread prosperity—such as good jobs with decent wages and generous benefits, publicly funded higher education, and a social safety net—because they wanted to prevent working people from turning to communism. The Right no longer fears communism, so they do not see the downside of attacking middle- and working-class people and particularly people of color. In addition, with the collapse of communism, the Left has lost it aspirational goal, as Jodi Dean has argued.[13]

The one-percent contingent attacked unions in the 1970s and '80s, social welfare programs in the 1980s and '90s, and public education in the 2000s and '10s, and now, post-2016, they have their sights set on the very pillars of the democratic republic itself—free and fair elections, the account-ability of representatives to the people, rational discourse, the possibility of principled dissent, checks and balances, a president subject to law, the impartiality of the courts, and the peaceful transition of power. The 1% seeks to block anything that stands in the way of its wealth accumulation. Even appeals to country over party no longer resonate because Capital has no country. Patriotism comes into consideration only to the extent that it can be manipulated—along with racist, misogynist, homophobic, and xenophobic fears and resentments—to keep white working people and the petit bourgeoisie (small business) on board with the Republican Party of immiseration that opposes their material interests. We essentially face a Hobbesian state of nature—characterized by power versus power unto death—and we have no zookeeper.

So, what is to be done? First of all, people are not going to sponta-neously come to an understanding of the dynamics currently unfolding, so we need political theorists and organizers—"organic intellectuals" in Gramsci's terms—to help thematize the whole. Second, we have to stop being reactionary and getting confused by hyper-partisanship. For example, the FBI and the CIA are not suddenly on our side, just because Trump hates them. Third, we need to understand that the progressive struggle must focus on political, economic, and social justice simultaneously; we cannot fall into the class versus race or class versus gender identity politics trap. Finally, while we need to carve out a realistic path forward, we must not limit ourselves to pragmatism, to focusing only on easily imaginable reforms. Remember, "It always seems impossible, until it is done." We need to start playing the long game, as well as the short game.

I will admit to having a dark view of the future. I do not believe in an earthly arc of history that inevitably bends toward justice. There is no guarantee that the changes we need to make will be made or made in time to save the republic, not to mention the planet. While I cannot offer solutions to all our problems or gin up the political will to force such changes to be made, I can offer some insights from my experiences working in the political realm. In short, we need to battle the little Prince wannabes who seek unaccountable power, we need to battle the metaphorical Prince inside our heads who commands our deference, and we need to force the 1% to battle the Modern Prince Collective. Let's address each one in turn.

LESSON 2: WE NEED TO KEEP BATTLING THE LITTLE PRINCE WANNABES, RISING UP WITHIN OUR REPUBLIC

To start, we need to resist creeping authoritarianism by refusing to bow down before demagogues and powermongers. While it is easy to locate examples of bullying within Trump's Republican Party, my experiences reveal that even Democrats are willing to support bullies, as long as they wear a Team D jersey. Remember, however, that just because "he's our son of a bitch" does not make a bully any less corrosive to democratic ideals. We need to *battle the little Prince wannabes.*

The Founders established a republic not a monarchy or principality. When the famous unnamed lady asked Benjamin Franklin about the kind of government he and the other political leaders had established, she mentioned two options, a republic or a monarchy, and Franklin replied, "A Republic, if you can keep it." Clearly, as everybody knew at the time, a republic is the opposite of a monarchy. Thomas Paine put it this way: "In America the law is king. For as in absolute governments the king is law, so in free countries the law *ought* to be king, and there ought to be no other."[14]

In a republic, the people rule in accordance with the *rule of law*—a political theoretical concept that means impartial laws applied equally to all, not just that there are laws—that put constraints on arbitrary power, whether exercised by government operatives (like racist police officers and ICE deportation agents) or forces within civil society (like tyrannical bosses and predatory landlords). Monarchies and principalities, on the other hand, unless constrained by a constitution, deploy authoritarian rule—the will of the king or prince being paramount—even if benevolently wielded, and in absolute monarchies, power remains unchecked because it supposedly derives from God. "Lock her up! Off with his head! Get the noose!"

When I worked to build support for impeachment proceedings against Donald Trump in early summer 2019, I argued that "the president is not a king, who is above the law." I insisted that looking the other way when faced with a criminal president or one who abuses his power—the Founders worried about both scenarios—would set a very dangerous precedent, and that is "how democracies die."[15] Most democracies do not end because of a military coup d'état but because elites willingly appease demagogues who then destroy democracy from within.[16] Unfortunately, many Democrats dragged their feet on impeachment, not because they doubted Trump's criminality and abuse of power, but because they thought impeachment might negatively affect the 2020 election. Indeed, Speaker Pelosi remained strangely resistant to growing calls for impeachment, until the whistleblower complaint essentially forced her hand. Since the Democrats had been calling on Republicans to put country before party for years, their refusal to do so themselves really rankled me. As you know from this narrative: I have a low tolerance for hypocrisy.

Why do Democrats refuse to stand up to presidential criminality? President Obama refused to file charges against people in the Bush-Cheney administration who committed war crimes.[17] Moreover, when the Democrats controlled both houses of Congress in 1986, they chose not to open an impeachment inquiry into the crimes of Reagan, after he repeatedly violated the law.[18] And of course, Nixon's crimes were pardoned, albeit by a Republican president. The reticence of political elites to hold their criminal peers to account probably arises partially from a reluctance to split the country with a divisive impeachment fight or criminal prosecution, but allowing the executive branch to violate the law puts our republic at risk. As David Swanson puts it, "The danger of abandoning . . . the rule of law is in fact nothing other than the danger of recreating a monarchy," our Founders' biggest fear.[19]

The Founders created Congress in the First Article of the Constitution as a coequal branch of government empowered to check the power of the president because they wanted to prevent a relapse into royalism, yet Congress has allowed the emergence of—to coin a term—a "Princely Presidency." As early as 1973, scholars worried about that situation. Arthur Schlesinger discussed the emergence an "imperial presidency" in 1973.[20] Nixon famously claimed the president has princelike powers: "When the president does it, that means it is not illegal," he claimed.[21] The George W. Bush administration, under the guidance of Dick Cheney and his courtiers, developed the idea of a "unitary executive," an absolutist concept antithetical to our antiroyalist constitution that gave the largest share of government power to Congress, a doctrine was first advanced under Reagan.[22] Boldly proclaiming himself "the decider," Bush single-handedly overrode the will of Congress by attaching "signing statements" to bills to reverse congressional decisions. Charlie Savage calls the Bush-Cheney regime "the return of the imperial presidency."[23]

Unfortunately, Obama continued to bolster executive power, rather than moving the country back toward legislative control, as mandated by the Constitution. In the first months of his presidency, Obama "committed to ceasing some of Bush's crimes and abuses, but claimed the power to continue others, opposed holding his predecessors accountable, worked hard to keep Bush and Cheney's crimes secret, and aggressively sought to maintain and expand presidential power, even continuing to use signing statements."[24] Obama's refusal to give up power is understandable to some extent. First, the Republicans play hardball power politics, maximizing every opportunity to push their agenda, so why should Democrats give up power when they get it? Second, given the absolute refusal of Republicans to work with Obama, he wanted to use whatever executive power he could to advance the Democratic agenda. Both motivations make sense, but further entrenching a Princely Presidency erodes republican self-rule, so it is ultimately counterproductive.

With the precedent of a Princely Presidency set by his predecessors' failure to support the Constitution and the rule of law, Trump took lawlessness to the next level. He openly praised dictators and glorified authoritarian tactics. His institutional and personal racism, xenophobia, and misogyny undermined the fundamental principle of equality, upon which any republic is based. He successfully confirmed over 150 judges to various courts, including the Supreme Court, who might be willing to advance the partisan and theocratic agenda of the Christian Right rather than protecting the impartial rule of law—but only time will tell. Finally, through his attorneys and executive branch courtiers, Trump went so far as to claim that not only can he not be charged with a crime while in office; he cannot even be investigated. "Article II allows me to do whatever I want," Trump repeatedly insisted.[25] Like an absolute monarch, he essentially proclaimed, "L'état c'est moi!" Fortunately, the Supreme Court determined in July 2020 that the president is not above the law and must respond to subpoenas like everybody else. It remains to be seen, however, at the time of this writing, whether the political class will even try to prosecute him for his crimes.

Sadly, Obama's refusal to hold Bush administration officials accountable for war crimes made it easier for Trump to appoint "Bloody Gina" Haspel, who ran one of the black sites where people were tortured and who participated in the destruction of videotapes of that torture, as CIA director—an appointment supported by six Senate Democrats, including Bill Nelson, who was my Florida senator. Most shockingly, Senator Dianne Feinstein, who led the torture investigation, actually praised Haspel during the confirmation. That reminds me of the woman who led the campaign against capital punishment in Sussex County endorsing Prince Speaker who championed the death penalty. It's hard to understand. Personally, I refused to vote for Nelson's reelection because he voted for Haspel, since I consider torture politically unforgiveable. Sadly, Rick Scott, a deeply corrupt, right-wing Republican, won that race.

Voters tend to spend an outsized amount of time focusing on the president, and indeed our society has developed a president-centric national political culture that undermines democratic practices. Many people now view the commander in chief as "the Decider" and members of Congress as partisan courtiers, instead of understanding that the legislature and the executive are coequal branches of government, and that We the People are sovereign. Swanson describes it this way:

> We have been trained to think of the president as our government, and of Congress and the courts as impediments to efficiency. We hear thousands of times a year on our television that bipartisanship is preferable to debate. . . . We hear that legislation is created by the White House and voted on out of loyalty or opposition to the White House, that keeping the workings of our government secret from us is necessary to protect us, that allowing presidents to seize unconstitutional

powers and even violate the laws is the only way to keep us safe, and that we all—not just members of the military—must obey our "commander in chief."[26]

These long-developing habits of deference toward the president undermine the possibility of democratic culture and participation.

Ever since the Democratic primary of 2016, I have observed on Facebook and heard at numerous party meetings repeated attempts to suppress differences of opinion within the party. If you criticize a Democrat, you will likely get accused of participating in a "circular firing squad." I should not have been shocked to learn from a friend who serves as executive director of a state Democratic Party that during the presidential selection process he received calls daily from Democrats, suggesting that the party eliminate the primary and just have party leaders chose the nominee. While it sounds absurd at first, the Republican Party actually cancelled some state primaries and caucuses to prevent anyone from challenging Trump.[27]

While the Princely Presidency must be opposed by all who want to maintain our republic over time—the challenge of this Machiavellian Moment—the president is not the only problem. All over the country, we see examples of lower-level legislators and executives who behave in a similar high-handed royalist manner, as illustrated in this text by my own experience with Prince Speaker. Tolerating their authoritarian behavior undermines democracy. As I told my party committee in 2015, we need to remember that our representatives work for us; we do not work for them, and we do not owe anyone our vote. Elected officials are accountable to us, and elections are the moment at which we evaluate their job performance. I have heard from party operatives in both Delaware and Florida that the mission of the Democratic Party is "incumbent protection." If you care at all about democratic self-rule, that contention could not be more wrongheaded.

LESSON 3: WE NEED TO KEEP BATTLING THE PRINCE INSIDE OUR HEADS

Next, we need to *battle the Prince inside our own heads* and resist taking the easy path of deferring to powermongers and going along with antidemocratic practices to make our own lives easier. Even if tolerating authoritarianism within the Democratic Party—that tries to silence dissent, expects fealty toward incumbents, badgers people to "vote blue no matter who," and rigs the system to prevent competition—helps maintain party power, the threat that a deferential or submissive mindset poses to democracy renders that approach counterproductive. It readies people psychologically to accept authoritarianism, whether royalist or otherwise.

When Prince Speaker ran a smear campaign against me for the better part of a year, most of my friends in the Democratic Party refused to defend me, some even taking his side. None of them were bad people, and most claimed to be strong progressives, so it has been challenging to figure out the reasons they acted as they did. I see multiple issues at play. First, some people do not have a strong commitment to democratic values. They had no problem with Prince Speaker's behavior, considering it par for the course. "Politics ain't beanbag," after all. Some thought I deserved the treatment I got for publicly embarrassing Prince Speaker with my op-eds and social media posts. Who the hell did I think I was? Just some "girl," according to the Speaker. Others excused authoritarian tactics because they thought they would help him get reelected or protect party power, whatever it takes.

Second, some people supported democratic values but lacked an understanding of the ways in which those values can be eroded by small acts of misbehavior. They did not see that tolerating authoritarianism in the Democratic Party, even for well-intentioned reasons, habituates people to a dynamic of powermongering and deference, more appropriate to a feudal or royalist hierarchy than to a government of equals. Not having a clear vision, they got confused by the manipulative rhetoric generated by Prince Speaker's minions or just went along with the crowd, trusting that the group was making sound decisions.

Third, some people probably had a strong commitment to democratic values and understood the corrosive effects of capitulating to a bully, but they lacked democratic courage. Sadly, our society provides few opportunities for people to develop their capacity for democratic courage; citizenship has been reduced to a legal category that requires nothing of us. Few people want to open themselves up to being the victim of a bully or being scorned by their friends and community. They do not want to obey power, but they fear disobeying. After all, look at the consequences of my disobedience. Those people are the ones who quit the party right after the committee endorsed Prince Speaker, uncomfortable with the events that occurred but not wanting to speak up.

While it might sound conservative to the ears of some, personal character makes a difference in a democratic society. People need to develop democratic virtues—critical thinking, caring about the common good, the courage to stand and fight. If you believe, as I do, that democratic self-rule by equals does not constitute the default condition of society but must be carefully cultivated and protected, then developing a democratic disposition must be part of the task. We must instill in children a commitment to democratic values and provide them with opportunities to develop their democratic capacities. In my case, taking civic education classes in public school gave me a set of expectations about American democracy that played a role in prompting me to get involved politically—but not in the way my anticommunist teachers envisioned.

Most parents do not run their homes in a democratic manner. I know mine didn't. While I believe we should protect children from subjection to harsh discipline and abuse—whether at home or school—that often turns people into nonempathetic, authoritarians, I am not necessarily advocating a parenting style that allows children to weigh in on every decision or make their own rules. Instead, I look to educational institutions, from kindergarten through college, to add to the lessons that parents teach and help prepare students for democratic participation, among other things.

Since the 1960s, civic education has weakened. While every state requires "some form of instruction in civics and/or government, and nearly 90 percent of students take at least one civics class," most states do not include civics on their standardized tests, so it does not count. Plus, "too often, factual book learning is not reinforced with experience-based learning opportunities like community service, guided debates, critical discussion of current events, and simulations of democratic processes."[28] Studies show that rote memorization is not an effective way to instill knowledge, much less prepare students for participation.[29] Consequently, "only 25 percent of US students reach the 'proficient' standard on the NAEP Civics Assessment."[30]

Regardless of the instruction being offered at home and in schoolrooms, however, I believe people can develop their democratic capacities at any point during their lives, but they need opportunities to do so. People learn by doing. People will hone their deliberative skills by participating in deliberative forums. People will practice standing up to power when they are invited to do so, as part of an organized action. And people will learn strategies for organizing by working with experienced organizers in neighborhoods and workplaces across the country.

Most critically, we must do everything we can to counteract the royalist mindset that can develop even within a democratic republic. That requires constant resistance to habits of powermongering and deference that often make people's lives easier. When the Democratic Party deploys authoritarian tactics to maintain power or to make the work of party operatives less complicated, we must resist. When elected officials refuse to respect the will of the people, we must speak out. And as the Left works to achieve and maintain power, we must carefully protect democratic processes within our new party. We must always respect the right of people to voice dissenting views. As Rosa Luxemburg put it, "Freedom only for the supporters of the government, only for the members of one party—however numerous they may be—is no freedom at all. Freedom is always and exclusively freedom for the one who thinks differently."[31]

LESSON 4: WE NEED TO MAKE SURE THE 1% IS BATTLING THE MODERN PRINCE COLLECTIVE

Finally, we need a strong party to support the side of the 99% in the class war—the Modern Prince Collective.[32] That party must provide a compelling analysis of the current political terrain, offer an ideological vision to unite and inspire people, fight for an agenda that serves the needs and interests of the 99%, and lead us into battle. We must let the 1%, its courtiers, and its minions know that they will soon be *battling the Modern Prince Collective*.

Gramsci builds his vision of a revolutionary party partly on the work of Machiavelli, who wanted to teach regular people the strategies for gaining and maintaining power that authoritarians seem to know in their gut.[33] Calling for a shift from individual to collective leadership, Gramsci says, "The modern prince, the myth-prince, cannot be a real person, a concrete individual. It can only be an organism, a complex element of society in which a collective will . . . begins to take concrete form. History has already provided this organism, and it is the political party."[34] Looking back through history, he views the Jacobins of the French Revolution as a link between Machiavelli's work and his own. According to Gramsci, "the essence of 'Jacobinism'" was unification of the people, which required the "the subordination of the 'countryside' to the 'city'."[35] In other words, creating a unified republic of equals required doing away with the feudal prerogatives that governed in rural areas. Even back then "rural consciousness" posed a problem.

Gramsci envisions a mass party of the people. He argues that "for a party to exist," it must have "a mass element, composed of ordinary men."[36] The party functions to unite a diversity of individuals from different sectors of society into a coherent whole based on a shared "consciousness" about the benefits of working together for progressive change. That is to say, it unites everyday people on the basis of class across industries but also connects them to "other subordinate groups, . . . bringing about not only a unison of economic and political aims, but also intellectual and moral unity."[37] Gramsci's party "must be and cannot but be the proclaimer and organizer of an intellectual and moral reform . . . [that] has to be linked with a programme of economic reform."[38] In other words, the party must articulate a vision and organize for both social and economic justice.

Gramsci stressed the importance of strong leaders to galvanize people. In my experience, it is incredibly hard to recruit folks to lead political organizations or run for office. For example, I easily got elected Progressive Caucus president because nobody else wanted the position, and when I stepped down, I could not find anyone who wanted to take over. Leadership matters. In her book on union organizing, Jane McAlevey stresses the importance of getting organic leaders on board with the union agenda, by which she means the people workers actually listen to, the real influencers, as opposed self-appointed captains or paid staff.[39]

The corollary of having to look for leaders is recognizing that most people are not leaders but followers, for whatever reason. Gramsci maintains that for a party's mass base to be effective, it needs "somebody to centralize, organize, and discipline" the mass base, but not in an authoritarian way. "When the party is progressive it functions 'democratically' (democratic centralism); when the party is regressive it functions 'bureaucratically' (bureaucratic centralism)."[40]

The fact that so many people are followers actually inspires hope in me because these foot soldiers could presumably be mobilized by the strong leadership of the Modern Prince Collective. While my former friends in the Sussex DP followed Lord County Chair in support of his agenda, when I was chair, they followed me in support of mine. The Right deals with the issue of followers by putting forward demagogues to lead the masses, but the Left cannot do that. We reject demagoguery. Thus, we need to create a collective entity to lead our people into battle, a democratically run political party that can unite all our disparate factions with a compelling ideological vision that makes sense of the whole. The Modern Prince Collective should also provide plenty of opportunities for political engagement, through which people can develop the democratic skills and virtues needed for republican self-rule.

The importance of having a coherent ideological vision cannot be overstated. Gramsci did not believe that class consciousness would develop spontaneously within the working class. Unions play an important role in organizing workers, but we also need intellectuals to provide an ideological vision to move people beyond their immediate interests.[41] Gramsci's concept of hegemony refers to the assumptions that people in a society internalize that lead them to support the status quo. Those hegemonic beliefs must be dislodged. Cultural change must precede, or at least accompany, political change.

In other words, Gramsci believed that before revolutionaries can take power, they must work to change people's consciousness to build support for democratic socialism. While Lenin wanted revolutionaries to seize political power first and then work on legitimation, which might sound appealing to some, we have to remember that he faced a context in which everyday people opposed the cruel Czarist regime, so undermining hegemonic beliefs were not his challenge. Today in the United States, however, we do not yet face that level of illegitimacy. The majority of people seem to consider our neoliberal, capitalist, oligarchic regime to be desirable or inevitable. We cannot successfully seize and maintain power by imposing our will on people invested in the current regime. Moreover, gaining power by imitating right-wing powermongers in the world of power politics that currently exists will ultimately fall short because people will continue to be caught in the same mindset of powermongering and deference that currently exists, which leaves them susceptible to royalism—or fascism. That is not a foundation upon which a democratic socialist society can firmly stand. "The master's tools can never dismantle the master's house."

For Gramsci, the struggle begins in civil society with consciousness-raising, before moving into the political realm where the Left tries to achieve and maintain power.[42] While I agree with him on the importance of changing culture, for the reasons just explained, I believe we also need to focus on the political piece. We must start right now formulating a long-term plan for taking political power, since the goals that need to be reached will probably take decades, and that political work must be done in a way that facilitates cultural change. Put differently, we need a long-term plan, and while we will need to play hardball at times, we must also remember that ultimately the means are the ends. While we might "need to put some of those motherfuckers in prison," as a left academic colleague recently remarked at a conference, the prisons we put them in cannot resemble the torture chambers that currently exist, despite how much our overlords might deserve that. We have to be better than that, more just and more humane.

A FINAL EXHORTATION:
LET'S RISE UP AGAINST AUTHORITARIANISM!

In the spirit of Machiavelli,[43] having taken account of everything discussed previously, and meditating on whether the time for the next democratic revolution is now, I do not know when there would be a more fitting time for the emergence of the Modern Prince Collective, the party of the 99%, to unify our movement. We live in dark times, but people have risen up from worse. Indeed, sometimes conditions of oppression give rise to great leaders and important movements. Out of slavery in Egypt emerged Moses, Miriam, and the Jewish people. Out of the Jim Crow South came Rosa Parks, Martin Luther King, and the civil rights movement. And out of Czarist Russia came Lenin, N. Krupskaya, and the revolutionary party.[44] Out of Trump's United States emerges Bernie Sanders, Alexandria Ocasio-Cortez, and a democratic socialist left on the rise. Who knows what comes next?

And although we have dared to hope before and been disappointed, we cannot give up. We must continue to have faith that we can redeem ourselves from the cruelty and arrogance of our political leaders and capitalist immiseration. Are we ready to follow the banner toward a more just political order? The task seems overwhelming but as Nelson Mandela put it, "It always seems impossible until it's done."

We need to do whatever it takes to create a just society, even if that means new political institutions, an economy that benefits all, and a truly democratic culture, and we need strong party leadership to unite our efforts.

We cannot let the opportunities arising from our current situation pass us by. We must throw off the cruel, capitalist system that stinks in our nostrils and move forward with democratic courage and hope. Together, we must work for a better society that is socially and economically just.

NOTES

PREFACE

1. This preface riffs on the preface to Machiavelli's *The Prince*, a book that shaped my vision of politics and that I reference throughout this text. See Niccolò Machiavelli, *The Prince and the Discourses*, trans. Luigi Ricci (New York: Random House, 1950), 3.

ACKNOWLEDGMENTS

1. Claire Snyder-Hall, "Battling the Prince: A Political Memoir," *New Political Science: A Journal of Politics and Culture* 39, no. 4 (2017): 687–696, https://doi.org/10.1080/07393148.2017.1379280.

THE BIG PICTURE: A THEORETICAL INTRODUCTION

1. See Elizabeth Hinton, *From the War on Poverty to the War on Crime: The Making of Mass Incarceration in America* (Cambridge, MA: Harvard University Press, 2017); Michelle Alexander, *The New Jim Crow: Mass Incarceration in the Age of Colorblindness* (New York: New Press, 2012); and Jane Mayer, *The Dark Side: The Inside Story of How the War on Terror Turned into a War on American Ideals* (New York: Anchor Books, 2009).

2. Steven Levitsky and Daniel Ziblatt, *How Democracies Die* (New York: Crown, 2018).

3. Zachary B. Wolf, "Yes, Obama Deported More People than Trump but Context Is Everything," CNN, July 13, 2019, https://www.cnn.com/2019/07/13/politics/obama-trump-deportations-illegal-immigration/index.html.

4. Laura Santhanam, "Trump's Immigration Policy Splits Americans in Half, Poll Says," *PBS News Hour*, December 11, 2018, https://www.pbs.org/newshour/politics/trumps-immigration-policy-splits-americans-in-half-poll-says.

5. Levitsky and Ziblatt, *How Democracies Die*, 21–22.

6. See Katie Rogers, Jonathan Martin, and Maggie Haberman, "As Trump Calls Protesters 'Terrorists,' Tear Gas Clears Path for His Walk to a Church," *New York Times*, June 1, 2020, https://www.nytimes.com/2020/06/01/us/politics/trump-governors.html?searchResultPosition=3.

7. Masha Gessen, "Donald Trump's Fascist Performance," *New Yorker*, June 3, 2020, https://www.newyorker.com/news/our-columnists/donald-trumps-fascist-performance.

8. Domenico Montanaro, "Poll: Two-Thirds Think Trump Made Racial Tensions Worse After Floyd Was Killed," NPR, June 5, 2020, https://www.npr.org/2020/06/05/870019283/poll-two-thirds-think-trump-made-racial-tensions-worse-after-george-floyds-death.

9. Suzanne Nuyen, "Federal Officers Used Unmarked Vehicles to Grab People in Portland, DHS Confirms," NPR, July 17, 2020, https://www.npr.org/2020/07/17/892277592/federal-officers-use-unmarked-vehicles-to-grab-protesters-in-portland.

10. Jason Hanna and Josh Campbell, "Trump Gloats about US Marshalls' Killing of Portland Antifa Suspect," CNN, October 15, 2020, https://www.cnn.com/2020/10/15/politics/trump-fugitive-shooting/index.html.

11. Everton Bailey, Jr., "Oregon Voters Disapprove of Portland Protests," *Oregonian*, September 10, 2020, https://www.oregonlive.com/politics/2020/09/oregon-voters-disapprove-of-portland-protests-feel-police-arent-using-enough-force-poll-finds.html.

12. Tucker Higgins, "Trump Retains Overwhelming Support from Republicans after Deadly U.S. Capitol Attack: NBC poll," CNBC.com, January 17, 2021, https://www.cnbc.com/2021/01/17/trump-retains-support-from-republicans-after-capitol-attack-nbc-poll.html.

13. Thomas Frank argues that the Democratic Party serves the interests of the professional class and lacks an agenda for working people in *Listen, Liberal: Or, What Ever Happened to the Party of the People?* (New York: Metropolitan Books, 2016).

14. Colin Campbell, "Donald Trump: 'I am the only one who can make America truly great again!,'" *Business Insider*, March 18, 2015, https://www.businessinsider.com/donald-trump-i-am-the-only-one-who-can-make-america-truly-great-again-2015-3.

15. The phrase comes from R. R. Palmer, *The Age of Democratic Revolution: The Challenge* (Princeton: Princeton University Press, 1950) and *The Age of Democratic Revolution: The Struggle* (Princeton: Princeton University Press, 1964). The age began with the Glorious Revolution of 1688 in England, in which parliament, with its rule of law, established dominance over the monarchy, with its rule of whimsy. The era continued with the American Revolution in 1776 and

the French Revolution in 1789, during which the people liberated themselves from monarchy and feudalism and established republics. These two eighteenth-century events were followed by the Haitian Revolution of 1794, the world's first and only successful slave uprising that became a model for anticolonial struggles in the twentieth century. A wave of smaller, unsuccessful revolutions all over Europe emerged during this time period as well. In both France and Haiti, the antiroyalist Jacobins led the people toward republicanism. See C. L. R. James, *The Black Jacobins: Toussaint L'Ouverture and the San Domingo Revolution* (New York: Random House, 1963), first published in 1938.

16. John Locke, *Second Treatise of Government,* in *Two Treatises of Government,* ed. Peter Laslett (Cambridge: Cambridge University Press, 1998).

17. Nancy Fraser uses the term *progressive neoliberal* instead of *centrist liberal* to refer to those who combine, "on the one hand, mainstream liberal currents of the new social movements (feminism, antiracism, multiculturalism, environmentalism, and LGBTQ rights); on the other hand, the most dynamic, high-end 'symbolic' and financial sectors of the US economy (Wall Street, Silicon Valley, and Hollywood)." She calls Republicans *reactionary neoliberals.* I do not follow her lead, however, because the term *progressive* in popular usage generally denotes people like Elizabeth Warren, not Bill Clinton, so calling the latter a *progressive neoliberal* in the context of this book would be confusing. For Fraser's take, see "From Progressive Neoliberalism to Trump—and Beyond," *American Affairs,* November 20, 2017, https://americanaffairsjournal.org/2017/11/progressive-neoliberalism-trump-beyond/.

18. Quint Forgy, "In Any Other Country, Joe Biden and I Would Not Be in the Same Party," *Politico,* January 6, 2020, https://www.politico.com/news/2020/01/06/alexandria-ocasio-cortez-joe-biden-not-same-party-094642.

19. Matt Grossman and David A. Hopkins, *Asymmetric Politics: Ideological Republicans and Group Interest Democrats* (Oxford: Oxford University Press, 2016).

20. Chris Cillizza, "Nancy Pelosi Just Threw Some Serious Shade at Alexandria Ocasio-Cortez's 'Green New Deal,'" CNN.com, February 8, 2019, https://www.cnn.com/2019/02/07/politics/pelosi-alexandria-ocasio-cortez-green-new-deal/index.html. For a discussion of Pelosi's support for neoliberal policies, see Robert Freeman, "Why on Earth Is Nancy Pelosi Protecting Donald Trump?," *Common Dreams,* September 24, 2019, https://www.commondreams.org/views/2019/09/24/why-earth-nancy-pelosi-protecting-donald-trump?fbclid=IwAR1Co4WfzdtLbdkqQIHBOYJnnR6grHmvE1y72SNALWmekmaDxExgNv_G5ic.

21. From *The Prince* in Niccolò Machiavelli, *Machiavelli: The Chief Works and Others, Volume 1,* trans. Allan Gilbert (Durham: Duke University Press, 1989), 10.

22. Maurizio Viroli, *Republicanism* (New York: Hill and Wang, 1999).

23. John P. McCormick, *Reading Machiavelli: Scandalous Books, Suspect Engagements and the Virtue of Populist Politics* (Princeton: Princeton University Press, 2018), 210.

24. McCormick, *Reading Machiavelli*, 9–17.

25. See Antonio Gramsci, "The Modern Prince," in *Selections from the Prison Notebooks of Antonio Gramsci*, ed. and trans. Quintin Hoare and Geoffrey Nowell Smith (New York: International, 1971), 126–127; Sebastian de Grazia, *Machiavelli in Hell* (New York: Vintage, 1989), 240; and R. Claire Snyder, *Citizen-Soldiers and Manly Warriors: Military Service and Gender in the Civic Republican Tradition* (Lanham, MD: Rowman & Littlefield, 1999), 15–43.

26. McCormick, *Reading Machiavelli*, 10.

27. Gramsci, *Prison Notebooks*, 129, 131.

28. See Philip Pettit, *Republicanism: A Theory of Freedom and Government* (Oxford: Oxford University Press, 1997); Michael Sandel, *Democracy's Discontents: America in Search of Public Philosophy* (Cambridge, MA: Belknap Press, 1998); Viroli, *Republicanism*; and Snyder, *Citizen-Soldiers*.

29. Snyder, *Citizen-Soldiers*.

30. James Madison, "Federalist 10," http://constitution.org/fed/federa10.htm.

31. Robert Dahl, *On Democracy* (New Haven: Yale University Press, 1998).

32. Madison, "Federalist 10," emphasis added.

33. J. G. A. Pocock, *The Machiavellian Moment: Florentine Political Thought and the Atlantic Republican Tradition* (Princeton: Princeton University Press, 1975).

34. For citation, see Bartleby.com, https://www.bartleby.com/73/1593.html.

35. James Madison, "Federalist 51," http://constitution.org/fed/federa51.htm.

36. Jean-Jacques Rousseau, *On the Social Contract and Other Later Political Writings*, ed. and trans. Victor Gourevitch (Cambridge: Cambridge University Press, 1997), 81.

37. Snyder, *Citizen-Soldiers*.

38. Carl Boggs, *Gramsci's Marxism* (London: Pluto Press, 1976), 39.

39. Terry Eagleton, *Ideology: An Introduction* (London: Verso, 1991), 114.

40. Eagleton, *Ideology*, 114.

41. Charles Derber and Yale R. Magress, *Bully Nation: How the American Establishment Creates a Bullying Society* (Lawrence: University Press of Kansas, 2016).

42. For examples, see the documentary *Immigration Nation*, on Netflix.

43. Richard Avramenko, *Courage: The Politics of Life and Limb* (Notre Dame, IN: University of Notre Dame Press, 2011).

44. Avramenko, *Courage*, 141.

45. Gabriel A. Almond and Sidney Verba, *The Civic Culture: Political Attitudes and Democracy in Five Nations* (Boston: Little, Brown, 1965), 3.

46. Almond and Verba, *Civic Culture*, 346.

47. Almond and Verba, *Civic Culture*, 347.

48. Almond and Verba, *Civic Culture*, 348.

49. See Russell J. Dalton and Christian Welzel, eds., *The Civic Culture Transformed: From Allegiant to Assertive Citizens* (New York: Cambridge University Press, 2014).

50. Barack Obama, "Farewell Address," https://www.nbcnews.com/story line/president-obama-the-legacy/president-obama-cap-long-goodbye-farewell-speech-n705381.

51. See David Daly, *Ratf**cked: The True Story Behind the Secret Plan to Steal America's Democracy* (New York: Liveright, 2016); Ari Berman, *Give Us the Ballot! The Modern Struggle for Voting Rights in America* (New York: Picador, 2016); Jake Johnson, " 'Even Worse than the DCCC Blacklist': Schumer Accused of Effort to Hamstring Progressives Trying to Unseat GOP Senators," *Common Dreams*, August 29, 2019, https://www.commondreams.org/news/2019/08/29/ even-worse-dccc-blacklist-schumer-accused-effort-hamstring-progressives-trying; Frank, *Listen, Liberal*; Michael J. Glennon, *National Security and Double Government* (Oxford: Oxford University Press, 2016); and Jane Mayer, *Dark Money: The Hidden History of the Billionaires Behind the Rise of the Radical Right* (New York: Doubleday, 2016).

52. While third parties currently face many legal barriers in our existing single-member plurality system, laws can be changed. The current two-party tyranny is not set in constitutional stone. In fact, it's a twentieth-century creation. For three different discussions of the ways in which changeable laws enshrine the two-party system in the United States, see Lisa Jane Disch, *The Tyranny of the Two-Party System* (New York: Columbia University Press, 2002); Seth Ackerman, "A Blueprint for a New Party," *Jacobin*, November 8, 2016, https://www.jacobinmag. com/2016/11/bernie-sanders-democratic-labor-party-ackerman/; and Lee Drutman, *Breaking the Two-Party Doom Loop: The Case for Multiparty Democracy in America* (New York: Oxford University Press, 2020).

53. For a discussion of the methodology of autoethnography, see Pat Sikes, ed., *Autoethnography* (Los Angeles: Sage, 2013); Heewong Chang, *Autoethnography as Method* (Walnut Creek, CA: Left Coast Press, 2008); and Barry Smart, *Sociology, Phenomenology and Marxian Analysis: A Critical Discussion of the Theory and Practice of a Science of Society* (London: Routledge and Kegan Paul, 2013).

54. Rousseau, *On the Social Contract*, 46.

55. From last paragraph of Karl Marx and Friedrich Engels, "Manifesto of the Communist Party," in *Marx: Later Political Writings*, ed. and trans. Terrell Carver (Cambridge: Cambridge University Press, 2000), 30. Original published in 1848.

CHAPTER 1. BECOMING AN ACTIVIST

1. Parts of this chapter rely on memories from decades ago. It is accurate to the best of my knowledge.

2. Maurice Isserman and Michael Kazin, *American Divided: The Civil War of the 1960s* (Oxford: Oxford University Press, 2000), 136; Frances Fox Piven and Richard A. Cloward, *Poor People's Movements: Why They Succeed, How They Fail* (New York: Vintage Books, 1979), 250.

3. Isserman and Kazan, *America Divided*, 138.

4. Isserman and Kazan, *America Divided*, 139.

5. For a recent discussion, see Jill Lepore, "The Riot Report: A Long History of Government Inaction," *New Yorker*, June 22, 2020, 24–29.

6. J. Patrice McSherry, *Predatory States: Operation Condor and Covert War in Latin America* (Lanham, MD: Rowman & Littlefield, 2005) gives details based on declassified government documents.

7. Esther Hautzig, *The Endless Steppe: Growing Up in Siberia* (New York: Harper Collins, 2018), originally published in 1968; James Houston, *Farewell to Manzanar* (New York: Houghton Mifflin, 1973).

8. Jean Hardisty, *Mobilizing Resentment: Conservative Resurgence from the John Birch Society to the Promise Keepers* (Boston: Beacon Press, 1999), 38–39.

9. Hardisty, *Mobilizing Resentment*, 49.

10. See Michael A. Milburn and Sheree D. Conrad, *Raised to Rage: The Politics of Anger and the Roots of Authoritarianism* (Cambridge, MA: MIT Press, 2016), and Marc J. Hetherington and Jonathan D. Weiler, *Authoritarianism and Polarization in American Politics* (Cambridge: Cambridge University Press, 2009).

11. David Mathews, Kettering Foundation Research Session, October 16, 2019.

12. "The D.A.R., as it is commonly called, is a historically white organization with a record of excluding blacks so ugly that Eleanor Roosevelt renounced her membership in protest." Sarah Maslin Nir, "For Daughters of the American Revolution, a New Chapter," *New York Times*, July 3, 2012, https://www.nytimes.com/2012/07/04/nyregion/for-daughters-of-the-american-revolution-more-black-members.html.

13. Peter N. Carroll, *It Seemed Like Nothing Happened: America in the 1970s* (New Brunswick, NJ: Rutgers University Press, 1990). Jacob Hacker and Paul Pierson, *Winner-Take-All Politics: How Washington Made the Rich Richer—and Turned Its Back on the Middle Class* (New York: Simon & Schuster, 2010), 99.

14. Hacker and Pierson, *Winner-Take-All*, 99.

15. Ryan Grim, *We've Got People: From Jesse Jackson to Alexandria Ocasio-Cortez, the End of Big Money and the Rise of a Movement* (Washington, DC: Strong Arm Press, 2019), 42.

16. Thomas Piketty, *Capital in the Twenty-First Century*, trans. Arthur Goldhammer (Cambridge, MA: Belknap Press of Harvard University Press, 2014).

17. For tax rate data, see Piketty, *Capital*. For the emergence of neo-feudalism, see Jodi Dean, "Communism or Neo-Feudalism," *New Political Science: A Journal of Politics and Culture* 42, no. 1 (February 2020): 1–17.

18. Kathleen Elkins, "Here's How Much You Have to Earn to Be in the Top 1% in Every US State," CNBC, July 27, 2018, https://www.cnbc.com/2018/07/27/how-much-you-have-to-earn-to-be-in-the-top-1percent-in-every-us-state.html.

19. See Aristotle, *Politics*, trans. Benjamin Jowett (Mineola, NY: Dover, 2000), 168–169.

20. Sara Diamond, *Roads to Dominion: Right-Wing Movements and Political Power in the United States* (New York: Guilford Press, 1995), 174, 234.

21. Carol T. Christ, "Inside the Clockwork of Women's Careers," Speech to the Chautauqua Institution, July 21, 2004, https://www.smith.edu/president-carol-christ/speeches-writings/inside-the-clockwork-of-womens-careers-a-speech-to-the-chautauqua-institution, 7.

22. Mary Daly, *Beyond God the Father: Toward a Philosophy of Women's Liberation* (Boston: Beacon Press, 1985), originally published in 1973.

23. Catharine A. MacKinnon, *Feminism Unmodified: Discourses on Life and Law* (Cambridge, MA: Harvard University Press, 1987).

24. Catherine MacKinnon, *Toward a Feminist Theory of the State* (Cambridge, MA: Harvard University Press, 1989), 124.

25. Caroline Bologna, "This Viral Rewrite of 'Baby It's Cold Outside' Emphasizes Consent," *Huffington Post*, December 10, 2018, https://www.huffpost.com/entry/baby-its-cold-outside-holderness-family-consent_n_5c0e7fd8e4b0edf5a3a6db8c.

26. SAMOIS, *Coming to Power: Writings and Graphics on Lesbian S/M*, 2nd ed. (Boston: Alyson, 1982), first published in 1980.

27. Cherrie Moraga and Gloria Anzaldúa, *This Bridge Called My Back: Writings by Radical Women of Color* (New York: Kitchen Table: Women of Color Press, 1981).

28. Alice Walker, *The Color Purple* (New York: Penguin, 2019).

29. Adrienne Rich, "Compulsory Heterosexuality and Lesbian Existence," in *Blood, Bread, and Poetry: Selected Prose 1979–1985* (New York: Norton, 1986).

30. David Cortright, *Peace: A History of Movements and Ideas* (Cambridge: Cambridge University Press, 2008), 141.

31. "There is a pretty high degree of congruence between senators' positions and the opinions of their constituents—at least when those constituents are in the top third of the income distribution. For constituents in the middle third of the income distribution, the correspondence is much weaker, and for those in the bottom third, it is actually negative. (Yes, when the poorest people in a state support a policy, their senators are less likely to vote for it.) . . . [And] while senators in both parties were more likely to vote for a policy when it was supported by better-off voters, Republicans were much more responsive to high-income voters than were Democrats." Hacker and Pierson, *Winner-Take-All*, 111.

32. Diamond, *Roads to Dominion*, 206.

33. Diamond, *Roads to Dominion*, 221.

34. For detailed documentation, see McSherry, *Predatory States*.

35. Christine A. Kelly, *Tangled Up in Red, White, and Blue: New Social Movements in America* (Lanham, MD: Rowman & Littlefield, 2001), 137–138.

36. Laura Wilkinson, "Smith College Students Continue Sit-In to Protest Apartheid," AP News, February 27, 1986, https://www.apnews.com/eb444f2a908a66d38db5669534e55f59.

37. Kelly, *Tangled Up*.

38. Laura Wilkinson, "Students at Smith, Brown Protest South African Investments," AP News, February 28, 1986, https://www.apnews.com/ebf8020c0e fa6d324d8a4842956514e6.

39. "Around the Nation: Smith College to End South Africa Investments," *New York Times*, October 28, 1986, https://www.nytimes.com/1986/10/28/us/ around-the-nation-smith-college-to-end-south-africa-investments.html.

40. Cecelie Counts, "Divestment Was Just One Weapon in the Battle Against Apartheid," *New York Times*, January 27, 2003, https://www.nytimes.com/roomfor debate/2013/01/27/is-divestment-an-effective-means-of-protest/divestment-was-just-one-weapon-in-battle-against-apartheid.

41. Kelly, *Tangled Up*, 142.

42. Faye J. Crosby, Ann Pufall, R. Claire Snyder, Marion O'Connell, and Peg Whalen, "The Denial of Personal Disadvantage among You, Me, and All the Other Ostriches," in *Gender and Thought*, ed. Mary Crawford and Margaret Gentry (New York: Springer-Verlag, 1989).

43. Diamond, *Roads to Dominion*, 219.

44. Audre Lorde, *Sister Outsider* (Trumansburg, NY: Crossing Press, 1984), 112.

45. Lorde, *Sister Outsider*, 112.

46. Sonia Johnson, *Going Out of Our Minds: The Metaphysics of Liberation* (Freedom, CA: Crossing Press, 1987), 21.

47. Johnson, *Out of Our Minds*, 21.

48. Johnson, *Out of Our Minds*, 35–36.

49. Johnson, *Out of Our Minds*, 36.

50. Johnson, *Out of Our Minds*, 38.

51. Johnson, *Out of Our Minds*, 36.

52. Johnson, *Out of Our Minds*, 38.

53. Cited in Johnson, *Out of Our Minds*, 43.

54. Cortright, *Peace*, 147.

55. Johnson, *Out of Our Minds*, 305.

56. Johnson, *Out of Our Minds*, 325.

57. Johnson, *Out of Our Minds*, 327.

58. Johnson, *Out of Our Minds*, 324.

59. Lorde, "The Transformation of Silence into Language and Action," in *Sister Outsider*, 41–42.

CHAPTER 2. MY FIRST CAREER: DEMOCRATIC THEORIST

1. Andrew Bacevich, *The New American Militarism: How Americans Are Seduced by War* (New York: Oxford University Press, 2005), 179.

2. Cortright, *Peace*, 150.

3. Malcolm Byrne, *Iran-Contra: Reagan's Scandal and the Unchecked Abuse of Presidential Power* (Lawrence: University Press of Kansas, 2014), 336. And yet under Trump it begins again, now that the Sandinistas are back in power. See Ben Norton, "US House Rams through Nicaragua Regime-Change Bill with Zero Opposition," *Gray Zone*, March 12, 2020, https://thegrayzone.com/2020/03/12/us-house-sanctions-nicaragua/?fbclid=IwAR0Gb1m9aWONAZO2Qv8HocfUvH3 judSPLKzRwyYiNly1WO-eEb_Na5O0H7w.

4. While generally attributed to Nelson Mandela, the source cannot be confirmed.

5. Bacevich, *New Militarism*.

6. Bacevich, *New Militarism*, 97, 118.

7. Max Weber, *The Protestant Ethic and the Spirit of Capitalism* (New York: Penguin, 2002).

8. Carol Blum, *Rousseau and the Republic of Virtue: The Language of Politics in the French Revolution* (Ithaca: Cornell University Press, 1989).

9. Rousseau, *Social Contract*, 46.

10. Rousseau, *Social Contract*, 56.

11. Rousseau, *Social Contract*, 54.

12. Thomas Paine, "Rights of Man, Part I," in *Paine: Political Writings*, ed. Bruce Kuklick (Cambridge: Cambridge University Press, 1997), 63.

13. Thomas Jefferson, "Letter to William Stephens Smith," November 13, 1787, https://www.loc.gov/exhibits/jefferson/jefffed.html#105.

14. See Francis Fukuyama, "The End of History?," *The National Interest* 16, no. 3 (Summer 1986): 3–18, https://history.msu.edu/hst203/files/2011/02/Fukuyama-The-End-of-History.pdf, 1. For an in-depth discussion of neoliberalism, see Wendy Brown, *Undoing the Demos: Neoliberalism's Stealth Revolution* (New York: Zone Books, 2015).

15. Benjamin R. Barber, *Strong Democracy: Participatory Politics for a New Age* (Berkeley: University of California Press, 1984).

16. Barber, *Strong Democracy*, 117.

17. Pat Buchanan, "1992 Republican National Convention Speech," August 17, 1992, https://buchanan.org/blog/1992-republican-national-convention-speech-148?doing_wp_cron=1478487975.2316689491271972656250.

18. Buchanan, "Convention Speech."

19. Buchanan, "Convention Speech."

20. See, for example, Josh Israel, "Public Television to Bring Back Racist, Anti-LGBTQ, Anti-Semite Pat Buchanan as Show Panelist," *Think Progress*, August 14, 2019, https://thinkprogress.org/public-television-to-bring-back-racist-anti-lgbtq-anti-semite-pat-buchanan-as-show-panelist-2eaab9f6dded/.

21. See, for example, Amy Gutmann and Dennis Thompson, *Democracy and Disagreement* (Cambridge, MA: Belknap Press of Harvard University Press, 1996).

22. For the public sphere, see Jürgen Habermas, *The Structural Transformation of the Public Sphere*, trans. Thomas Burger (Cambridge, MA: MIT Press, 1989), originally published in German in 1962.

23. See, for example, Iris Marion Young, *Justice and the Politics of Difference* (Princeton: Princeton University Press, 1990).

24. David Mathews, *With the People: An Introduction to an Idea* (Dayton: Kettering Foundation, 2020).

25. David Mathews, *Politics for People: Finding a Responsible Public Voice* (Urbana: University of Illinois Press, 1999), 11. The book was first published in 1994.

26. Mathews, *Politics for People*, 12.

27. For a discussion of how participatory democracy does not reduce to volunteerism, see Benjamin R. Barber, *The Truth of Power: Intellectual Affairs in the Clinton White House* (New York: W.W. Norton, 2001), chapter 6.

28. Mathews, *Politics for People*, 221.

29. Robert Putnam, *Bowling Alone: The Collapse and Revival of American Community* (New York: Simon & Schuster, 2000), 19. For the original article, see "Bowling Alone: America's Declining Social Capital," *Journal of Democracy* (January 1995): 65–78.

30. See Amanda Litvinov, "Forgotten Purpose: Civic Education in Public Schools," *NEA Today*, March 16, 2017, http://neatoday.org/2017/03/16/civics-education-public-schools/, and Kei Kawashima-Ginsberg, "The Future of Civic Education," http://www.nasbe.org/wp-content/uploads/Future-of-Civic-Education_September-2016-Standard.pdf.

31. Barber, *Strong Democracy*.

32. While some conservatives view service learning as simply volunteerism, which they hope could replace government, Barber conceptualizes it as a way to create partnerships between active citizens and the government they authorize to work on their behalf. "For progressives," he explains, "voluntary service activity represented a strengthening of democracy, a devolution of power not to individuals and private corporations but to local democratic institutions and self-governing communities. It was a way to share responsibility and build partnerships between citizens and their elected officials, a way to pull down rather than put up walls between government and the rest of us." Barber, *Truth of Power*, 174.

33. Jerry Brown quote cited in Barber, *Truth of Power*, 56.

34. Stephen Eric Bronner, *Socialism Unbound* (New York: Routledge, 1990) was the first of many books on the subject of socialism.

35. Bronner, *Socialism Unbound*, 2.

36. Bronner, *Socialism Unbound*, xi.

37. Ivan Krastev and Stephen Holmes, *The Light That Failed: Why the West Is Losing the Fight for Democracy* (New York: Pegasus Books, 2019).

38. Stephen Eric Bronner, *Bitter Taste of Hope: Ideals, Ideologies, and Interests in the Age of Obama* (Albany: State University of New York Press, 2017), 97.

39. Erica L. Green and Stephanie Saul, "What Charles Koch and Other Donors to George Mason University Got for Their Money," *New York Times*, May 5, 2018, https://www.nytimes.com/2018/05/05/us/koch-donors-george-mason.html. For the history of right-wing operations at Mason, particularly related to James Buchanan, see Nancy McLean, *Democracy in Chains: The Deep History of the Radical Right's Stealth Plan for America* (New York: Penguin Books, 2017).

40. R. Claire Snyder, *Gay Marriage and Democracy: Equality for All* (Lanham, MD: Rowman & Littlefield, 2006).

41. For a detailed account, see Naomi Klein, *Fences and Windows: Dispatches from the Front Lines of the Globalization Debate* (New York: Picador, 2002), and Manfred Steger, "Confrontations: Antiglobalist Demonstrations from the 'Battle of Seattle' to the Collapse of Cancun," in *Globalism: Market Ideology Meets Terrorism*, 2nd ed. (Lanham, MD: Rowman & Littlefield, 2005).

42. Peter Dreier, "The Campus Anti-Sweatshop Movement," *The American Prospect*, December 19, 2001, https://prospect.org/education/campus-anti-sweatshop-movement/.

43. See Thomas Frank, *One Market Under God: Extreme Capitalism, Market Populism, and the End of Economic Democracy* (New York: Doubleday, 2000).

44. Benjamin R. Barber, *Jihad vs. McWorld: How Globalism and Tribalism Are Reshaping the World* (New York: Ballantine Books, 1995). It was later reissued in 2001 with the subtitle "Terrorism's Challenge to Democracy." Barber uses the term *jihad* to denote particularism that fragments societies, a definition that does not accord with the religious meaning of the term and also ignores the fact that Islam is a universalizing religion.

45. Laurence Ralph, *The Torture Letters: Reckoning with Police Violence* (Chicago: University of Chicago Press, 2020).

46. See "About ADP," https://www.aascu.org/programs/ADP/.

47. Kathleen Davis, "The One Word Men Never See in Their Performance Reviews," *Fast Company*, August 27, 2014, https://www.fastcompany.com/3034895/the-one-word-men-never-see-in-their-performance-reviews.

48. Laura Doyle, *The Surrendered Wife: A Practical Guide to Finding Intimacy, Passion, and Peace with a Man* (New York: Fireside, 2001), 201. For my article, see "The Ideology of Wifely Submission: A Challenge for Feminism?," *Politics and Gender* 4, no. 4 (December 2008): 563–586.

49. Christ, "Clockwork," 4.

50. Sara McLaughlin Mitchell and Vicki L. Hesli, "Women Don't Ask? Women Don't Say No? Bargaining and Service in the Political Science Profession," *PS: Political Science and Politics* (April 2013): 355–369.

51. Christ, "Clockwork," 2.

52. Tara Mohr, "Learning to Love Criticism," *New York Times*, September 27, 2014.

53. Maria Konnakova, "Lean Out: The Dangers for Women Who Negotiate," *New Yorker*, June 11, 2014; Sheryl Sandberg, *Lean In: Women, Work, and the Will to Lead* (New York: Alfred A. Knopf, 2013).

54. Liz Elting, "The High Cost of Ambition: Why Women Are Held Back for Thinking Big," *Forbes*, April 24, 2017, https://www.forbes.com/sites/lizelting/2017/04/24/the-high-cost-of-ambition-why-women-are-held-back-for-thinking-big/#1482d5671ee6.

55. Elting, "Ambition."

56. Davis, "One Word."

57. Kate Manne, *Down Girl: The Logic of Misogyny* (New York: Oxford University Press, 2019), 68.

58. Manne, *Down Girl*, 68.

59. Lisa Belkin, "The Opt-Out Revolution," *New York Times Magazine*, October 26, 2003, https://www.nytimes.com/2003/10/26/magazine/the-opt-out-revolution.html.

60. Anne-Marie Slaughter, "Why Women Still Can't Have It All," *Atlantic*, July/August 2012, http://www.theatlantic.com/magazine/archive/2012/07/why-women-still-can-8217-t-have-it-all/9020/2.

61. Slaughter, "Still Can't Have It All."

62. Slaughter, "Still Can't Have It All."

63. Kathi Weeks, *The Problem with Work: Feminism, Marxism, Antiwork Politics, and Postwork Imaginaries* (Durham: Duke University Press, 2011).

CHAPTER 3. TALES FROM THE CAMPAIGN TRAIL

1. Kara Nuzback, "200 Rally at Occupy Rehoboth," *Cape Gazette*, November 8, 2011, https://www.capegazette.com/node/19240.

2. Snyder, *Gay Marriage and Democracy*.

3. Bill Turque, "Five Things to Know about State Senator Jamie Raskin," *Washington Post*, April 6, 2016, https://www.washingtonpost.com/local/md-politics/five-things-to-know-about-state-sen-jamie-raskin/2016/04/06/713160ae-f10c-11e5-89c3-a647fcce95e0_story.html.

4. Susan J. Carroll and Kira Sanbonmatsu, *More Women Can Run: Gender and Pathways to the State Legislatures* (Oxford: Oxford University Press, 2013), 48–53.

5. Snyder, *Citizen-Soldiers*.

6. According to a new study, most state legislators, especially new ones, run for office with no platform or agenda. Alexander Hertel-Fernandez, *State Capture: How Conservative Activists, Big Businesses, and Wealthy Donors Reshaped the American States—and the Nation* (New York: Oxford University Press, 2019), 9–10.

7. Liliana Mason, *Uncivil Agreement: How Politics Became Our Identity* (Chicago: University of Chicago Press, 2018).

8. Hertel-Fernandez, *State Capture.*

9. Wellstone Action, *Politics the Wellstone Way: How to Elect Progressive Candidates and Win on Issues*, edited by Bill Lofy (Minneapolis: University of Minnesota Press, 2005).

10. David Mathews, *Is There a Public for the Public Schools?* (Dayton: Kettering Foundation, 1996).

11. According to the FEC, "an independent expenditure is an expenditure for a communication that expressly advocates the election or defeat of a clearly identified candidate and which is not made in coordination with any candidate or his or her campaign or political party." Because the Supreme Court case *Citizens United v. FEC* declared spending constitutionally protected free speech, independent expenditures can be unlimited. See Federal Elections Commission, "Understanding Independent Expenditures," https://www.fec.gov/help-candidates-and-committees/candidate-taking-receipts/understanding-independent-expenditures/.

CHAPTER 4. GOOD OLE BOYS VS. NASTY WOMEN: CULTURAL POLARIZATION IN US POLITICS

1. In chapter 3, I define good ole boys as the bipartisan, fraternity-like network of white men with family roots in the state who valorize masculinity, particularly in its working-class form, as evidenced by the esteem they show for police officers, firefighters, corrections officers, and veterans.

2. Quote from Caroline Light, gender studies professor at Harvard University, cited in Danielle Paquette, "Donald Trump and the Disturbing History of Calling Women 'Nasty'" in *Washington Post*, October 20, 2016, https://www.washingtonpost.com/?utm_term=.963bcf699ae6. See also Manne, *Down Girl.*

3. Rob Goodman, "What the King of Hawaii Can Teach Us About Trump," *Politico*, January 4, 2017, http://www.politico.com/magazine/story/2017/01/what-trump-taught-us-about-american-democracy-214596.

4. Almond and Verba, *Civic Culture*, 3.

5. Campbell Robertson and Robert Gebeloff, "How Millions of Women Became the Most Essential Workers in America," *New York Times*, April 18, 2020, https://www.nytimes.com/2020/04/18/us/coronavirus-women-essential-workers.html.

6. Katelyn Fossett, "Why Are So Many White Americans Dying?," *Politico Magazine*, April 5, 2017, https://www.politico.com/magazine/story/2017/04/anne-case-angus-deaton-study-214987. See also Jonathan M. Metzl, *Dying of Whiteness: How the Politics of Racial Resentment Is Killing America's Heartland* (New York: Basic Books, 2019).

7. Quoted in Bread and Roses, "Tasks for 2019," https://tinyurl.com/y35qnyyq.

8. For a full accounting of white male rage, see Michael Kimmel, *Angry White Men: American Masculinity at the End of an Era* (New York: Nation Books, 2013).

9. Arlie Russell Hochschild, *Strangers in Their Own Land: Anger and Mourning on the American Right* (New York: New Press, 2016), 137.

10. David Masciotra, "'Real Americans' vs. 'Coastal Elites': What Right-Wing Sneers at City Dwellers Really Means," *Salon*, November 20, 2016, https://www.salon.com/2016/11/20/real-americans-vs-coastal-elites-what-right-wing-sneers-at-city-dwellers-really-mean/. See also Barbara Ehrenreich, "Dude, Where's That Elite?," *New York Times*, July 1, 2004, https://www.nytimes.com/2004/07/01/opinion/dude-where-s-that-elite.html.

11. For an op-ed that makes this point, see Sarah Sobieraj, "With a Snarl, Trump Ratifies His Supporters' Rage," *New York Times*, August 9, 2016, https://www.nytimes.com/roomfordebate/2016/08/09/what-is-with-those-crowds-at-trump-rallies/with-a-snarl-trump-ratifies-his-supporters-rage.

12. Joan Williams, "We Need to Redefine What Working Class Means," *Time Magazine*, http://time.com/4899906/donald-trump-white-working-class/. For a longer version of her argument, see *White Working Class: Overcoming Class Cluelessness in America* (Boston: Harvard Business Review Press, 2017). The social science literature generally defines a working-class person as someone who does not hold a four-year college degree, using education as a proxy for class.

13. Williams, "Working Class."

14. Williams, "Working Class."

15. Williams, "Working Class."

16. Williams, "Working Class."

17. Williams, *White Working Class*, 31.

18. Williams, *White Working Class*, 106.

19. David Goodhart, *The Road to Somewhere: The Populist Revolt and the Future of Politics* (London: C. Hurst, 2017).

20. Katherine J. Cramer, *The Politics of Resentment: Rural Consciousness in Wisconsin and the Rise of Scott Walker* (Chicago: University of Chicago Press, 2016), 6.

21. Cramer, *Politics of Resentment*, 212.

22. Cramer, *Politics of Resentment*, 7.

23. Mason, *Uncivil Agreement*.

24. @DarrigoMelanie, October 26, 2019.

25. Intersectionality originated as a methodology created by Black women who wanted to explore the ways in which race and gender work simultaneously to form identity, but it has been expanded to include other axes of identity as well.

Patricia Hill Collins and Sirma Bilge say that "most" scholars "would probably accept the following general description: Intersectionality is a way of understanding and analyzing the complexity in the world, in people, and in human experiences. The events and conditions of social and political life and the self can seldom be understood as shaped by one factor. They are generally shaped by many factors in diverse and mutually influencing ways. When it comes to social inequality, people's lives and the organization of power in a given society are better understood as being shaped not by a single axis of social division, be it race or gender or class, but by many axes that work together and influence each other. Intersectionality as an analytic tool gives people better access to the complexity of the world and of themselves." Patricia Hill Collins and Sirma Bilge, *Intersectionality* (Cambridge, MA: Polity Press, 2016), 2.

26. Collins and Bilge, *Intersectionality*, 8.

27. Caroline Heldman, Meredith Conroy, and Alissa R. Ackerman, *Sex and Gender in the 2016 Presidential Election* (Santa Barbara: Praeger, 2018), 11.

28. Heldman, Conroy, and Ackerman, *Sex and Gender*, 11, 9.

29. Empirical studies document the presence of sexism in the 2016 presidential race. See Heldman, Conroy, and Ackerman, *Sex and Gender*.

30. For a discussion of double standards and misogyny in the Clinton campaign, see Judith Grant, "A Left Feminist Comment on Supporting Hillary Clinton," *Politics and Gender* 14 (2018): 106–131. For how misogyny punishes women for defying patriarchal norms, see Manne, *Down Girl*.

31. Buchanan, "Convention Speech."

32. For an alternative view, see Heldman, Conroy, and Ackerman, *Sex and Gender*.

33. Danny Hayes and Jennifer L. Lawless, *Women on the Run: Gender, Media, and Political Campaigns in a Polarized Era* (New York: Cambridge University Press, 2016), 6.

34. Hayes and Lawless, *Women on the Run*, 130.

35. Hayes and Lawless, *Women on the Run*, 7.

36. Hayes and Lawless, *Women on the Run*, 93.

37. George Lakoff, *Don't Think of an Elephant! Know Your Values and Frame the Debate* (White River Junction, VT: Chelsea Green, 2005), 4.

38. Hetherington and Weiler, *Authoritarianism and Polarization*, 1.

39. Hetherington and Weiler, *Authoritarianism and Polarization*, 1.

40. Hetherington and Weiler, *Authoritarianism and Polarization*, 2.

41. Transcript of Donald Trump's State of the Union address, delivered to Congress on January 30, 2018, NPR, https://www.npr.org/2018/01/30/580378279/trumps-state-of-the-union-address-annotated.

42. Heldman, Conroy, and Ackerman, *Sex and Gender*, 12, and Ashley Jardina, *White Identity Politics* (Cambridge: Cambridge University Press, 2019).

43. Pew, "An Examination of the 2016 Electorate, Based on Validated Voters," August 9, 2018, https://www.people-press.org/2018/08/09/an-examination-of-the-2016-electorate-based-on-validated-voters/.

44. Hillary Clinton, interview with Rachel Martin, NPR, September 12, 2017, transcript, http://www.npr.org/2017/09/12/549430064/transcript-hillary-clinton-s-full-interview-with-npr-s-rachel-martin. Hillary Rodham Clinton, *What Happened* (New York: Simon & Schuster, 2017).

45. Supporters of both Sanders and Clinton, however, were less sexist than the general population (36.2%) and also than Donald Trump supporters (58%). "The Impact of 'Modern Sexism' on the 2016 Presidential Race: A Report from the 2016 Blair Center Poll Prepared by Angie Maxwell, Ph.D. and Todd Shields, Ph.D." See https://blaircenter.uark.edu/the-impact-of-modern-sexism/. The measure of "modern sexism" is based on agreement with the following statements: "Many women are actually seeking special favors, such as hiring policies that favor them over men, under the guise of asking for 'equality'; Most women interpret innocent remarks or acts as being sexist; Feminists are seeking for women to have more power than men; When women lose to men in a fair competition, they typically complain about being discriminated against; Discrimination against women is no longer a problem in the United States."

46. Cooper Allen, "Gloria Steinem: Young Women Support Sanders Because 'The Boys Are with Bernie,'" *USA Today*, February 6, 2016, https://www.usatoday.com/story/news/politics/onpolitics/2016/02/06/gloria-steinem-bernie-sanders-women/79943264/.

47. Alan Rappeport, "Gloria Steinem and Madeleine Albright Rebuke Young Women Backing Bernie Sanders," *New York Times*, February 7, 2016, https://www.nytimes.com/2016/02/08/us/politics/gloria-steinem-madeleine-albright-hillary-clinton-bernie-sanders.html.

48. Jennifer Hansler, "Michelle Obama: 'Any woman who voted against Hillary Clinton voted against her own voice,'" CNN, September 27, 2017, http://www.cnn.com/2017/09/27/politics/michelle-obama-women-voters/index.html.

49. Jonathan Vankin, "LISTEN: Steve Bannon Calls Women 'Bunch of Dykes' in Radio Interview," *Heavy*, November 14, 2016, http://heavy.com/news/2016/11/steve-bannon-dykes-donald-trump-strategist-what-is-white-nationalism-alt-right-2016-presidential-election/.

50. @LopezforDE, December 25, 2016.

51. Rob Burton, "A Sussex Democrat Is Voting for Ernie Lopez," *Cape Gazette*, September 26, 2014, https://www.capegazette.com/article/sussex-democrat-voting-ernie-lopez/71747.

52. Parija Kavilanz, "Only 7% of Firefighters Are Women. She Wants to Change That," CNN Money, June 7, 2016, http://money.cnn.com/2016/06/07/smallbusiness/female-firefighter-erin-regan/index.html.

53. Justin Jouvenal, "Female Firefighter's Suicide Is a 'Fire Bell in the Night,'" *Washington Post*, August 22, 2016, https://www.washingtonpost.com/local/public-safety/female-reghters-suicide-is-a-re-bell-in-the-night/2016/08/22/11c 73a16-3956-11e6-a254-2b336e293a3c_story.html?hpid=hp_hp-more-top-stories_firefighter-935pm%3Ahomepage%2Fstory&utm_term=.ce24134de4a2.

54. Jouvenal, "Female Firefighter's Suicide."

55. Alex Seitz-Wald, "How Fire Fighters Help Explain the Outcome of 2016 Election," NBC News, December 23, 2016, https://www.nbcnews.com/storyline/democrats-vs-trump/how-firefighters-help-explain-outcome-2016-election-n699 196.

56. Jouvenal, "Female Firefighter's Suicide."

57. Seitz-Wald, "Fire Fighters Help Explain."

58. Seitz-Wald, "Fire Fighters Help Explain."

59. Seitz-Wald, "Fire Fighters Help Explain."

60. Richard D. Lyons, "1,097 Men Shut the Fire House Door; 990 Women See No Cause for Alarm," *New York Times*, March 8, 1992, http://www.nytimes.com/1992/03/08/news/1097-men-shut-the-firehouse-door-990-women-see-no-cause-for-alarm.html.

61. Glenn Rolfe, "Georgetown's Oyster Eat: A Pearl in History," *Sussex Post*, February 20, 2017, https://sussexpost.com/news/georgetowns-oyster-eat-pearl-history/.

62. Lyons, "Fire House Door."

63. For a video of the event, see "Behind the Scenes: Georgetown Fire Company 80th Annual Oyster Eat," https://video.search.yahoo.com/search/video;_ylt=A0geK.itpAhf6wMAO1JXNyoA;_ylu=X3oDMTB0N2Noc21lBGNvbG8DYmYxBHBvcwMx BHZ0aWQDBHNlYwNwaXZz?p=oyster+eat+delaware&fr2=piv-web&fr=mcafee#id =1&vid=ea4f8ae8e258c559a3d72461391c38dc&action=view.

64. For a description, see Glenn Rolfe, "Oyster Eat Slides into Georgetown Tonight," *Cape Gazette*, February 22, 2018, https://delawarestatenews.net/entertainment/oyster-eat-slides-georgetown-tonight/.

65. Lyons, "Fire House Door.

66. Lyons, "Fire House Door.

67. Lindsey Gruson, "Delaware Oyster Eat Calls Wanderers Home," *New York Times*, March 2, 1986, http://www.nytimes.com/1986/03/02/us/delaware-oyster-eat-calls-wanderers-home.html.

68. Rolfe, "Georgetown's Oyster Eat."

69. Staff writers, "Oysters and Beer Make Fundraising Easy for Georgetown Fire Department," *Delmarva Life*, February 29, 2016, http://www.delmarvalife.com/delmarvalife/oysters-and-beer-make-fundraising-easy-for-georgetown-fire-department/.

70. Gruson, "Delaware Oyster Eat."

71. Franny Andrews, "Becky Breasure Recognized for Service as Great Pocahontas," Press Release, *Cape Gazette*, December 10, 2016, http://www.cape

gazette.com/article/becky-breasure-recognized-service-great-pocahontas/1216
31.

72. See "Improved Order of Red Men," https://en.wikipedia.org/wiki/
Improved_Order_of_Red_Men, and "Degree of Pocahontas," https://en.wikipedia.
org/wiki/Degree_of_Pocahontas.

73. Andrews, "Great Pocahontas."

CHAPTER 5. THE ROYALIST MINDSET

1. I wrote about this issue before changing my last name, in R. Claire
Snyder, "The Allure of Authoritarianism: Christian Right Marriage and the
Reconsolidation of Patriarchy," in *W Stands for Women: How the George W. Bush
Presidency Shaped a New Politics of Gender*, ed. Michaele Ferguson and Lori
Marso (Durham: Duke University Press, 2007). See also Claire Snyder-Hall, "The
Ideology of Wifely Deference: A Challenge for Feminism?" *Politics and Gender*
4, no. 4 (December 2008): 563–586.

2. Levitsky and Ziblatt, *How Democracies Die*, 23–24.

3. Madison, Federalist 51.

4. Rousseau, *Social Contract*, 101–102, emphasis mine.

5. Peter Dreler, "Go Out and Make Me Do It," *Huff Post*, November 9,
2009, https://www.huffpost.com/entry/go-out-and-make-me-do-it_b_281631.

6. Sarah Gamard, "Meet the Most Powerful Ex-Police Officer in the Delaware
General Assembly," *New Journal*, June 15, 2020, https://www.delawareonline.com/
story/news/politics/2020/06/15/meet-most-powerful-ex-police-officer-delawares-
general-assembly/5329483002/.

7. Quoted in Gamard, "Powerful Ex-Police Officer."

8. Jeff Neiburg, "Delaware Fraternal Order of Police Endorses Trump; President
Responds," *New Journal*, September 5, 2020, https://www.delawareonline.com/story/
news/2020/09/05/delaware-fraternal-order-of-police-endorses-trump-president-
responds/5728007002/.

9. For a description of the authoritarian mindset, see Hetherington and
Weiler, *Authoritarianism and Polarization*, and Milburn and Conrad, *Raised to Rage*.

10. Gamard, "Powerful Ex-Police Officer," and Hochschild, *Strangers in
Their Own Land*.

11. Gamard, "Powerful Ex-Police Officer."

12. Gamard, "Powerful Ex-Police Officer," and Karl Baker, Jeanne Kuang,
and Esteban Parra, "How Delaware Officials Tried to Persuade Organizers to
Postpone Friday's Protest," *News Journal*, June 4, 2020, https://www.delawareonline.
com/story/news/2020/06/04/how-delaware-officials-tried-persuade-organizers-post-
pone-fridays-protest/3142946001/.

13. *Citizens United* is the Supreme Court case that essentially allows unlimited money in politics.

14. Jonathan Starky and Jon Offredo, "Amid Budget Grief, Big Raises for Dover Political Aides," *News Journal*, September 22, 2015, https://www.delaware online.com/story/news/local/2015/09/22/amid-budget-grief-big-raises-dover-political-aides/72634124/.

15. Liza Featherstone, "You're Fired: Political Discourse in the Age of Trump," *Baffler*, February 6, 2017, https://thebaffler.com/blog/youre-fired-featherstone.

16. Hetherington and Weiler, *Authoritarianism and Polarization*, 55.

17. Morris P. Fiorina, *Culture War? The Myth of Polarized America*, 2nd ed. (New York: Pearson Education, 2006), 204–205.

CHAPTER 6. SOFT AUTHORITARIANISM IN THE DEMOCRATIC PARTY

1. See Grim, *We've Got People*.

2. Carl Boggs, *Fascism Old and New: American Politics at the Crossroads* (New York: Routledge, 2018), 204. Boggs argues that the United States could be heading toward fascism but not because of Trump, who has not fundamentally changed anything.

3. Alexander Burns, "Biden Pursues Ideas to Match Scale of Crisis," *New York Times*, May 18, 2020, A1.

4. See American Presidency Project for statistics, https://www.presidency. ucsb.edu/statistics/data/voter-turnout-in-presidential-elections.

5. Viroli, *Republicanism*.

6. Carol Anderson, "Republicans Could Use the Coronavirus to Suppress Votes Across the Country. This Week We Got a Preview," *Time Magazine*, April 8, 2020, https://time.com/5817380/voter-suppression-coronavirus/.

7. Anderson, "Republicans Could Suppress Votes."

8. Claire Snyder-Hall, "We Need to Stop the 'More Money in Politics Bill,'" *News Journal*, January 22, 2016, https://www.delawareonline.com/story/opinion/contributors/2016/01/22/we-need-stop-more-money-delaware-politics-bill/7916 7302/.

9. Under Article V of the US Constitution, petitions supported by two-thirds of the states (34) can force Congress to call a constitutional convention.

10. For details see Jonathan Allen and Amie Parnes, *Shattered: Inside Hillary Clinton's Doomed Campaign* (New York: Crown, 2017), and Donna Brazile, *Hacks: The Inside Story of the Break-Ins and Breakdowns That Put Donald Trump in the White House* (New York: Hachette Books, 2017). See also Michael Sainato, "Court Concedes the DNC Had the Right to Rig Primaries Against Sanders," *Observer*, August 6, 2017, https://observer.com/2017/08/court-admits-dnc-and-debbie-wasserman-schulz-rigged-primaries-against-sanders/.

11. Frank, *Listen, Liberal*.

12. Joseph O'Neill, "Brand New Dems?," *New York Review of Books*, April 29, 2020, 44–47, 47.

13. Summer Meza, "Biden Doesn't Want to Hear Millennials Complain: 'Give Me a Break,'" *Newsweek*, January 12, 2018, https://www.newsweek.com/joe-biden-says-millennials-dont-have-it-tough-780348.

14. Will Weissert, "In Reversal, Clinton Says She'd Back Sanders If He's Nominee," Associated Press News, 1/21/20, https://apnews.com/92c5b7f05fd6ea3b94 98d3b9ab2a9506.

15. Zac Anderson, "Impeachment Dividing Dems and GOP, but Not Vern Buchanan and Margaret Good," *Sarasota Herald Tribune*, September 26, 2019, https://www.heraldtribune.com/news/20190926/impeachment-dividing-dems-and-gop-but-not-vern-buchanan-and-margaret-good.

16. Zac Anderson, "Vern Buchanan's Impeachment Balancing Act," *Sarasota Herald Tribune*, October 27, 2019, https://www.heraldtribune.com/news/20191027/vern-buchanans-impeachment-balancing-act.

17. Phillip Bailey, "Amy McGrath: 'If President Trump Has Good Ideas, I'll Be for Them,'" *Louisville Courier Journal*, July 10, 2019, https://www.usatoday.com/story/news/politics/2019/07/10/amy-mcgrath-outlines-why-kentucky-should-ditch-mitch-mcconnell/1698463001/.

18. Quoted in Chris Cillizza, "What Barack Obama Gets Exactly Right about Our Toxic 'Cancel' Culture," CNN, October 30, 2019, https://cnn.it/2N1XQj7.

19. Marc Caputo and Matt Dixon, "Florida Democrats Return PPP amid Scandal," *Politico*, July 9, 2020, https://www.msn.com/en-us/news/politics/florida-democrats-return-ppp-money-amid-scandal/ar-BB16vGGp.

CONCLUSION: WHAT IS TO BE LEARNED?

1. My Kettering Foundation colleague, Peter Levine, who used that phrase for the title of his book, traces the origins to June Jordan's "Poem for South African Women" in his blog post, "who first said 'We are the ones we have been waiting for,'" March 9, 2011, https://peterlevine.ws/?p=6105. Peter Levine, *We Are the Ones We Have Been Waiting For: The Promise of Civic Renewal in America* (Oxford: Oxford University Press, 2013).

2. Grim, *We've Got People*, 63.

3. For one example, see Ralph Nader, "Don't Blame Third Parties," Letter to the Editor, *New York Times*, October 5, 2016, https://www.nytimes.com/2016/10/06/opinion/from-ralph-nader-dont-blame-third-parties.html.

4. Nate Cohn, "How United Are Democrats? A 96–0 Data Point Offers a Hint," *New York Times*, July 8, 2020, https://www.nytimes.com/2020/07/08/upshot/democrats-united-poll-election.html

5. Cohn, "How United?"

6. Cohn, "How United?"

7. John Whitesides and Ellen Wolfhorst, "Clinton Endorses Obama," Reuters, June 6, 2008, https://www.reuters.com/article/us-usa-politics-idUSN31443685 20080607.

8. Grim, *We've Got People*, 62.

9. Grim, *We've Got People*, 63.

10. Grim, *We've Got People*, 63.

11. Grim, *We've Got People*, 66.

12. Grim, *We've Got People*, 66.

13. Jodi Dean, *Communist Horizon* (New York: Verso, 2012).

14. Thomas Paine, *Common Sense*, in *Paine: Political Writings*, ed. Bruce Kuklick (Cambridge: Cambridge University Press, 1997), 28.

15. Levitsky and Ziblatt, *How Democracies Die*.

16. Levitsky and Ziblatt, *How Democracies Die*.

17. For a recent overview of Bush war crimes, see Mehdi Hasan, "Dear Ellen: The Problem with George W. Bush Is Not His Beliefs—It's His War Crimes," *Intercept*, October 9, 2019, https://theintercept.com/2019/10/09/ellen-degeneres-george-bush/?fbclid=IwAR1Maob0HZW7bvdOaPd_W3r9LNXJNu_rGC63PLYsz0DJFxeDhmem RJHQqOw. For a full report on them, see Consumers for Peace, "War Crimes Committed by the United States in Iraq and Mechanisms for Accountability," October 10, 2006, http://www.consumersforpeace.org/pdf/war_crimes_iraq_101006.pdf. See also David Swanson, *Daybreak: Undoing the Imperial Presidency and Forming a More Perfect Union* (New York: Seven Stories Press, 2009), and Mayer, *Dark Side*.

18. See Byrne, *Iran-Contra*.

19. Swanson, *Daybreak*, 8.

20. Arthur M. Schlesinger Jr., *The Imperial Presidency* (Boston: Houghton Mifflin, 2004).

21. Quoted in Marc Fisher, "He Ignores the Law When He Doesn't Like It," *Washington Post*, September 23, 2019, https://www.washingtonpost.com/politics/when-the-president-does-it-that-means-its-not-illegal/2019/09/22/62559ea6-dcb8-11e9-ac63-3016711543fe_story.html.

22. Swanson, *Daybreak*, 16.

23. Charlie Savage, *Takeover: The Return of the Imperial Presidency and the Subversion of American Democracy* (New York: Little, Brown, 2007).

24. Swanson, *Daybreak*, 8–9. Full a detailed account of the ways in which the Obama administration not only continued but in some cases expanded Bush administration policies and executive power grabs, see Charlie Savage, *Power Wars: Inside Obama's Post-9/11 Presidency* (New York: Little, Brown, 2015).

25. Michael Brice-Saddler, "While Bemoaning Mueller Probe, Trump Falsely Says Constitution Gives Him 'the Right to Do Whatever I Want,'" *Washington Post*, July 23, 2019, https://www.washingtonpost.com/politics/2019/07/23/trump-falsely-tells-auditorium-full-teens-constitution-gives-him-right-do-whatever-i-want/.

26. Swanson, *Daybreak*, 7.

27. Savannah Behrmann and John Fritze, "Republicans in 4 States May Cancel Their 2020 Primaries to Support Trump," *USA Today*, September 7, 2019, https://www.usatoday.com/story/news/politics/elections/2019/09/07/republicans-may-cancel-2020-presidential-primaries-back-trump/2235859001/.

28. Amanda Litvinov, "Forgotten Purpose: Civic Education in Public Schools," *NEA Today*, March 16, 2017, http://neatoday.org/2017/03/16/civics-education-public-schools/.

29. Kawashima-Ginsberg, "Future of Civic Education."

30. Litvinov, "Forgotten Purpose."

31. From Rosa Luxemburg, "The Problem of Dictatorship," in *The Russian Revolution*, https://www.marxists.org/archive/luxemburg/1918/russian-revolution/ch06.htm.

32. Jodi Dean calls for a return to a strong party from a different perspective in *Crowds and Parties* (New York: Verso, 2016).

33. Gramsci, "Modern Prince," 129. McCormick, *Reading Machiavelli*.

34. Gramsci, "Modern Prince," 129.

35. "Introduction," by Hoare and Smith, to Gramsci's "Notes on Italian History," in *Prison Notebooks*, 45.

36. Gramsci, "Modern Prince," 152.

37. Gramsci, "Modern Prince," 181.

38. Gramsci, "Modern Prince," 133.

39. Jane F. McAlevey, *No Shortcuts: Organizing for Power in the New Gilded Age* (Oxford: Oxford University Press, 2016).

40. Gramsci, "Modern Prince," 155.

41. Gramsci, *Prison Notebooks*.

42. Benedetto Fontana, *Hegemony and Power: On the Relations between Gramsci and Machiavelli* (Minneapolis: University of Minnesota Press, 1993), 150.

43. This final exhortation riffs on the famous last chapter in Machiavelli, *The Prince*.

44. Lenin and his wife Krupskaya shared political and intellectual commitments. Tamas Krausz, *Reconstructing Lenin: An Intellectual Biography*, trans. Balint Bethlenfalvy with Mario Fenyo (New York: Monthly Review Press, 2015), 43–49. For more on Krupskaya's political work, see Paul Le Blanc, *Lenin and the Revolutionary Party* (Chicago: Haymarket Books, 1993).

BIBLIOGRAPHY

Alexander, Michelle. *The New Jim Crow: Mass Incarceration in the Age of Color-blindness*. New York: New Press, 2012.

Allen, Cooper. "Gloria Steinem: Young Women Support Sanders Because 'The Boys Are with Bernie.'" *USA Today*, February 6, 2016. https://www.usa today.com/story/news/politics/onpolitics/2016/02/06/gloria-steinem-bernie-sanders-women/79943264/.

Almond, Gabriel A., and Sidney Verba. *The Civic Culture: Political Attitudes and Democracy in Five Nations*. Boston: Little, Brown, 1965.

Anderson, Carol. "Republicans Could Use the Coronavirus to Suppress Votes Across the Country. This Week We Got a Preview." *Time Magazine*, April 8, 2020. https://time.com/5817380/voter-suppression-coronavirus/.

Anderson, Zac. "Vern Buchanan's Impeachment Balancing Act." *Sarasota Herald Tribune*, October 27, 2019. https://www.heraldtribune.com/news/20191027/vern-buchanans-impeachment-balancing-act.

Anderson, Zac. "Impeachment Dividing Dems and GOP, but Not Vern Buchanan and Margaret Good." *Sarasota Herald Tribune*, September 26, 2019. https://www.heraldtribune.com/news/20190926/impeachment-dividing-dems-and-gop-but-not-vern-buchanan-and-margaret-good.

Andrews, Franny. "Becky Breasure Recognized for Service as Great Pocahontas." Press Release. *Cape Gazette*, December 10, 2016. http://www.capegazette.com/article/becky-breasure-recognized-service-great-pocahontas/121631.

Aristotle. *Politics*. Translated by Benjamin Jowett. Mineola, NY: Dover, 2000.

"Around the Nation: Smith College to End South Africa Investments." *New York Times*, October 28, 1986. https://www.nytimes.com/1986/10/28/us/around-the-nation-smith-college-to-end-south-africa-investments.html.

Avramenko, Richard. *Courage: The Politics of Life and Limb*. Notre Dame: University of Notre Dame Press, 2011.

Bacevich, Andrew. *The New American Militarism: How Americans Are Seduced by War*. New York: Oxford University Press, 2005.

Bailey, Phillip. "Amy McGrath: 'If President Trump Has Good Ideas, I'll Be for Them.'" *Louisville Courier Journal*, July 10, 2019. https://www.usatoday.com/story/news/politics/2019/07/10/amy-mcgrath-outlines-why-kentucky-should-ditch-mitch-mcconnell/1698463001/.

Baker, Karl, Jeanne Kuang, and Esteban Parra. "How Delaware Officials Tried to Persuade Organizers to Postpone Friday's Protest." *News Journal*, June 4, 2020. https://www.delawareonline.com/story/news/2020/06/04/how-delaware-officials-tried-persuade-organizers-postpone-fridays-protest/3142946001/.

Barber, Benjamin R. *Jihad vs. McWorld: How Globalism and Tribalism Are Reshaping the World*. New York: Ballantine Books, 1995.

Barber, Benjamin R. *Strong Democracy: Participatory Politics for a New Age*. Berkeley: University of California Press, 1984.

Barber, Benjamin R. *The Truth of Power: Intellectual Affairs in the Clinton White House*. New York: W.W. Norton, 2001.

Behrmann, Savannah, and John Fritze. "Republicans in 4 States May Cancel Their 2020 Primaries to Support Trump." *USA Today*, September 7, 2019. https://www.usatoday.com/story/news/politics/elections/2019/09/07/republicans-may-cancel-2020-presidential-primaries-back-trump/2235859001/.

Belkin, Lisa. "The Opt-Out Revolution." *New York Times Magazine*, October 26, 2003. https://www.nytimes.com/2003/10/26/magazine/the-opt-out-revolution.html.

Boggs, Carl. *Fascism Old and New: American Politics at the Crossroads*. New York: Routledge, 2018.

Boggs, Carl. *Gramsci's Marxism*. London: Pluto Press, 1976.

Bologna, Caroline. "This Viral Rewrite of 'Baby It's Cold Outside' Emphasizes Consent." *Huffington Post*, December 10, 2018. https://www.huffpost.com/entry/baby-its-cold-outside-holderness-family-consent_n_5c0e7fd8e4b0edf5a3a6db8c.

Brice-Saddler, Michael. "While Bemoaning Mueller Probe, Trump Falsely Says Constitution Gives Him 'the Right to Do Whatever I Want." *Washington Post*, July 23, 2019. https://www.washingtonpost.com/politics/2019/07/23/trump-falsely-tells-auditorium-full-teens-constitution-gives-him-right-do-whatever-i-want/.

Bronner, Stephen Eric. *Bitter Taste of Hope: Ideals, Ideologies, and Interests in the Age of Obama*. Albany: State University of New York Press, 2017.

Bronner, Stephen Eric. *Socialism Unbound*. New York: Routledge, 1990.

Buchanan, Pat. "1992 Republican National Convention Speech." August 17, 1992. https://buchanan.org/blog/1992-republican-national-convention-speech-148?doing_wp_cron=1478487975.2316689491271972656250.

Burns, Alexander. "Biden Pursues Ideas to Match Scale of Crisis." *New York Times*, May 18, 2020, A1.